THE COUNTY LIEUTENANCIES AND THE ARMY

1803-1814

The County Lieutenancies and the Army

1803-1814

BY

THE HON. J. W. FORTESCUE

PREFACE

The present volume may be described as an "overflow" from the *History of the British Army*. It owes its existence principally to the Secretary of State for War, who, recognising the importance of the subject at the present time, kindly granted the writer a small subsidy to insure him against loss through its publication. But for this help, for which I desire to express my grateful thanks, the matter here printed must have been packed into some twenty or thirty pages only. As things stand, the twenty or thirty pages have been expanded into ten times that number; and if, as I fear, the ordinary reader finds them impossible to read, I can only assure him that I have found them maddening to write.

The subject of the recruiting of the Army during the Great War has, so far, been left in complete obscurity; nor, in my belief, could it be fully cleared up without examination of the papers (if they still exist) of every Lord-Lieutenant and of a great many Deputy-Lieutenants, of masses of municipal archives, and of tons of provincial newspapers. Such a task would occupy the best part of any one man's lifetime; and I need not say that I have not attempted it. I have, however, done my best to exhaust the official records which bear upon the question ; and these in themselves are neither few nor unimportant. The most instructive of them is the series preserved at the Record Office under the title of *Home Office*, *Internal Defence*, which consists of three hundred and twenty-six bulky volumes and bundles of manuscript correspondence received by the Secretary of State from the Lords-Lieutenant. Of these the first two hundred and fifty embrace the period 1803-1814, and being arranged by counties and in order of date, are convenient and intelligible. The remaining seventy-six are imperfect and in a state of chaos, covering all dates (exclusive of the years above named) from 1793 to 1814, with loose papers of several subsequent years even to 1826. For this disorder not the Record Office must be held responsible, for it has no sufficient staff to rearrange such papers, but former clerks at the Home Office, to whom it is an abiding reproach.

The letters from the Secretary of State to the Lords-Lieutenant and other local authorities, military and civil, are comprised in a series of entry books, under the heads of Circulars, Militia, Local Militia, and Volunteers. Many of them have been very imperfectly kept, particularly the Circulars ; and it has been frequently necessary for me to divine the contents of the Secretary of State's letters from the answers returned to them by his correspondents.

The archives of the Home Office, however, are concerned only with what are termed the Auxiliary Forces. The records of the Horse Guards and War Office for the same period are unfortunately by no means so full. In the first place, the Duke of York's papers seem to have vanished beyond recall, which is a grievous loss. In the second, the letters and orders concerning recruiting are not to be found, unless by chance transcribed in the two series of entry books known as the Secretary at War's Common Letter Books and the Commander-in-Chief's Letter Books. The Duke of York, however, caused to be compiled and printed for his Office brief accounts of the various recruiting Acts, and of their working and results, together with comments and returns. Though these accounts, which are entitled *Military Transactions of the British Empire*, do not extend beyond the year 1809, when he was driven from office, they are of the greatest value and fill up many gaps which are left open by the lack of original manuscript material. It is greatly to be regretted that the compilation of these *Military Transactions* should have been allowed to cease by the Duke's successor, Sir David Dundas.

Upon the whole, I reckon that the manuscript authorities, which I have perused for the compilation of the present brief narrative, include about 100,000 documents of one kind and another bearing upon my subject. One very voluminous and most important return, of which no copy exists at the Record Office, I was so fortunate as to find at Windsor Castle ; and I have to express my humble thanks to His Majesty the King for his gracious permission to make use of it.

Of printed authorities the most important are the *Journals* of the House of Commons, which contain some most useful and interesting returns, and Hansard's *Parliamentary Debates*, together with the Acts of Parliament passed in the period 1803-1814. Acts, Debates, and Journals alike are, in great measure, unintelligible without the gigantic commentary supplied by the two hundred and fifty manuscript volumes already referred to.

I must return my warmest thanks, as usual, to Mr. Hubert Hall for invaluable help afforded during my researches at the Public Record Office.

J. W. F.

CONTENTS

CHAPTER I

CHAPTER II

CONTENTS

CHAPTER III

CHAPTER IV

CHAPTER V

TABLE OF APPENDICES

ABBREVIATIONS USED IN THE CITATION OF AUTHORITIES

A.G.	Adjutant-General.
C.C.L.B.	Commander-in-Chief's Letter Books.
C.G.M.	Clerk of the General Meeting (of a Lieutenancy).
C.J.	Commons Journals.
C.S.M.	Clerk of Subdivision Meeting (of a Lieutenancy).
D.L.	Deputy-Lieutenant.
H.D.	Hansard's Parliamentary Debates.
H.O.	Home Office (one division of the Military Records at the Record Office).
I.D.	Internal Defence. (See Preface.)
I.F.O.	Inspecting Field-Officer.
L.L.	Lord-Lieutenant.
L.M.	Local Militia.
L.M.E.B.	Local Militia Entry Books.
M.E.B.	Military Entry Books.
Mila. E.B.	Militia Entry Books.
O.C.	Officer Commanding.
S.C.L.B.	Secretary at War's Common Letter Books.
S.S.	Secretary of State.
S.W.	Secretary at War.
V.L.	Vice-Lieutenant.
W.O.	War Office.

ABBREVIATIONS USED IN THE CITATION OF AUTHORITIES

CHAPTER I

I

The military system of England from the close of the Middle Ages to the nineteenth century was practically, though with superficial differences, the same. To every place which required a garrison, whether at home or abroad, a small permanent force was indissolubly attached, and for purposes of war an army was improvised.

The institution and increase of the Standing Army affected this system far less than might be supposed. For if the Army grew, so also did the population of the British Isles, to say nothing of British possessions abroad; and the regular forces were the only police of the slightest efficiency either at home or beyond sea. Owing to the jealousy of the House of Commons, these forces were never numerous enough for their work; and, owing to the general hostility of the nation towards the service, even the meagre establishment voted for the various corps was rarely maintained at its proper strength. Hence, if troops were required for an expedition over sea, it was necessary to draft three or four battalions into one, and to recreate, or, in plain words, to improvise new battalions to take the place of those that had been drained to the dregs.

The improvisation of an army during the eighteenth century was generally effected in three ways: by ordinary recruiting, by raising new corps, and by raising men for rank.

Ordinary recruiting was a regimental matter, which kept two or three officers and a small party of men constantly absent from regimental duty. It was usually stimulated at the outbreak of a war by adding two troops or companies to every regiment or battalion, which gave a step without purchase to a limited number of officers.[1]

The raising of new regiments is a thing that explains itself. Practically it offered commissions to any enterprising gentleman or gentlemen who, by hook or crook, could get together a body of men; and in its essence it differed very little from raising men for rank, which signified the grant of a step of promotion to all officers and of a commission to all civilians who would collect a given number of recruits. An increased bounty, of course, necessarily accompanied the whole of these arrangements; and though, in certain instances, men of rank and station could raise whole regiments of excellent soldiers, yet the backbone of an improvised army was the crimp.

The replacing of casualties suffered on active service, that is to say the maintenance as distinguished from the formation of an army, was left wholly to ordinary recruiting; and it need hardly be said that in a long war this meagre resource invariably failed. Increased bounties led always to increased desertion; and even in Queen Anne's time it was necessary to enlist men for short service, instead of, as usual, for life, and to make a levy of so many men from every parish in the country. As time went on, the difficulty of keeping corps in the field up to strength constantly increased. In Marlborough's day every regiment sent its recruiting parties home as soon as the Army went into winter quarters; but when winter quarters ceased to be, and campaigns were no longer bounded by the seasons, the problem became almost insoluble. Towards the end of the Seven Years' War new levies were raised as fast as men could be found to undertake them, but the

[1] This mode of augmentation lasted till the Crimean War.

recruits furnished thereby to the Army in Germany were of miserable quality. In fact, greatly though the sudden peace of 1763 was blamed, it came none too soon for the British Army.

That war, however, brought with it one great and solid advance in our military system, namely, the Militia Act of 1757. This measure provided for passing the entire manhood of the country through the Militia by ballot, in terms of three years; but it was never properly executed, and hence lost very much of its value. The ballot itself was never enforced[1] until the American trouble became serious in 1775, and then, since substitution was allowed, the traffic in substitutes interfered gravely with recruiting for the Regular Army. The price of a substitute rose to ten guineas before the close of the war, which meant that recruits for the Line could not be obtained for less than eleven or twelve guineas. This was the first serious symptom of a very grave mischief.

From 1784 until 1792 Pitt allowed the military forces of the country to sink to the lowest degree of weakness and inefficiency; and in 1793 he found himself obliged to improvise not merely an army, but, owing to the multiplicity of his enterprises, a very large army. He fell back on the old resources of raising men for rank and calling into existence new levies, allowing the system to be carried to such excess that the Army did not recover from the evil for many years. Never did the crimps reap such a harvest as in 1794 and 1795; and never was a more cruel wrong done to the Army than when boys fresh from school, in virtue of so many hundred wretched weaklings produced by a crimp, took command of battalions, and even of brigades, over the heads of good officers of twenty and thirty years' service. In 1793 the bounty offered to men enlisting into the Line was ten guineas; within eighteen months the Government was contracting with certain scoundrels for the delivery of men at twenty guineas a head, and,

1 *H.D.* Speech of W. Windham, 21st Feb. 1805.

long before that, the market price of recruits had risen to thirty guineas.

One cause of the extreme dearness of recruits was dread of service in the West Indies, where Pitt had decided to make his principal military effort. Nor was this repugnance unreasonable, for West Indian duty in those days was practically synonymous with death. But, apart from this, the Government, by its own military policy, had done its utmost to hinder recruiting for the Line. The Militia was, very properly, at once embodied and made up to strength as soon as the danger of war became serious; but substitutes were allowed, and these substitutes were precisely the men who, but for the heavy bounty which they could gain from serving comfortably at home, would gladly have enlisted in the Army. Furthermore, by enrolling many scores of thousands of Volunteers as independent units, dissociating them, contrary to all precedent, from the Militia, and exempting them from the ballot, Ministers diminished seriously the number of men who were liable to be drawn for the Militia, threw the obligation upon a smaller class of the population, and, as a natural consequence, increased the demand for substitutes. Then again, they had raised several thousand Fencible regiments, both horse and foot. These, being engaged for home service alone, differed from Militia only in that they were not chosen by the ballot, and, consequently, they absorbed thousands of men who would otherwise have taken service with the Regulars. Meanwhile the mortality among the troops in the West Indies was appalling; and yet, for military reasons, it was urgently necessary to obtain more men by some means for both Navy and Army. An Act was therefore passed for levying men from every parish in the United Kingdom, after the precedent of Queen Anne. The measure was a total failure so far as the Army was concerned, and in the Navy it was generally considered, from the bad character of the men produced, to have been a chief cause of the Mutiny of 1797.

By 1796, therefore, the Government was at its wits' end, and in that year there was serious danger of invasion. In spite of all its Fencibles and Volunteers, it did not feel safe, and so fell, during the next two years, to raising more Fencibles, a Supplementary Militia, more Volunteers, and, last of all, a force called the Provisional Cavalry, which was supposed to include all mounted men not already gathered into the Fencible and Yeomanry Cavalry. The Provisional Cavalry was a crying failure. "It passed," in Windham's words, "over the country like a blight. It was a pleasant "conceit to make every man ride another's horse, till "at length when the men and horses were all brought "together, no man knew how to mount, and so they all "separated." So short-lived was this force, that the foregoing caustic sentence is almost all that is discoverable concerning it; but it is very evident that the class which the Government desired to enlist in it contrived to evade service by procuring substitutes, though paying dearly for them. The Supplementary Militia was more successful. Ministers had the good sense not to grant any exemption to the Volunteers until the ballot had been held. But even so, between these various calls for men, bounties, or, more accurately speaking, the cost of recruits and substitutes, rose in 1798 to sixty, seventy, and even eighty guineas.[1]

It was very plain that such a state of things could not continue; wherefore, in 1798 Ministers passed an Act to enable ten thousand Militiamen to enlist in the Army for a bounty of ten pounds. The Lords-Lieutenant set their faces against it, not wishing to see their men shipped off to the West Indies; and the measure was a failure. But, fortunately, the demand for men in the West Indies ceased about this time, and the Government was able to reintroduce the Act in 1799, with the additional provision that the service of the enlisted Militiamen should be confined to Europe. Then the ten thousand, most of whom had already

[1] *H.D.* New Series, iii. 599.

received large sums as substitutes, swarmed joyfully to the colours, and having received their bounty, by some extraordinary folly, in advance, reeled round them in a state of crapulous insubordination for some days until the money was spent. After that, they proved to be good men, decidedly superior, by Sir Ralph Abercromby's testimony, to the ordinary class of recruit. Many of them volunteered for service in Egypt, though their engagement did not bind them to do so; and in fact the Army depended chiefly on Militiamen for its recruits until the signature of the preliminaries of peace in October 1801.

II

The Treaty of Amiens was admittedly only an experiment, and an experiment so doubtful that it could deserve no higher title than a suspension of arms. In such circumstances it was impossible for Addington to reduce the military force to a peace establishment, and the lowest number of regular troops for which he dared to estimate was 132,000. On the other hand, the Fencibles, both horse and foot, were totally disbanded, which diminished the force for home defence by at least 20,000 men. It had been hoped that most of these men, who from long divorce from any but military employment were practically soldiers, would have enlisted in the Line; but they did not. The nation seemed, not unnaturally, to be sick of warlike exercises, and recruits were by no means plentiful. True prudence and forethought would have dictated special efforts to make up the Regular Army to its full establishment, for if war was to come again, the surest method of defence was certainly to take the offensive. Such a policy, however, would have been construed as lack of faith on Addington's part towards his own experiment, though it was less for this reason than from sheer want of foresight and ignorance of war that the Ministry turned all its energies, as shall presently be seen, towards purely defensive preparations.

An attitude of passive and inert defence is very rarely sound, and was never more false than in 1803. It has generally been assumed that, in the circumstances, it was impossible for England to think of taking the offensive. Yet this is at least open to question. The enemy to be encountered was indeed most formidable; but before rushing to the conclusion that the initiative must necessarily have been yielded up to him, some account at least should be taken of his position. 1803.

Napoleon was not prepared for war. He was entangled in costly and most difficult operations at St. Domingo when hostilities began; and the intervention of the British fleet turned them into utter disaster. Of forty-eight ships of war which he had sent off to the West Indies, only seven ever returned to Europe[1] except as British prizes; while the soldiers captured by the British amounted to over seven thousand, quite apart from thirty to forty thousand men who had already perished of yellow fever or deserted to the enemy. The British fleet, owing to the mistaken economies of St. Vincent, was by no means so efficient as it should have been, but the French fleet was so contemptible in numbers and unreadiness as to be hardly worth mentioning. It may be asserted without hesitation that the British Government could, so far as the safety of the sea was concerned, have sent any force that it pleased to any point that it pleased; and thirty thousand, or even twenty thousand, men despatched to Sicily or to Naples in the summer of 1803 must almost certainly have broken up the camp at Boulogne. Napoleon had violated Neapolitan territory by occupying Brindisi, Tarento, and Otranto with a small force. The appearance of a formidable British expedition would have compelled him to reinforce it and the whole of his Italian garrisons very heavily; for he could hardly have withdrawn this detachment without endangering his reputation in France, or, indeed,

[1] They could not even return to France, but were obliged to take refuge in Spanish ports.

1803. without seeing the force harassed to destruction on its retreat. Calabria and Apulia were ripe for revolt against him, and the rest of Italy was by no means so quiet that he could afford to leave it weakly occupied when there was a chance of a reverse to his arms. The British force could have been doubled or trebled as the augmentation of the Army progressed, and Napoleon would thus have been forced to fight us amid a hostile population, at the end of a long line of communications, in a country which favoured the action of our fleet even more than Spain.

It may be urged that a policy so audacious was too much to expect of British Ministers in the presence of such a man as Napoleon; and such an objection must not be lightly dismissed. Addington was such a proverb for mediocrity that, though he was popular among the country gentlemen, the nation felt little confidence in him; and if he had attempted such a stroke as is outlined in the preceding paragraphs, he might well have brought a storm about his ears and have been compelled to cancel any offensive expedition, even if he had designed it. But this is not the main point. The real question at issue is whether in the particular circumstances he should have devoted his principal effort to reinforcing the Army, which could serve abroad, or to creating a huge defensive force, which could only serve at home. Obviously, regular troops, which from their nature are superior to half-trained levies as well for internal defence as for foreign attack, were preferable if they could be raised in sufficient numbers and at reasonable expense. Indeed, though the fact is occasionally obscured, the Regular Army is, and always has been, the only land force that we can depend upon for any description of war. All inquiries, therefore, into our military preparations at any period must be conducted, primarily and above all, to ascertain how they affected, for good or evil, the strength, numbers, and efficiency of the Regular Army.

War was declared, as has been told, on the 16th of

May 1803. Exact returns of the effective strength of the Regular Army on the 1st of June are fortunately to hand,[1] and it will be profitable to begin by abstracting them here. It must be premised that the Regular Army consisted at that time of three regiments of Household Cavalry; seven regiments of Dragoon Guards; twenty-five regiments of Dragoons; seven battalions of Foot Guards; ninety-six regiments of the Line, all of one battalion apiece, except the First Royals, which had two battalions, and the Sixtieth, which had six; seven Garrison Battalions; a small independent corps at Goree; another of five hundred men in New South Wales; seven foreign corps (about 3500 of all ranks) of infantry; the Royal Waggon Train, numbering just over two hundred men; and the Staff Corps, or War Office Engineers, which had been called into being during the last war because the established Engineers under the Office of Ordnance acknowledged no master but their own Master-General, and made difficulties about obeying the orders of the Commander-in-Chief. The above were all white troops, and it will be convenient to reckon them all together, for the men of the Sixtieth were for the most part as truly foreign as De Roll's or De Watteville's. Besides these there were four thousand native troops in Ceylon, all of them useless and some of them dangerous, and six West Indian regiments, which for West Indian service were excellent and invaluable troops.[2] 1803.

The effective strength of the whole (deducting the Ceylonese) was 14,734 cavalry and 79,508 infantry, *effective rank and file*, that is to say, corporals and privates only. Adding one-eighth for drummers, sergeants, and officers, we obtain, in round numbers, a total of 15,600 cavalry, and 89,500 infantry, or as nearly as may be

[1] *Military Transactions of British Empire, 1803-1807.* Printed for the Commander-in-Chief's office.

[2] The return shows nine West India regiments, but not one of them was 600 strong; and they were in process of reduction into six. They were, and of course still are, composed of negroes of African origin, and frequently of African birth.

1803. 104,000 men. To this figure must be added further the two regiments of Life Guards, 700 of all ranks, which for some reason were omitted from the return, and the Artillery, which may be taken at between 9000 and 10,000 of all ranks.[1] The effective strength of the British Army, therefore, on the 1st of June 1803 may be set down with tolerable correctness at 114,000 of all ranks. The establishment fixed by the estimates of 1802 was 132,000 men of all ranks, exclusive of the foreign corps. Hence at the outbreak of the war the Army was over twenty thousand men, or nearly one-sixth, short of its proper strength.

Of the effective rank and file 9046 cavalry and 22,814 infantry were in Great Britain, 3215 cavalry and 16,556 infantry in Ireland. The remainder were abroad or on passage. It so happened that the force in the West Indies was very large, for the garrisons of the French islands, which had been captured in the late war and given back at the peace, had not yet returned home. The Government at once employed them in recovering some of the restored islands and settlements. St. Lucia, Tobago, Demerara, Essequibo, Berbice, and Surinam were taken before the end of the year with little difficulty or bloodshed; and, since many of the Dutch prisoners from the four places last named took service with the British, the net loss of men was trifling—possibly, indeed, was turned for a few weeks into gain. But the whole of these new acquisitions required garrisons, and most of them were extremely unhealthy, so that Addington's single offensive movement necessarily involved an increased drain upon the Regular Army, and that for a station which was loathed and dreaded as the grave of some twenty or thirty thousand men during the last war.

However, Pitt's policy of "filching sugar islands" was undoubtedly popular with the mercantile classes;

[1] Its establishment was 10,296, and, like the Guards and the Cavalry at that time, the Artillery had no difficulty in obtaining recruits.

and Addington may be pardoned if, with the great man's shadow always across his path, he fell into the same evil ways. But when, in these circumstances, Mr. Yorke introduced the Army Estimates on the 6th of June 1803, not a few members of the Commons were staggered to find that he proposed, and plumed himself on proposing, no further increase in the Regular Establishment than from 132,000 to 138,000 men. On the other hand, he pointed with pride to the figures of nearly 84,000 men which he assigned to the Militia. This complacency brought upon him a furious attack from Windham, who asked how men could be expected to enlist in the Regulars for life, with liability to serve in any part of the globe, when they could receive far larger bounties to serve for a few years comfortably at home. "How," he added, "without a Regular Army can there be a possibility of any but a passive and defensive policy, which must be alike ruinous and dishonourable?" Pitt echoed Windham's criticism, the meaning of which will presently be made clear, and joined in his condemnation of a purely defensive attitude; but Addington disarmed opposition by asserting that, though he had indeed dealt with defensive measures first, owing to the vast preparations of the enemy, yet the country would doubtless afford means for offensive operations as soon as a favourable opportunity should arise. Beyond question Addington spoke in good faith, probably with a thought for a certain Army of Reserve Bill which was already in preparation; but he was completely at fault over the possibility of turning his defensive measures to offensive account. To estimate the causes and consequences of his error, it is now necessary to see what those defensive measures were.

1803.

CHAPTER II

I

1802. UPON the peace of Amiens, Addington made it his first business to pass an Act[1] to enable Yeomanry and Volunteer corps to continue their service if they were willing to do so; for the various Acts passed by Pitt's Administration had provided for the maintenance of Volunteers only until the close of the war. The whole organisation and system of Volunteers under Pitt had been vicious and false. The corps made their own conditions of service, were supported by private subscriptions, and were directed by committees of subscribers who were not necessarily holders of commissions. These committees addressed the Secretary of State directly, and it was an open question whether they or the officers were the true commanders of the corps.[2] But no effort was made by Addington to reduce chaos to order, nor in any way to correct what was amiss. Sections 2, 3, and 4 of the English Act provided that Volunteers and Yeomanry should be exempt from the Militia Ballot[3] on attending five days' exercise every year, forfeiting that privilege if discharged from their corps. For the rest, Volunteers were relieved, under section 7, from the duty on hair-powder, and Yeomanry from the duty on

[1] 42 Geo. III. cap. 66 for Great Britain; cap. 68 for Ireland.

[2] The documents concerning the Volunteers of 1794 to 1801 are so scanty and imperfect that it is impossible to speak of them except in general terms. So much as I have written above is, however, certain.

[3] It must be noted that as there was practically no ballot in Ireland, there was no exemption.

one horse, in addition. Corps which, when called on, consented voluntarily to march out of their counties to repel invasion or to suppress riots were, under section 10, entitled to receive the same pay as regular troops, and were subjected to military discipline, with the proviso that they could be tried only by courts-martial composed of officers of Yeomen or Volunteers. Under section 11 officers and men disabled on active service were entitled to half-pay or to a Chelsea pension respectively; and therewith the enactment was complete. Not a word was said as to the preservation of discipline during the days of exercise; not a word to prevent the multiplication of small corps, a thing which had been the curse of the Volunteers from 1794 to 1801; finally, not a word as to pay and allowances, except in case of invasion. 1802.

The Act having been passed, the Secretary of State for War, on the 2nd of July, sent round a circular to the Lords-Lieutenant inviting offers of service, and tendering the following allowances: £2 a year to every Volunteer for his clothing and appointments; £60 a year for every troop of Yeomanry which counted not fewer than forty rank and file.

A fair number both of cavalry and infantry accepted these terms, more often as isolated troops and companies than as regiments or battalions; but a great many refused further service, not seeing any occasion for such patriotic display in time of peace.

The Irish Volunteers Act differed not a little from the British. Therein it was enacted that the men should receive clothing, arms, and pay from Government while out on exercise, which exercise was not to exceed two days in each month. Permanent pay also was allowed to one sergeant in each troop; and the provisions seemed to point to real desire for efficiency, until the third section stated expressly, with startling abruptness, that neither enrolment nor the receipt of pay or allowances should subject either Volunteers or Yeomen to military duty or discipline.

1802. The next measure of Addington's Government was a new Militia Act,[1] whereby several previous Militia Acts were repealed, and the purport of them, with some amendments, re-enacted. The population of the United Kingdom at this time was, roughly speaking, 14,500,000, namely, England, 9,000,000; Scotland, 1,500,000; Ireland, 4,000,000. The Act (together with its affiliated Acts[2]) provided for raising altogether 51,489 men, between the ages of eighteen and forty-five, in Great Britain, according to a regular quota for every county, and for giving the King's authority to augment that number by one-half on calling Parliament together within fourteen days. This augmentation was known as the Supplementary Militia, the original 51,489 being distinguished as the Old Militia—technical terms which should be borne in mind.

All Militiamen were to be chosen by ballot, and by no other means whatever, and were positively forbidden, under penalties (sec. 4), to enlist in the Regular Army. The regular period of training was fixed at twenty-one days annually (sec. 88).

The machinery for the levy was as follows:—For the purposes of the Militia each county as a whole was governed by "General Meetings of the Lieutenancy," that is to say, by a Council of the Lord-Lieutenant and of his Deputies. The Lord-Lieutenant himself was appointed by the Sovereign; the Deputies, of whom a qualification in respect of property was required, were appointed by the Lord-Lieutenant, subject to the Sovereign's approbation. In the absence of the Lord-Lieutenant, the Sovereign could give three deputies a commission to act in his stead. With the Council of the Lieutenancy was a Secretary, known as the Clerk of the General Meeting, who was appointed by the Lord-Lieutenant and removable by him (sec. 18).

Each county was further parcelled out into sub-

[1] 42 Geo. III. cap. 90.

[2] The Affiliated Acts mean those for the City of London, the Cinque Ports, and the Stannaries, which were dealt with separately.

divisions, under the control of two or more Deputy- 1802.
Lieutenants, who held subdivision meetings under the orders of the General Meeting, and had likewise a Secretary known as the Subdivision Clerk. Upon the approach of a ballot the General Meeting gave orders to the constables of the hundreds (or other administrative divisions of the county) to draw up lists of all men between the ages of eighteen and forty-five, with a statement of their claims, if any, to exemption. This order was passed on to the parish constables for execution in each parish; and the lists when completed were affixed to the door of the church, so that every man could see them and have the opportunity of appealing to the next subdivision-meeting, in case his claims to exemption should have been omitted. The decision of the subdivision-meeting upon such appeals was final, and the lists as amended by it were then transmitted by the Clerk of the General Meeting to the Privy Council, which was charged with the duty of fixing and, from time to time, revising the quota of men to be found by each county.

The numbers of his county's quota having been reported to the Lord-Lieutenant, a General Meeting decided upon the number to be produced by each subdivision; and the subdivision-meetings in their turn distributed these numbers among the various parishes. The men liable to service were drafted into five classes (sec. 54): (1) Men under thirty and childless; (2) men over thirty and childless; (3) all men having no children living under fourteen years of age; (4) all men having but one child under fourteen; (5) all other men whatsoever. Notice was then given in each subdivision that all men liable to be drawn should attend at a certain place on a certain day within three weeks of the subdivision-meeting; and on that day the Deputy-Lieutenants again met and held the ballot.

If a part only of the Militia was to be embodied, and if the number of men to be called out was equal to the number of the first, or first and second, or other

1802. succeeding classes in their order, then the Deputy-Lieutenants might take those classes complete, without ballot, and use the ballot only for the remainder (sec. 134).

The Deputy-Lieutenants were required to discharge, without further claim, all ballotted men under the height of five feet four inches, and all men physically unfit, provided that they were not possessed of property to the value of £100. Exemption was granted (sec. 43) to peers; to all officers on full or half pay in the Army, Navy, and Marines; to all non-commissioned officers and men serving in any of the King's other forces; to any officer who was serving or who had served for four years in the Militia; to resident members of the universities, clergymen, duly registered teachers, constables and other peace-officers, articled clerks, apprentices, seafaring men and men employed in the royal arsenals, dockyards, or factories; to men free of the Company of Watermen of the Thames; and finally, to any poor man (which was construed under sec. 53 to mean a man possessing less than the value of £100) who had more than one child born in lawful wedlock.[1] Besides these, the Volunteers could claim their exemption under the Volunteer Act.

Ballotted men, or, as they were frequently called, lot-men, if they accepted personal service, were sworn in to serve as privates for a term of five years (sec. 41), after which time they were exempt until their turn came in rotation to be ballotted again. They were known technically as *principals*, to distinguish them from *substitutes*, the persons who must next engage our attention, for there were various means provided by the Act for commutation of personal service. In the first place,

[1] A nice point was raised as to the exemption of a man whose second legitimate child was born after he had been ballotted, but before he had been enrolled. It was decided that in this case he was exempt; but that if the child was born *after* he had been enrolled, then he was not exempt (*W. O. Mila. Books*, S. W. to Tho. Wright, 26th Jan. 1803). How far this decision may have affected the domestic arrangements of poor families we are not told.

any man chosen or ballotted was empowered (sec. 41) to produce a man "of the same county, riding, or place, or from some adjoining county or place, able and fit for service," and having not more than one child born in lawful wedlock, to serve in his stead. Such men were called *personal* substitutes, and were sworn in to serve for five years, or, if the Militia were embodied within that period, then for such further time as it might remain embodied; or, in fewer words, till the close of the war. 1802.

Again, the churchwardens or overseers of any parish might, by consent of the inhabitants, produce voluntary candidates for the Militia to the subdivision-meeting, to be accepted in lieu of men chosen by ballot, and might levy a parochial rate to pay them a bounty not exceeding £6 apiece (sec. 42).[1] Such men were known and named in the Act, by an extremely unfortunate confusion of speech, as volunteers. They were really *parochial* substitutes, and for the sake of clearness I shall call them throughout by the name of parochial substitutes. These likewise were enrolled for five years, or until the Militia should be disembodied; and under sec. 43 previous service as a substitute, whether parochial or personal, did not entitle a man to immunity from the ballot. No ballotted man nor substitute of any description whatever could be enrolled for service unless first approved by a surgeon (sec. 52).

Again (sec. 136), any man on the list of ballottable men might offer himself to serve in lieu of a ballotted man, and might be accepted by the Deputy-Lieutenants, provided that he were not over thirty-five years of age and had no children living under fourteen years of age. The service of such men was subject to the same conditions as if they had been actually ballotted.

Yet again (sec. 45), any ballotted man could purchase exemption for five years by payment of a fine of £10; or, to put the matter in different words, could

[1] From this rate men who were serving in the Militia, in person or by substitute, were excused.

1802. commute his term of five years' service for that sum of money. But this privilege was not extended to Quakers, who were required either to serve or to find a substitute; and if any Quaker failed to do so, two or more Deputy-Lieutenants were empowered to hire a substitute for him and to levy distress upon his goods for payment of the same (secs. 45, 50). The fines thus collected were applied by the Deputy-Lieutenants to the purchase of substitutes for those persons who had paid them; and any surplus remaining thereafter was handed over to the commanding officer of the County Militia Regiment to be included in the regimental stock-purse (sec. 66).

For the relief of the poorer inhabitants there was a provision that any man worth less than £500 who might be ballotted should, whether he elected to serve in person or by substitute, receive from the Deputy-Lieutenants a sum equal to half the current price of a substitute at the time, the money being raised by a parochial rate (sec. 122).

The general and designed result of the foregoing enactments, though it may not appear on the face of the Act, was as follows:—All men between the ages of eighteen and forty-five were liable to serve in person or by substitute, or to pay a fine, unless they combined the disabilities of being physically unfit (including a shorter stature than five feet four inches) and of possessing less than the value of £100 in property. A man might be blind, deaf, dumb, handless and legless. He was none the less liable to serve by substitute or to pay a fine, so long as he were of the right age and worth more than £100; and this is the explanation of the relief granted by sec. 122, quoted in the preceding paragraph. The provisions respecting the numbers and age of children in the cases of principals and substitutes were due to the fact that the wives and families of Militiamen were entitled to parochial support while the men themselves were serving in the ranks. Hence the criticism of this Act, by a well-known commentator on the Army, that as a tax it was local and personal, instead of general and imperial, and, as such, necessarily levied with great inequality.[1] 1802.

The only form of evasion against which the Act pretended to guard was that of persons who fraudulently bound themselves apprentices to qualify themselves for exemption. Such persons could be compelled to serve, if detected, and the masters to whom they bound themselves were liable to a fine of £10 (sec. 49).

To provide against malingering, it was enacted that though men who became physically unfit might be discharged, yet such discharge must be confirmed by two Deputy-Lieutenants (sec. 55). Vacancies by death or discharge were filled up by a fresh ballot from the subdivision, and presumably (though it was not laid down by the Act) within the parish from which the dead or discharged man had been originally drawn (sec. 56).

Vacancies through the promotion of privates to be non-commissioned officers were, however, not filled up by ballot, the parish being conceived to have fulfilled its duty by producing a non-commissioned officer (sec. 57). The point is worth noting, for the position of non-commissioned officers and drummers of Militia was peculiar. They were sworn in to serve until legally discharged by their colonel, that is to say, practically for life, though after twenty years' service in the Militia they were qualified for a Chelsea pension (sec. 86). If reduced to the ranks by a court-martial, non-commissioned officers and drummers were liable to serve as privates for fifteen months at ordinary times; but if the Militia was embodied they were not entitled to discharge until its disembodiment (sec. 105). In the event of the death or discharge of any one of them, the Deputy-Lieutenants for the subdivision from which they were drawn might apply to Quarter Sessions for the average price of a substitute in the parish concerned, and so provide a man to take his place (sec. 58).

[1] Clode, i. 289. But Clode's analysis and comprehension of the Militia Acts are extremely imperfect.

1802. Privates whose time was within four months of expiring could give notice if they were willing to prolong their service, stating the bounty for which they asked. If accepted, they were treated as parochial substitutes, and their bounties were raised by a parochial rate (secs. 123, 124). A guinea was also allowed to them for renewal of their necessaries at the close of their five years, part of which was expended by their captain for their benefit, and the rest—by custom one moiety—handed over to them. This was known as renewal money. The like sum was paid also to substitutes at the end of their first five years' service, and also at the end of every three years over and above the original five years (sec. 126). Substitutes who deserted or absented themselves from duty could be sentenced by court-martial to serve in the Militia for a limited period, or in the Regular Army for life (sec. 127). Militiamen generally, who absented themselves or deserted, were liable to a fine of £20 upon conviction before a Justice of the Peace, or six months' imprisonment in default (sec. 99).

If any county failed to produce its quota of men within six months after the passing of the Act, or within three months of notice given by the officer commanding the Militia regiments of the county, it was liable to a fine of £10 annually for every man deficient. For the payment of this sum Quarter Sessions were required to make an assessment upon parishes at large or upon the particular parishes that were responsible for the deficiencies. The money thus raised was retained in the hands of the County Treasurers for three months, during which time the Deputy-Lieutenants were permitted to agree with men to enlist voluntarily in the Militia for a bounty not exceeding £10. The balance of the money was then paid to the Receiver-General of the county, and by him to the Imperial Exchequer; and after the Receiver-General's receipt for the same the county was acquitted of its default for that year (secs. 158-166). If any county failed to raise the fines thus imposed, the Solicitor to the Treasury was required to put the law into force against it (sec. 169). 1802

Thus, outside the cost of pay and equipment, the Imperial Treasury was not concerned with the Militia save by the acceptance, in the last resort, of money in lieu of men.

A second Act (42 Geo. III. cap. 91) applied the same principle *mutatis mutandis* to Scotland, at the same time increasing its quota of Militia from 6000 to nearly 8000 men. Its ten regiments, which had been raised in 1797 for the duration of the last war only, were grouped anew and reorganised into fifteen battalions.[1]

[1] Old Organisation of the Scottish Militia:—

1st or Argyll	*i.e.* Argyll, Dumbarton, Bute, Inverness.
2nd or Ross-shire	*i.e.* Ross, Elgin, Nairn, Cromarty, Sutherland, Caithness.
3rd or Lanark	*i.e.* Lanark.
4th or Dumfries	*i.e.* Dumfries, Selkirk, Peebles, Roxburgh, Kirkcudbright, Wigtown.
5th or Fife	*i.e.* Fife, Stirling, Kinross, Clackmannan.
6th or Aberdeen	*i.e.* Aberdeen, Banff.
7th or Ayr	*i.e.* Ayr, Renfrew.
8th or Forfar	*i.e.* Forfar, Kincardine.
9th or Perth	*i.e.* Perth.
10th or Edinburgh	*i.e.* Edinburgh, Linlithgow, Haddington, Berwick.

New Organisation of the Scottish Militia :—

No.	Regiment.	Colonel.
1.	Aberdeen.	Lord Aboyne.
2.	Ayr.	Lord Montgomerie.
3.	Fife.	Lord Crauford.
4.	Lanark.	Marquis of Douglass.
5.	Perth.	Duke of Athol.
6.	Renfrew.	Earl of Glasgow.
7.	Argyll and Bute.	John Campbell.
8.	Berwick, Haddington, Linlithgow, Peebles.	Earl of Home.
9.	Ross, Caithness, Sutherland, Cromarty.	Lord Seaforth.
10.	Dumfries, Roxburgh, Selkirk.	Earl of Dalkeith.
11.	Edinburgh City and Co.	Duke of Buccleuch.
12.	Forfar, Kincardine.	M. Douglass.

1802. Both Acts received the Royal assent on the 26th of June 1802.

Subsidiary to these was an Act to regulate the Militia of the Stannaries (42 Geo. III. cap. 72), wherein the general procedure was the same, but the fine for commutation of five years' service was £15 instead of £10.

The Militia of Ireland was not dealt with until the following session, in December 1802, when an Act (43 Geo. III. cap. 2) was passed "for the more speedy and effectual enrolment of the Militia of Ireland." The preamble set forth that "the mode of ballot hath not been generally adopted in Ireland, and that it might therefore be attended with inconvenience to proceed by that mode only"; the "inconvenience" being an euphemism for desperate riots. The Lord-Lieutenant was therefore empowered to recruit men by voluntary enlistment for the Militia during the space of four months, offering a bounty of two guineas a man. The men so raised were sworn to serve upon the same terms as the substitutes in England, that is to say, for five years, or if the Militia were embodied within those five years, then until disembodiment. £40,000 was set apart for the payment of bounties, whence it may be inferred that the Government desired to raise about 20,000 recruits, though the ordinary strength of the Irish Militia was 15,000 men. It is important to note that the Irish Act, unlike the British Act, contained no authority to raise Supplementary Militia.

II

1803. Before the New Year had come, the prospects of prolonging the truce of Amiens became very doubtful;

New Organisation of the Scottish Militia :—

No.	Regiment.	Colonel.
13.	Inverness, Banff, Elgin, Nairn.	Sir F. Grant.
14.	Kirkcudbright, Wigtown.	Sir J. Dal. Hay.
15.	Stirling, Dunbar, Clackmannan, Kinross.	Duke of Montrose.

and as the spring advanced the near approach of war was more and more apparent. On the 11th of March 1803—the very day, curiously enough, upon which Napoleon issued his first orders for the formation of a flotilla—the Government directed the Militia to be embodied; and thenceforward measure followed measure with astonishing rapidity upon the Statute-book. 1803.

The first was an Act of one section (43 Geo. III. cap. 19; 24th March 1803), prolonging the annual training of the Militia from twenty-one to twenty-eight days. The next was an Act (43 Geo. III. cap. 33; 7th April 1803) for doubling the bounty for Irish Militiamen, a sure proof that the men were not coming forward in sufficient numbers. Then came an Act to relax the qualifications of property required of Militia officers in Great Britain until the 25th of March 1804, sufficient officers of the wealth demanded by the Act of 1802 being impossible to obtain.

It was none too soon, for war was declared on the 16th of May, and on the 28th the Lords-Lieutenant were directed to enrol the Supplementary Militia, that is to say, the additional number, amounting to one-half of the established Militia, authorised by the Act of 1802. On the previous day, the 27th of May, an Act had been passed to provide for the usual parochial relief of families of Embodied Militiamen (43 Geo. III. caps. 47, 89); and this was followed three weeks later by an Act for the more speedy completion of the Militia (43 Geo. III. cap. 50, 11th June 1803). This last provided that within ten days the Deputy-Lieutenants should meet and fill up all vacancies in the Militia without inquiry as to their cause; that Commandants of Regiments should from time to time notify to the Clerks of General Meetings the number of men wanting to their full establishment; and that the Deputy-Lieutenants should meet and supply all deficiencies within seven days after receiving notice from the Clerk (sec. 1). Further, the fine of £10 for every man deficient in the quota of each county was ordained to be repeated

1803. cumulatively every quarter until the deficiency should be made good (sec. 4). A new oath was also required of a Militiaman to the effect, among other matters, that he had no rupture, nor ever was troubled with fits, and was no ways disabled by lameness or otherwise (sec. 9 and Schedule B). The fine for commutation of five years service was also raised, from the 28th of May onward, from £10 to £15 (sec. 10). Lastly, at the very end came a section threatening high constables and constables, as well as adjutants or non-commissioned officers, with a fine of £50 if they should insure, or in any way be concerned in insuring, any persons for the provision of substitutes—a very significant matter which shall be duly explained in its place.

So much for the Militia; it is now necessary to turn for a moment to the Volunteers. On the 31st of March the Government issued circulars inviting the services of more Volunteers under the Volunteer Act of 1802, setting forth the pay and allowances which they were prepared to grant to them as well as the number of days' training required of them, and promising exemption from the Militia ballot to those who fulfilled these conditions. This, as shall be told later, caused some increase in the number of Volunteers; and the Government followed this up by producing an Act to provide more effectually for the defence and security of the realm (43 Geo. III. cap. 55, 11th June 1803), a measure which I shall call by the name of the First Defence Act.

Hereby the Lords-Lieutenant of the United Kingdom were required to procure returns of all able-bodied men between the ages of fifteen and sixty, distinguishing those who were already serving in the Yeomanry or Volunteers, those who were willing to serve in defence of the country (stating their terms), those who were willing to serve gratuitously or for hire as waggoners, pioneers, and the like, and those who from age, infirmity, or extreme youth were incapable of service. The Lieutenants were further ordered to furnish particulars as to vehicles, horses, boats, cattle, food, and forage, so as to enable them to be removed or utilised in case of invasion (sec. 1). The King was empowered to command the Lords-Lieutenant to appoint officers, approved by him, to train men who were willing to be armed (sec. 2). General Meetings and subdivision-meetings could be held, as under the Militia laws, to enforce the Act (secs. 3-6). The King was empowered to order the destruction of buildings and the destruction or removal of waggons, cattle, etc., in case of emergency (sec. 7). Persons enrolled in Volunteer corps after the passing of the Act were not to be called out except according to their offers of service, nor except in case of invasion or imminent danger of invasion (sec. 8). The King was authorised to treat for the purchase of land necessary for military purposes; and, in case of urgent need, machinery was provided for compelling its sale (sec. 10). Provision was also made for compensation to the owners of property destroyed in case of invasion or threat of invasion (sec. 11). 1803.

This Act was apparently designed to encourage men to enrol themselves in the Volunteers; but it was, on the face of it, a half-hearted measure, and it is difficult to see why the Lieutenants should have been put to the trouble of ascertaining whether men were willing to serve in defence of their country, when the King had the undoubted right to call on them to serve whether willing or unwilling. However, the Act was circulated in the counties on 24th June for what it might be worth.

Then came a new complication. Sailors were wanted for the Navy, and a good many seafaring men had been enrolled in the Militia, probably as substitutes, being tempted either by the bounty or by this opportunity of escaping impressment. An Act (43 Geo. III. cap. 62)[1] was passed on the 24th of June authorising all such men to be discharged from the Militia into the fleet, provided that not more than one-tenth of the full number of

[1] A similar Act for Ireland (43 Geo. III. cap. 76) was passed on 4th July 1803.

1803. privates in any regiment were so discharged at any one time. The men on being taken into the Navy were to receive the usual bounty granted to seamen, and were bound to serve till the end of the war and until three months after the ratification of a definitive treaty of peace. Their late colonels were authorised to fill their places by the enlistment of voluntary recruits,[1] by beat of drum or otherwise, and were to receive ten guineas a man for the purpose, which sum was to be ultimately charged to the account of the Navy. Thus to the three different descriptions of recruits already supplied to the Militia under the Militia Act, viz. lotmen, personal substitutes, and parochial substitutes, there was added a fourth—voluntary enlisters for an increased bounty. Moreover, as the Militiamen transferred to the Navy were not required to disgorge the bounty which they had received upon entering the Militia, the country was put to the expense of paying twice over for their services. It will be remembered that seamen and seafaring men were exempted from the Militia ballot under section 43 of the Militia Act of 1802; but there was no provision to prevent them from being enrolled either as principals or as substitutes.

Yet another little Act was rendered necessary by the fact that, though the Militia Act of 1802 duly provided for raising the Supplementary Militia, it had omitted the means of supplying the increased numbers with a due proportion of officers. This defect was accordingly made good by an Act for Augmenting the Number of Field Officers and other Officers of Militia within Great Britain (43 Geo. III. cap. 71, 8th July 1803.

III

Meanwhile the Government had decided, or thought that it had decided, upon a definite plan for Volunteers. The Secretary of State accordingly informed the Lords-

[1] They are called volunteers under the Act, but I have avoided the word to save confusion.

Lieutenant of the fact in a circular of the 20th of June, intimating at the same time that no Volunteers accepted after the 16th of June should be exempt from the ballot for a new force, which was about to be called into existence. On that same day, the 20th of June, Mr. Yorke introduced the measures for the creation of this new force. These, though entitled the Additional Force Acts, became better known as the Army of Reserve Acts (England, 43 Geo. III. cap. 82; Scotland, cap. 83; Ireland, cap. 85; 6th July 1803). The Acts ordained that there should be raised by ballot, under the Militia laws, 34,000 men for England, 6000 for Scotland, and 10,000 for Ireland.[1] Exemption, over and above the exemptions granted by the Militia Acts of 1802, was given to poor men who had more than one child born in lawful wedlock under ten years of age, or who were infirm; and the Deputy-Lieutenants were further empowered to discharge any ballotted man who was unfit for service through infirmity or otherwise, if his worldly possessions did not amount to the value of £100 (secs. 6, 13).[2] Exemption was also granted to any who had served personally or by substitute in the Militia (unless their turn to be ballotted should in rotation have come round again), and to all Volunteers and Yeomanry who had been enrolled and had entered their names on the muster-roll before the 22nd of June 1803; provided that, in the case of country corps, their offer of service extended, in event of invasion, to the whole of their military district, or in the case of London, Bristol, Exeter, Liverpool, Chester, Manchester, Hull, Norwich, Leeds, York, Sheffield and Birmingham, Edinburgh and Glasgow, to the defence of these cities and their respective vicinities. Men who had served in the Army, or as substitutes, personal or parochial,[3] in

1803.

[1] Besides these, the City of London, which by charter was exempt from furnishing men for military service, volunteered to raise 800 men for the Army of Reserve, and was empowered to do so by 43 Geo. III. cap. 101; 27th July 1803.

[2] The references are to the English Act.

[3] The words of the Act are "substitutes or volunteers," as usual

1803. the Militia, and had been discharged therefrom, were expressly excepted from this exemption (sec. 8).

The standard of height for the Army of Reserve was five feet two inches only, if the man were "otherwise able-bodied and fit for service" (sec. 9); and it was enacted that notice to a ballotted man's wife, family, or servant was to be sufficient to subject him to the penalties of desertion if he did not present himself within fourteen days of such notice.

Service could be commuted in two ways: (1) by producing a substitute of the same or some adjoining county, the limitation placed by the Militia Act upon the number of a substitute's children being removed (sec. 14); (2) by payment of a fine of £20, which, however, did not purchase immunity from the ballot for more than one year. Ballotted men who neglected to pay this fine or to find a substitute could be compelled to serve (sec. 15). Of each fine of £20 one-half was paid to the overseers to provide a parochial substitute (sec. 17), and the remainder to the Paymaster-General of the Army; and, as in the case of the Militia, parishes were empowered to evade a ballot, in whole or in part, by producing "volunteers," that is to say, parochial substitutes, and paying them the "average price of a substitute" out of the parochial rates. If the number of parochial substitutes presented before the ballot by any subdivision amounted to two-thirds of its quota, the ballot could be suspended for six days, and these days of grace could be still further prolonged by the Royal consent, to give time for the production of the remaining third (sec. 22). It was also ordained that half the current price of a substitute, according to the estimate of the Deputy-Lieutenants, should be paid to every man who served in person or by substitute,

without defining what description of Volunteer is intended, though (as the reader may have remarked) the word Volunteer has already, in the Acts already cited, been used in three different senses. I take the purport of the Act, however, to have been that no service in the Militia, except in person or by (not *as*) a substitute, was to grant exemption.

provided that his worldly estate was less than £500 in value (secs. 23, 25). Moreover, every principal upon accepting service was to receive two guineas bounty, and every substitute one guinea, from the general funds of the county, the money being paid to the captains of the companies and accounted for by them to the men (secs. 25, 26). It may be reckoned that each man received one-half of this sum after deduction of half a guinea for necessaries. 1803.

All men enrolled under the Act were sworn to serve in the United Kingdom and Channel Islands only, principals for five years, substitutes for five years or until six months after a definitive peace. All enrolled men, whether principals or substitutes, were further required to swear that they were not ruptured nor subject to fits, nor otherwise physically disabled, and that they were not apprentices, seamen, members of the Army, Navy, Marines, or Militia (sec. 19). After enrolment they could either be formed into new corps or embodied in old regiments, though never outside the United Kingdom and Channel Islands, and they were to be subject to the Mutiny Act (sec. 29). Vacancies through death or discharge were to be filled up, as in the Militia, by ballot (sec. 31); and the wives and families of Army Reserve men were entitled to parochial support in the same way as Militiamen (sec. 33). They were allowed to enlist into the Regular Army if they wished; and in this case the parishes were not compelled to fill the vacancies thus made (sec. 33). Colonels of regiments were required to furnish lists of vacancies to the Quarter Sessions of each county on the 29th of September 1803; and for every man deficient of the quota a fine of £20 was to be imposed, a further fine of the same sum being added cumulatively every quarter until the deficiency should be made good (sec. 35). It was specially added that the raising of men under this Act was to be no excuse for not levying men as usual for the embodied Militia.

The Scottish Act was the same *mutatis mutandis*,

1803. except that the fines for commutation of service were to be made over entirely to the parish authorities for the provision of substitutes, any remaining surplus being remitted to the Paymaster-General of the Army.

The Irish Act enacted that the ballot should be employed to raise the Army of Reserve (sec. 11), but if five members of any General Meeting were of opinion that the men could be more expeditiously raised by beat of drum, the Lord-Lieutenant might authorise them to dispense with the ballot (sec. 38). If within five weeks of authorisation the county raised two-thirds of its quota by voluntary enlistment, the Lord-Lieutenant could grant it three weeks' grace to raise the remainder. If without such authority from the Lord-Lieutenant the full quota was not raised in six weeks, or if the three weeks of grace proved to be unavailing, then appeal must be made to the ballot.

Judging from the surface of this Act, the Government's intention was to raise by ballot 50,000 additional Militiamen. The points wherein members of the Army of Reserve mainly differed from Militiamen were that they could be drafted into second battalions of the Regular Regiments at home; that they could enlist from these for general service in the Regular Army; that they need not be more than five feet two inches in height; and that substitutes could be men with any number of children.

This measure had not been law for a fortnight when, on the 18th of July, the Government brought in yet another bill to amend the Defence Act of the 11th of June, "and to enable His Majesty more speedily and effectually to exercise his ancient and undoubted prerogative in requiring the military service of his liege subjects in case of invasion of the realm." This bill passed on the 27th of July, and was known as the Levy en Masse Act (43 Geo. III. cap. 96), the execution of which was as usual thrown upon the Lords-Lieutenant and their Deputies, under the machinery of the Militia Laws. They were required first to obtain lists of all men between the ages of seventeen and fifty-five (sec. 3), and to sort them into four classes : viz. (1) unmarried men under thirty, with no child living under ten years of age ; (2) unmarried men between thirty and fifty, with no child as aforesaid ; (3) married men from seventeen to thirty, with not more than two children living under ten years of age ; (4) all other persons (sec. 4). Exemption was granted to the Judges of the Courts of Law, to persons too infirm for service, clergymen, schoolmasters, Quakers, officers and men actually serving in the Army, Navy, Marines, Militia, and Volunteers, Lords-Lieutenant, Deputy-Lieutenants, and peace officers (sec. 12). But ministers, churchwardens, and parochial officers at large were all required to help in making out the lists (sec. 13). This done, the King could direct any parishes to be provided with arms, which arms were to be stored in the church or other convenient place under the care of the churchwardens, acting under the directions of the Deputy-Lieutenants (sec. 25). The King could order the three first classes to be trained in the use of arms for two hours at least on every Sunday (or other convenient day) in the week, for the entire period between the 25th of March and the 25th of December, the Deputy-Lieutenants being held responsible for such training (sec. 27). In case of emergency the King could further require them to be trained, before Christmas 1803, on successive days during three or more weeks as the Deputy-Lieutenants might arrange, the total number of successive days not to fall below fourteen or rise above twenty (sec. 28). The Deputy-Lieutenants could further appoint a captain, two lieutenants, and an ensign to every 120 men (subject to removal by the King), and the captains could appoint non-commissioned officers (sec. 30). The Deputy-Lieutenants were also empowered to hire out-pensioners to train their men, and to pay them not more than half-a-crown a day out of the parochial rates (sec. 32) ; but a constable was also

1803.

1803. required to be present, under pain of ten shillings fine. The Deputy-Lieutenants were to appoint days of exercise, and residents within four miles of the place of muster were subject to a fine of five shillings in the case of the rich, and one shilling in the case of the poor, if they failed to attend; the above fines being raised respectively to forty shillings and five shillings for non-attendance on three successive days. If the classes should be called up for extraordinary training under sec. 28, the labouring men were to be entitled to pay of one shilling for each attendance (sec. 37). Any man misconducting himself during exercise could be haled before a Deputy-Lieutenant or Justice of the Peace, and fined five shillings or, in default, imprisoned for a week (sec. 44). In case of invasion, or imminent danger of invasion, the King [1] was to direct the whole or part of the men enrolled under the Act, either to be embodied and placed in existing regiments of Regulars, Militia, and Fencibles, or to be formed into new corps. When thus embodied the levies were liable to march to any part of Great Britain and were subject to the Mutiny Act (sec. 44). The King was also empowered to give provisional orders for embodiment previous to invasion (sec. 48); but no man serving under the Act could, under any pretence whatever, be compelled to serve outside Great Britain. The Lieutenants were further required to fix places of assembly and to arrange signals for drawing out the men; and such persons as disobeyed the order or signal to assemble were to be deemed deserters (sec. 50). If any man presented himself on horseback, armed and equipped at his own expense, he was to be attached to some corps of cavalry, and not compelled to serve with the infantry.

If only a part of the classes was to be embodied, the Deputy-Lieutenants were to choose the required number by ballot (sec. 52); but in places where Volunteer corps were formed, or where a number of

[1] The words are "His Majesty *shall* order and direct." (The italics are mine.)

men of any age between seventeen and fifty, equal to three-fourths of the first class, engaged themselves to serve as Volunteers, and to march to any part of Great Britain, the King was empowered to suspend the training prescribed by the Act. For the rest, two guineas were to be paid to every man when called out to repel invasion, in order to provide him with necessaries, and one guinea to enable him to return home after expulsion of the enemy (secs. 59, 60). Their wives and families were also entitled to parochial relief during their absence, as under the provisions of the Militia Act (sec. 61). Meanwhile it was expressly provided that this Act should not exempt men from the ballot for the Militia or the Army of Reserve (sec. 62). 1803.

On the same day (27th July) there was passed another Act for the more speedy completion of the Militia and the Army of Reserve (43 Geo. III. cap. 100), making men who refused to be examined for their fitness for the Militia liable to compulsory service, if found physically able, and lowering the standard of substitutes for the Militia to the height of five feet two inches. Both provisions showed clearly enough that men were difficult to obtain.

Then, though the Levy en Masse Act was the second of its kind, it had hardly been passed before it was found to need amendment. No provision had been made for exonerating persons who changed their parish, or who went abroad, from the penalties imposed by the Act. The King had been empowered to remove officers appointed by the Lords-Lieutenant, but no power had been given to the Lords-Lieutenant to supply the vacancy by a fresh appointment. The number of non-commissioned officers allowed under the Act was insufficient, and, finally, section 32 forbade the Deputy-Lieutenants to hire any sergeant-instructors except out-pensioners of Chelsea. All these matters were set right by the Levy en Masse Amendment Act (43 Geo. III. cap. 120; 11th Aug. 1803). One important alteration was also added, namely, that if the

1803. number of Volunteers in any county were satisfactory to the King, he could suspend the operation of the Levy en Masse Act, even though they did not amount to the prescribed tale of three-fourths of the first class (sec. 1).

On the same day, however, the 11th of August, yet another Act was passed, which was fraught with consequences far more serious. This bore the innocent appellation of an Act to authorise the billeting of Yeomanry and Volunteers when assembled for training, and was known as the Billeting Act (43 Geo. III. cap. 121). The measure certainly contained provisions to justify its title; but it contained also much more. For it ordained the qualification of an effective Yeoman to be twelve days' exercise, and of an effective Infantry Volunteer to be twenty-four days' exercise in the year; and it exempted all such effective men from the ballot not only under the Army Reserve Act, but under any future Act to raise an Additional Force (secs. 1 and 2). The measure contained also two important provisions of another kind. Section 9 subjected the Yeomanry and Volunteers to the Mutiny Act, when called out to repel invasion; while section 11 removed them from the control of the Lords-Lieutenant in the same emergency, and placed them under the Generals commanding districts. Section 13 vested funds subscribed for Volunteer and Yeomanry corps, as well as arms and stores purchased therewith, in the officers commanding those corps; and section 14 made it lawful for such Volunteers as refused to pay sums required from them under the rules of their corps to be haled before a Justice of the Peace, who had power to cause the same, together with a fine of double the amount, to be levied by distress, if necessary, and to be paid to the general stock of the corps.

The meaning of these two last provisions shall in its place be more fully explained. For the present it is enough to draw the reader's attention to them, and to point out that section 14 gave the only power that existed, so far, for enforcing discipline among Volunteers until called out to repel invasion. 1803.

Yet another Act of the same date (43 Geo. III. England, cap. 123; Scotland, cap. 124; 11th Aug. 1803) rectified a mistake in section 5 of the Army of Reserve Acts, and exempted men who were serving personally or by substitute in the Militia from being ballotted for the Army of Reserve, unless their turn to be ballotted had come back in rotation, and conversely delivered those who were serving personally or by substitute in the Army of Reserve from the ballot for the Militia.

With this enactment the session closed; and the wearisome statement of the Acts of Parliament being for the present complete, we must look next to the men who were required to enforce them.

IV

The execution of the Militia Act and its affiliated Acts was committed, as we have seen, to the Lords-Lieutenant of Counties. Necessarily, therefore, much depended upon their goodwill, their zeal, and their capacity. Speaking generally, it may be said that they performed their duties with admirable intelligence, energy, and tact. There were, of course, men of all descriptions among them. A few like Lord Eglinton, Lord Townsend, the Duke of Northumberland, and the Duke of Richmond were military officers of wide experience, considerable technical knowledge, and original ideas; but the majority were simply sensible, industrious, and capable country gentlemen, whose rank and character gave them deserved influence among their peers, and whose weight was sufficient to bear down anything like captious criticism or opposition among their subordinates. A certain number were of course fussy, self-important, and inclined to multiply hard questions and to lengthen out correspondence; but these were not many nor, for all their defects, the least

1803. patriotic or efficient. Three only in the whole of the United Kingdom seem to have been thoroughly unfit for their place; and of these one was a sensitive magnate of slender intellect, who delighted in raising difficulties, the second was disabled by age and infirmity, and the third was accused of giving commissions in the Volunteers to uncertificated bankrupts in order to annoy a brother landlord who was politically opposed to him.[1] In Scotland, where Lords-Lieutenant and Militia were new things, the jealousies of county against county often found expression through their administrative chiefs, but this fault really lay rather in the body of the Scottish people than in the individuals directly concerned.

Probably the greatest trouble of the Lords-Lieutenant all over Great Britain lay with brother magnates of as high position as themselves who, though to the last degree loyal, patriotic, and generous, often wanted to conduct matters according to their own ideas, to erect the corps which they had raised, and which no one but themselves could have raised, into independent units, and to employ them only upon such service as they themselves considered appropriate. Such men required to be handled with much delicacy and tact. If their political opinions differed from those of the Lieutenant, they scented a job in every order and every appointment; and it was only by timely concessions and judicious flattery that they were kept in comparative subordination and good-humour. One of their worst failings was their preference for addressing the Secretary of State direct, instead of through the Lord-Lieutenant, a fault which it was not always easy for the latter, if he happened to be a personal friend, to correct or reprove.

The work thrown upon the Lords-Lieutenant was in many cases extremely heavy. Devon, Lancashire, Hampshire, and the West Riding of Yorkshire were

[1] *I.D.* vol. ii. Berks, *passim*; vol. xxxiv. Worcestershire, *passim*; vol. xii. Edinburgh, C. Hope to S.S. 25th Aug. 1803.

the counties in which, owing to density of population, or extent of territory, or difficulty of communication, or to all three combined, the demands upon them were greatest; but in none of the maritime counties were their duties light. Curiously enough, nearly all of them —even such great men as the Duke of Portland and Lord Fitzwilliam—wrote the whole of their numerous letters with their own hands. A very few always employed a clerk, either because they were crippled by gout or, in at least one case, because the Lieutenant's own handwriting was illegible. The Lieutenant of Devon frequently used his wife as his amanuensis, and it is probable that others did the same.

1803.

Apart from their correspondence, the Lords-Lieutenant of necessity were constantly making journeys to their provincial capitals, to other centres of population, and to the most important of their neighbours and friends, either to consult them or to reconcile differences and put an end to quarrels. In many counties, where the roads followed the old tracks chosen to suit the peculiar requirements of pack-horses, riding was practically the only means of travelling from place to place; and it must have been no uncommon thing for the Lieutenants to be in the saddle at dawn in order to ride thirty or forty miles to a county meeting and return before dark.[1] The postal arrangements were very primitive, and the Post Office, strangled in red-tape, was often a hindrance rather than an aid to the practical transmission of correspondence. It will hardly be believed that as late as November 1803 Lieutenants and Deputy-Lieutenants were called upon to pay postage-fees for letters delivered on the business of the State. Complaints to the Secretary of State brought no relief, until a Deputy-Lieutenant of Sussex wrote to

[1] A generation has arisen which has no idea of the part that riding played formerly in the life of a country gentleman. The present writer, as a boy, was brought up, according to the old traditions, to order out a pony and ride for distances so short that it would have saved time to walk; but to make the shortest journey on foot was unheard of.

1803. his chief that he had recently paid seven shillings for two packets, and that he would receive in future no letters on the public service that did not arrive free of charge.[1]

Of the Deputy-Lieutenants, who formed altogether a very large body, it is less easy to speak. Some of their failings will appear in the ensuing narrative of the administration of the various Acts under the Militia Laws; but in England it seems that the majority did their work with intelligence, loyalty, and goodwill. In some of the wilder parts of the country they had long distances to travel; stupid and inefficient parochial officers to instruct; ignorant, prejudiced, and occasionally lawless peasants to soothe, convince, reconcile or overpower. The work must have made great demands upon their time, their patience, and even their physical endurance, yet as a rule they seem not to have shrunk from it, though their sympathy with their people was often greater than their respect for the law.

V

1802-3. Let us now pass from the letter of the laws, and from those who executed them, to the actual history and effect of their working in the years under review. It will be remembered that the Militia and Volunteer Acts of 1802 were passed in time of peace. The first ballot of the Militia under the new law was likewise held in time of peace, in the course of the winter of 1802, when the defects of the measure very soon became apparent. The purport of the Act was to make a levy of men in just proportion to its population from every parish in the three Kingdoms. The very essence of the force in theory was that the contingent of each county should be drawn from that county, or at least from the border of a neighbouring county. Whether the men were principals or substitutes, and

[1] *I.D.* vol. xxxii. L.L. Sussex, to S.S. 11th Dec. 1803; Lord Gage to L.L. Sussex, 18th Dec. 1803.

whether as substitutes they were personal or parochial, there were special clauses designed to safeguard the local character of the Militia; and though, in the case of substitutes provided by the Deputy-Lieutenants from the proceeds of exemption-fines, there were no special words to enact that these men should be drawn from the district or county, yet the whole spirit of the Act intimated that this was its intention. 1802-3

It must be said at once that, even before war broke out, the bare allowance of the principle of substitution sufficed to nullify these particular provisions of the Militia Act completely. This was due to two principal causes; first, to the want of uniformity in the method of conducting the ballot, and, secondly, to the practice of insurance.

The ballot has been for so long obsolete that the traditions concerning it have utterly perished; and it is now exceedingly difficult to discover anything about it. The one thing that appears certain is that the Deputy-Lieutenants of every subdivision were at liberty, so far as the Act was concerned, to arrange matters as they found most convenient, and that they availed themselves of that liberty with edifying readiness. It is, indeed, probable that there were almost as many methods as counties.

It should seem, however, that the commonest procedure was as follows. First the lots were drawn,[1] and the men upon whom they fell furnished their substitutes or paid the fine which entitled them to five years' exemption. A second ballot was then held, in which the names of the men who had been chosen by the first ballot were omitted; and the victims of the second ballot, upon enrolling themselves or finding a substitute, received the proceeds of the fines paid by the men of the first ballot.[2] The method was curious, and though

[1] The approved method was to write the names of ballottable men on slips of paper, place the slips, folded, in a bag or box, and draw them out one by one in public.

[2] *W.O. Mila. Book*, S.W. to C.G.M. Yorks, 26th July 1803.

1802-3. it was apparently recognised and approved for a time at headquarters,[1] it is easy to see that it was unfair to poor men and tended of itself to raise the price of substitutes. Thus if a really poor man were drawn by the first ballot, he had practically no choice but to accept six guineas and serve. If, on the other hand, he escaped the first ballot, he could be sure of at least ten pounds on being drawn for the second; and if, on the second ballot, additional men paid the fine, and it was necessary to proceed to a third ballot upon the same principle, the men then drawn might well receive £15 or £20.[2]

But throughout the whole of the vast correspondence upon the subject the most remarkable point is, that no one, from the parish overseer to the Secretary of State, ever expected a principal to accept service in the Militia. It was assumed in every quarter that substitutes would be provided practically in every case; and, in fact, in 1803-5, the ballot was simply an instrument for compelling the parishes to organise at their own expense recruiting depôts for the Militia. The means contrived to attain this end were various. The Act itself prescribed one by allowing parishes to produce their quota of so-called volunteers in anticipation of the ballot. In Carnarvonshire[3] the practice was as follows. The Deputy-Lieutenants grouped the parishes together by twos and threes "to make the choice of men as equal as possible"; and the ballot was duly held. But before the ballot it was customary

[1] But Mr. Bragge, when Secretary at War, opined that the practice was illegal, unless the fines paid for exemption were insufficient for the purchase of substitutes. Sec. at War to S.D.C. Essex, 2nd Sept. 1803. It is most improbable that the practice was discontinued in spite of this opinion.

[2] But these sums must not be accepted as exact, for the price of substitutes of course varied according to the demand; and though £6 was by law the extreme fee to be granted to the parochial substitutes known as volunteers, yet section 122 of the Militia Act, as has been seen, gave ballotted men, worth less than £500, half the current price of a substitute.

[3] *I.D.* vol. vi. C.G.M. Carnarvon, to S.S. 29th Jan. 1803.

for the men liable to service to collect money (from what source is not specified) to pay the fine in lieu of personal service. Instead, however, of paying this money to the Deputy-Lieutenants as a fine, pursuant to the directions of the Act, they handed it to the parish overseers, who agreed with them to find their substitutes. The advantage of the plan was this. The mere payment of the fine to the Deputy-Lieutenants would have brought exemption to a man for five years only, whereas the provision of a substitute gave him permanent immunity from the ballot. If the price of a substitute exceeded the means in the hands of the overseers, the overplus was paid by the parish on which the lot happened to fall, on the understanding that the other parishes should in due time contribute their share. The other parishes, however, sometimes declined to pay their contribution when called upon ; and owing to this accident the history of this particular method of applying the ballot has been preserved. For the Deputy-Lieutenants, dismayed at finding the peculiar machinery of their county thrown out of gear, and doubtless stimulated by the cries of the parish which had so imprudently trusted to the good faith of its fellows, actually appealed to the Secretary of State to know if they had any legal remedy against the parishes which had declined to pay the money expected of them. 1802-3.

The whole transaction was, on the face of it, of an extremely doubtful character, for the overseers under the Act were responsible for the preparation of the Militia lists ; yet none of the county authorities saw any harm in converting them into contractors for the supply of recruits. It is hardly to be imagined that the overseers failed to make money out of the business, so that in point of fact they were neither more nor less than official crimps. Section 15 of 43 Geo. III. cap. 50, was of course designed to check this evil, but it could be so easily evaded that it can hardly be treated with serious consideration.

More commonly, however, precisely the same end

1802-3. was attained by different means, namely insurance. In Scotland the practice was "carried to a great height"; but the Militia was so new a thing in North Britain that the country had not learned the higher application of insurance. The policy of a Scottish society insured men only for the price of the exemption fine. The English institutions provided their clients with a substitute or the price of a substitute. In their inception these insurance societies arose in the most natural manner possible. In any given parish or town there was a given number of men liable to be ballotted, of whom in normal times only a small fraction—probably less than one-tenth—was required at one time for service. So many of these as could afford a small outlay met together and agreed to subscribe so much apiece to purchase substitutes for such of their number as might be drawn for service. This was the simplest form of insurance; and hence in the Parliamentary debates the words subscription society and insurance society are used synonymously. In many cases the parochial authorities took the lead in the management of these societies, made the necessary calculations, collected the subscriptions, transacted the whole of the necessary business, and doubtless remunerated themselves, with the full consent of their subscribers, with a small commission for their pains. In Lichfield we learn that at ordinary times the subscription for substitutes was no more than five shillings,[1] though for reasons presently to be shown, it rose to four times that amount before the end of 1803.

In Blackburn, later on in the same year, a still more curious instance came to light which, though it deals with a later phase of affairs, enables us to study the question of insurance in closer detail. After the ballot-list had been published, but before the ballot had taken place, a subscription was set on foot in the town which was open to all whose name appeared on that

[1] *I.D.* vol. xxix. Magistrates of Lichfield to L.L. 19th Nov. 1803.

list. The men to be supplied numbered 36; the subscribers amounted to 512. A contribution of £1 a head was reckoned to be sufficient to enable the subscribers to hire parochial substitutes for the beneficiaries of the society at large, and to pay bounties to men who provided substitutes for themselves. The sum of £189 : 10s. was thus paid out on account of ten of the subscribers, in bounties varying from £16 to £20. As these amounts were equal to the full current price of substitutes, and any additional expenditure on the part of the ballotted men was therefore voluntary and unnecessary, the Deputy-Lieutenants considered that any surplus, remaining after repayment to them of their subscription of £1 and of any little additional expenses, should go to the general fund for the benefit of all the subscribers. The ten men, however, thought differently. Under section 122 of the Militia Act of 1802 ballotted men, worth less than £500, were entitled to receive half the current price of a parochial substitute; and this they claimed as their right. The Deputy-Lieutenants flatly refused to pay it. The men had found their substitutes at a trifling cost, they had also gained exemption from the parish rate levied for the payment of bounties, and the Deputies were furious at the idea of their making also £7 or £8 out of the transaction. It was contrary to all precedent in Lichfield, where the rule was that men who served personally should alone receive back their subscription and half the current price of a substitute. Thereupon the ten men concerned carried their appeal to the Secretary of State, and demanded their half bounty as a right. The matter was referred to the law officers, who were fain to confess that the law was on the side of the claimants, and that the money must be paid.[1] The Secretary of State gave orders accordingly, and the Deputy-Lieutenants were left to take such satisfaction as they might from these very ingenious men. 1803.

[1] *I.D.* vol. cliv., Twelve Liverpool men to S.S. 4th March; Mr. W. Carr to C.G.M. Lancs, 28th Jan. 1804.

1803. The above is the only instance which I have disinterred of men actually making money out of the evasion of service in the Militia; but it is in other ways instructive, since it shows that a subscription club was the ordinary method of raising parochial substitutes, and that it was not only countenanced but actually administered by the Deputy-Lieutenants, the very persons who were responsible for the execution of the Act. There can be little doubt but that the same practice obtained, with superficial differences, in the majority of the parishes in Great Britain. The people made a law for themselves for the conduct of the ballot; and when that law was transgressed, they did not hesitate to invoke the aid of the Secretary of State to enforce it. It seems never to have occurred to them that their local customs, erected as it were behind the back of the law, could have less force than the law itself. Nor indeed apparently did the Secretary of State attempt to override local custom, unless his authority was called in actually to defy the law. Any attempt to do so would probably have made the ballot impossible.

But the petty local insurance clubs and societies were a small matter compared with the much more important institutions which already existed in 1802, and which were destined to extend their operations enormously as ballot succeeded ballot in the years that followed. Their agents were ubiquitous and vigilant. Even in 1802 three men who were travelling north with the certainty of being appointed sergeants of Militia, were intercepted on their way by the emissaries of an insurance society and tempted by large bounties to end their journey and to enlist as substitutes and privates.[1] The great centre of insurance was, of course, London; and there were bitter complaints from all counties around the metropolis that its societies offered their policy-holders either the amount of the fine for exemption or a substitute who invariably deserted.[2] These institutions

[1] *W.O. Mila. Books*, Sec. at War to Lord Galloway, 19th Jan. 1803.
[2] *I.D.* vol. cvi. L.L. Bucks, to S.S. 23rd Oct. 1807.

extended their branches as far as Warwick, probably indeed further, and it seems that they made enormous profits.[1] Sometimes the insurance society consisted of a single enterprising individual, who openly advertised his readiness to provide substitutes at a figure which seemed extravagantly low but beyond question brought him a very handsome income. A Mr. Pearce of Hackney thus filled the ranks of the Tower Hamlets Militia for twelve years, until in 1808 the parish officers, finding that they received no share of his gains, decided to reject every man that he offered, and so ruined his business. Pearce was, of course, hardly, if at all, other than a crimp; yet, amazing as it may seem, his friends appealed to the Secretary of State to support him against the parish officers.[2] 1803.

Thus it has been made sufficiently plain that all the energy and intelligence of the nation, not wholly without countenance by the Legislature, was directed from the very first to evasion of personal service in the Militia. The result was to stultify all legislative provision for making the Militia a strictly local force. In the first place, the Act, as has been seen, did not enact that the parochial substitutes, to be provided by the Deputy-Lieutenants out of the fines for exemption, should be of the same or the adjoining county. In the second place, the main object of the Deputy-Lieutenants, who were but human, was to produce the men required of them and to free themselves from the heavy, irksome, and often distressing duty imposed upon them by the Act. Men did not travel far afield in those days, and the squires, great and small, knowing all that was to be known about every family in their parishes, could appreciate how hardly the ballot would bear upon this man or that. Moreover, the ballottable men were often their own workmen, whom, for their own sakes, they would naturally be unwilling to lose. Hence it is hardly matter of surprise if, after harrowing interviews with

[1] *I.D.* vol. cli. C.G.M. Warwick, to S.S. 23rd Jan. 1808.

[2] *Ibid.* vol. cli. J. Bugby to S.S. 18th Feb. 1808.

1803. tearful mothers, wives, and daughters, they should have listened to plausible persons who offered to provide any number of substitutes at a moderate charge, without ascertaining too particularly whether the said substitutes really came from the same or an adjoining county. It was always easy for a crimp or an insurance agent to say that they were from the county town, and very difficult to prove that they were not. The wording of the Act also permitted much laxity of interpretation, for it did not provide that substitutes should be men *on the ballot-lists* of the same or an adjoining county, which they certainly ought to have been if they were to be properly qualified. The desire, then, for a quiet life and for the sight of happy faces about them did much to make Deputy-Lieutenants disregard the enactments for making the Militia a local force.

In the large towns a different set of causes produced precisely the same effect. About London the five Militia battalions of Middlesex and Surrey, after many ballots and many disappointments, abandoned in despair the task of raising men upon the spot and sought them elsewhere. Any number of men were forthcoming in London itself, but they disappeared with amazing speed as soon as their bounty was in their pockets. The Lord-Lieutenant did his best to meet this evil by marching the men out of the county as soon as they were enrolled, so as to make desertion more difficult; and he actually suspended the ballot until he could obtain permission to do so. But even so, his success was small.[1] In September 1803, after eight or nine months of effort, the West Middlesex and Westminster battalions had not yet made up the numbers of their original establishment, and had not raised a man of their Supplementary Militia.[2] The East Middlesex battalion was stronger, but this was because the commanding officer had early sent recruiting parties to Norwich to

[1] *I.D.* vol. xxiii. L.L. Middlesex, to S.S. 6th and 9th July 1803.

[2] *Ibid.* vol. xxiii. L.L. Middlesex, to S.S. 15th Sept. 1803.

collect men. The Westminster battalion followed his example by sending a party to Birmingham, nominally to arrest deserters, but really to enlist recruits. The practice was plainly illegal, and the Secretary at War repeatedly pointed out that it was so; but Colonel Wood of the East Middlesex let the letters from the War Office pass unheeded and went his own way, knowing that if he were to conform to the law he would have not a man in his battalion.[1] Moreover, as the Secretary at War was fain to confess, there was no penalty provided in any Act to check this particular breach of the law, which meant that there was no protection for any district against any other district which chose to steal its men. It is an actual fact that in the ranks of the Middlesex Militia, whose quota (including the Supplementary Militia) was over 4500 men, there was but one principal to be found; and when his time of service expired in 1808, the Lord-Lieutenant begged to be allowed to keep him as a curiosity.[2] 1803.

On the south side of the Thames the case was precisely the same. Substitutes were presented as fast as they were called for, only to disappear beyond hope of recall within forty-eight hours. At the beginning of April 1803, after endless ballotting, the southward district of Surrey had produced only 22 men out of its quota of 288; and the Clerk of the General Meeting declared the task of raising the rest to be hopeless unless the substitutes could be at once carried off to headquarters, dressed, powdered, and furnished with queues, so as to make them easily recognisable.[3] It is not recorded that the difficulty was overcome in the same way as in Middlesex, but it is reasonable to assume so; and with all London open to them for substitutes, it is impossible

[1] *W.O. Mila. Entry Books*, Sec. at War to T. Kerrison, Esq., 1st June, to O.C., E. Middlesex Mila. 15th June, 3rd Oct. 1803; 6th Jan., 22nd June 1804; 14th Feb. 1805; to O.C., Westminster Mila. 28th June 1803; to O.C., E. Middlesex Mila. 11th Feb. 1808.

[2] *I.D.* vol. cxlii. L.L. Middlesex, to S.S. 24th March 1808.

[3] *Ibid.* vol. xxxi. C.G.M. Surrey, to L.L. 4th April 1803.

1803. to suppose that the Surrey Militia can have included many Surrey men.

VI

The reader will naturally ask whether the reluctance to serve in the Militia was so general as the foregoing narrative would lead one to suppose. The answer is certainly in the affirmative; and the prime reasons undoubtedly were that, contrary to the spirit of the elder Pitt's original Act, personal service was not insisted upon and the Militia was not made a truly national force. There was, however, far less reluctance in England than in Scotland, where the Militia had been unknown until 1797. From almost every county in Scotland, even before the war broke out, came the same tale of difficulty in obtaining not only men but officers, and of perfunctory conduct, or worse, on the part of Deputy-Lieutenants. In Aberdeen ballotted men invariably paid the fine for exemption, and no gentleman would accept even a captain's commission when offered to him.[1] In Banff, again, only one duly qualified gentleman could be persuaded to become a captain.[2] In Haddington there was the like dearth of officers, and in Peebles the like unwillingness of men.[3] In Bute there were only five men in the Militia who had not been drawn from other counties, and not one single ballotted man had been enrolled.[4] From Ross came the report that the Highlanders would have nothing to do with the Militia; that the most mountainous district had not produced a man; that the Militia laws were ill understood by magistrates and Deputy-Lieutenants, and that, being an innovation, they were detested by the Highlanders as an intolerable grievance.[5] In Stirling the

[1] *I.D.* vol. i. L.L. to S.S. 15th Jan., 22nd July 1803.

[2] *Ibid.* vol. iii. L.L. to S.S. 4th April 1803.

[3] *Ibid.* vol. iv. L.L. Haddington, to S.S. 16th March; C.G.M. Peebles, to S.S. 19th June 1803.

[4] *Ibid.* vol. xxxvii. L.L. Argyll and Bute, 5th Sept. 1804.

[5] *Ibid.* vol. vi. V.L. Ross, to S.S. 1803.

Lieutenancy had done its work so ill that in several cases the same man had been enrolled and had received bounty for several different subdivisions.[1] In Selkirk the Lord-Lieutenant despaired of providing his quota of twelve men for the Supplementary Militia, though he could count upon payment of the fines.[2] Forfar could show but one principal to every six substitutes, and to every five men that paid the fine for exemption.[3] From Kirkcudbright the Lord-Lieutenant reported that almost the whole of the Militia would be substitutes, and that the insurance societies had been largely patronised in the towns.[4] In Perth it was a case of few enrolments and many fines.[5] In fact, the service was not only unpopular but suspected; for it was bound up with an oath and a red coat, and it was hard to make the cautious Scots believe that this combination did not signify compulsory military service for life. 1803.

In England, though there were a few places in which the same superstition existed, there was generally no dread of unfair treatment of Militiamen; and yet the Service was disliked, and not only disliked, but not unfrequently despised. This was due, no doubt, to the practice, consecrated by Pitt, of permitting men to serve their country as Volunteers, or, in other words, of allowing the mass of the citizens to substitute undisciplined for disciplined service. The Militia, during embodiment, was subjected to the same penal code as the Army, not excluding the lash. Had personal service been enforced, the character [6] of the men would have been so superior that the cat-o'-nine-tails would have fallen almost into disuse except in rare cases, when, in the judgment of that day, it was the only possible penalty. For it must be

1 *I.D.* vol. viii. L.L. Stirling, to S.S. 3rd June 1803.

2 *Ibid.* vol. xi. L.L. Selkirk, to S.S. 15th June, 3rd July 1803.

3 *Ibid.* vol. xiv. L.L. Forfar, to S.S. 4th July 1803.

4 *Ibid.* vol. xvii. L.L. to S.S. 23rd Jan. 1803.

5 *Ibid.* vol. xxvii. L.L. to S.S. 24th June 1803.

6 It will be remembered that Abercromby pronounced the Militiamen under his command in 1799 to be of a superior class to the ordinary recruits.

1803. remembered that flogging formed as essential a part of civil as of military punishment at that period. The officers of the Militia, especially in the higher ranks, bore some of the greatest names in England; and even if occasionally petty squires and their sons were disposed to be tyrannical, there were probably always men of higher social position in the same battalion to keep them in restraint. But when the ranks of the Militia were filled with men who, if they had not become substitutes, would have enlisted in the Army, the case was completely changed. The lash was absolutely necessary for the enforcement of discipline; and flogging, though unknown in some battalions, was certainly not unknown in others. The waged class in those days, it must also be remembered, was far more lawless, violent, and reckless than in these, and, unless subjected to some born leader of men, did not understand gentle measures.

But, in the writer's opinion, the prevailing prejudice and contempt towards the Militia, which is as strong to-day as it was then, was only a part of the general dislike and distrust which Englishmen had for generations been trained to cherish against a Standing Army. Before the elder Pitt took the Militia in hand in 1757, the force was popular but utterly useless. When it was founded upon an effective basis its popularity rapidly waned; and when, after long years of disuse, the ballot was applied to it, it became hateful. The truth is that the ballot hit the class which has always been most averse from military service, and loves nothing of war except its trappings, because it may possibly gain money by them. It was this class that, by its superiority of education and its greater power and facility of self-protection, formed subscription societies and insurance companies, and made the largest fortunes by crimping. Its members, which could have best afforded to pay dearly for substitutes, obtained the first call upon them and bought them at the cheapest rate. Even failing a substitute, the purchase of five years' exemption for £10, which was prohibitive to a labouring man, was well within their means. Had the fine been £100 instead of £10, the distribution of the burden would have been infinitely more equitable. 1803.

Yet another cause which brought the Militia into general dislike was the principle of paying for a national object out of strictly local taxation. To take the simplest instance of its injustice, a battalion of Militia stationed in an unhealthy quarter, or detailed for duty in exposed situations, necessarily suffered greater losses from sickness and death than others in more favourable circumstances. Yet the burden of making good the casualties was thrown upon the unfortunate county, and in that county upon the unfortunate parishes, which had provided the dead or disabled men. And closely bound up with the inequality of this taxation was the extreme crudity of the system of exemptions. To give but one example, any man who had served for four years as an officer in the Militia was exempt. But a man who had served for twenty years in the Regular Army and had, it might be, sold his commission and retired to the country broken down by wounds or disease after active service in pestilent climates, was still liable to enter the ranks, pay a fine, or purchase a substitute, provided that he was, as he very well might be, under forty-five years of age. There was no point upon which the Secretary of State insisted more strongly than that neither officers nor men who had served in the Regular Army were, or ever had been, exempt from the Militia ballot solely on that account.[1] It is easy to conceive of cases in which this decision was perfectly just; but it is not less easy to see that it might be both unfair and oppressive. Moreover, it was false policy to put a soldier, who might have given the best years of his life to his country's service, on the same level with petty attorneys and tradesmen, who had never worked for any interest except their own, and never intended to do so. It was

[1] *W.O. Mila. Books*, Mr. Lewis to Col. Matthew, 28th Oct.; S.W. to Captain Hardwicke, 13th June; to F. Davies, 28th June 1803.

1803. a weak point throughout the Act that it conferred no advantages for previous good service to the State. There was a case in which the last remaining son of a poor old couple in Northamptonshire was ballotted. They had given two sons to the Guards, and had lost them both on active service, and they had at the moment three more sons serving in the Militia. Yet it was only by appeal of the Lord-Lieutenant to the Secretary of State that any consideration could be obtained for them ; and meanwhile they were unavoidably kept for many days in miserable suspense.[1]

Another most amazing fact is that though parish officers, being concerned with the ballot, were exempt from it, Deputy-Lieutenants were not. The question was actually raised through the ballotting of a Deputy-Lieutenant by his brethren, and the matter was referred to the Secretary of State. His answer was that he would make inquiry as to the general practice in the kingdom ; to which the Lord-Lieutenant rejoined that the practice varied, and that the Law-Officers of the Crown ought to settle the question once for all without loss of time. The Law-Officers opined that Deputy-Lieutenants were *not* exempt from the Militia ballot. To this the Deputy-Lieutenant concerned made answer that in that case he would resign. If, he said, there were no exemption at all, he would not complain, but if peers were exempted, why not Deputy-Lieutenants? Officers of Militia were required and bound to obey the orders of the Deputy-Lieutenants ; and any three Deputy-Lieutenants, commissioned to act as the Lord-Lieutenant, could review the Militia. How could ballotted privates give commands to their own officers? The Secretary of State wisely made no attempt to meet these unanswerable arguments, but replied in true official style, that the Government would not submit to Parliament any bill to exempt Deputy-Lieutenants from the ballot ; and there the matter ended. There

[1] *I.D.* vol. xxv. Mr. de C. Brooke to L.L. Northants, 28th Sept. 1804.

can be little doubt as to who was in the right of the question.[1] 1803.

It was unfair, again, that such a misfortune as physical infirmity should in no case have given relief from the Militia ballot unless a man were worth less than £100. Of course, the Deputy-Lieutenants could always reject a man for the Militia if he were below five feet four inches in height; and no doubt this rule was frequently stretched in the interests of humanity to give deliverance in many hard cases. But it is to be noted that the Deputy-Lieutenants were not *bound* to reject men who fell below that stature; and that the deficiency of inches of itself gave no immunity from the ballot and its consequences.[2] By the letter of the law, therefore, a hunchback from three to four feet in height, under forty-five years of age, and worth £101, was liable to pay a fine of £10 for five years' exemption, provide a substitute, or serve in person; and the fine could be extorted from him by distraint upon his goods.[3] It is noticeable too, in reference to the position of the sick and infirm under the Militia Act, that not a word was said as to the exemption of practising doctors, an omission which was resented in those days, and would be still more resented in these, from the hardship which it meted out both to members of a singularly self-denying profession and to their unfortunate patients.

VII

Enough has been said to show, without further analysis of the list of exemptions, that apart from all

1 *I.D.* vol. clxvii. L.L. Leicestershire, to S.S. 9th Nov.; S.S. to L.L. 15th Nov., 18th Dec.; Mr. Burnaby to S.S. 28th Dec. 1809; S.S. to Mr. Burnaby, 29th Jan. 1810.

2 *W.O. Mila. Books*, S.W. to F. Davies, 28th June 1803.

3 *Ibid.* S.W. to R. Else, 26th July 1811. "The Law officers have decided that a man worth more than £100, ballotted and willing to serve, but physically unfit, is obliged to find a substitute, under sections 45 and 52 of 42 Geo. III. cap. 90."

1803. prejudice against the Militia, and from all ignoble shirking of national duty, there was sound reason why many should find the Act of 1802 both unfair and oppressive. There was, therefore, much real justification for subscription societies, insurance companies, and all the other apparatus of evasion; and the result was that the poor, upon whom the law was not intended to bear with peculiar hardness, suffered from it beyond all others. There was a general demand for substitutes to make up the original establishment of the Militia under conditions of peace, and prices soon began to rise. In Hampshire there was a rush to obtain temporary employment in the dockyards in order to gain immunity from the ballot.[1] In the East Riding of Yorkshire the Lord-Lieutenant declared that unless the entire area of Yorkshire was thrown open to him for substitutes, he would be unable to fill the ranks of the county regiment. Men could not be bought even in March 1803 for the amount of the £10 fine, nor at "scarce any price."[2] Details of the price of substitutes at the outbreak of the war are unfortunately rare, for the Lieutenancies were still in full struggle with their first difficulties when the proclamation of the 28th of May threw upon them the duty of raising the Supplementary in addition to the Old or Established Militia. By that day there had been raised of the Old Militia 34,302 men out of a quota of 43,539 in England; 5965 out of 8000 in Scotland; 12,369 out of 15,000 in Ireland. Thus after fully six months of incessant ballotting and general exertion there were still 13,903 men wanting out of a total establishment of 66,539, making a total deficiency of fully twenty per cent; and now there was demanded in Great Britain a further contingent of rather more than 25,000 men. Moreover, on the 15th of June, almost before the

[1] *I.D.* vol. xvi. L.L. Hants, to S.S. 7th Jan. 1803.

[2] *Ibid.* vol. xxxvi. L.L. Yorks E.R. to S.S. 9th March; O.C., E. York Mila. to S.S. 13th March; Resolution of the Lieutcy. Yorks E.R. 26th March.

Lords-Lieutenant had had time to set the necessary machinery in motion, the Act for completing the Militia (43 Geo. III. cap. 50) became law, which raised the fine for exemption to £15, and inflicted on the counties a cumulative penalty of £10 quarterly for every man deficient of their quota. 1803.

This augmentation naturally increased the demands for substitutes; for the provision of a substitute, it must be remembered, entitled a ballotted man to exemption for life, whereas a fine gave him immunity only for a term of years. Naturally the price of the article rose rapidly in the market, with all other prices that were dependent on it. In Anglesey in May 1803 substitutes cost from £12 to £13. In Denbigh not one could be bought in June for less than £20. In Berkshire during the same month they received from £15 : 15s. to £21 : 10s, and were difficult to obtain even at that price.[1] In Middlesex the Lord-Lieutenant, by throwing all his Supplementary Militia into one of his three battalions, was able to complete that one to its ordinary establishment, and was obliged to leave the remaining two far below theirs.[2] In fact, the Supplementary Militia in the metropolis was merely a name, for the Old Militia was still far below its strength. In Scotland the raising of additional Militiamen was almost as great a farce as in London.[3] In Essex, and possibly in other counties,

[1] *I.D.* vol. i. L.L. Anglesey, to S.S. 21st May; vol. ii. L.L. Berks, to S.S. 23rd June; vol. ix. L.L. Denbigh, to S.S. 31st July 1803.

[2] *Ibid.* vol. xxii. L.L. Middlesex, to S.S. 15th Sept. 1803.

[3] I subjoin a return, probably more favourable than the ordinary, of the progress of the ballot in Forfar. It shows how many men had to be ballotted to produce a small quota. Unfortunately such returns are all too rare in the correspondence.

Men ballotted for Supplementary Militia on 13th June, 88	
Of which enrolled, Principals, 3; Substitutes, 33	36
Paid the £15 penalty	17
Unfit or exempt, for which others were ballotted	33
Failed to attend	2
Total	88

1803. a new method of evasion was discovered. Some ingenious person on studying the Act found out that if he refused to swear that he was not ruptured, nor subject to fits, nor physically disabled, the Deputy-Lieutenants had no power to enrol him even if they knew his objection to be false. Instantly the epileptic and the afflicted with hernia were multiplied manifold in Essex, and the Secretary of State could only make a memorandum to omit this clause from future enactments.[1]

Such new enactments, as we have seen, were not long in coming. Before the Lieutenancies had well digested the proclamation for the Supplementary Militia and the Militia Completion Act, they were required to swallow the Army of Reserve Act, bidding them levy before Michaelmas yet another forty thousand men by ballot in Great Britain, on pain of a cumulative quarterly fine of £20 for every man deficient. This brought up the total of men to be raised in Great Britain within less than twelve months to 117,000. Moreover, by comparison of the Acts of Parliament it will be seen that the Lieutenants had practically to collect this number under three different sets of conditions. Men ballotted for the Militia before the 28th of May (the date of summons to the Supplementary Militia) were exempt for five years on payment of £10; men ballotted after that date could not gain the

Final Ballot

Total enrolled for County of Forfar, Principals, 12; Substitutes, 76	88
Unfit or exempt, for whom others were ballotted	88
Paid the £15 penalty	60
Allowed time to find Substitutes	2
Failed to appear (warrants issued)	18
Total	256

(*I.D.* vol. xiv. Forfar, 4th July 1803).

[1] *I.D.* vol. xiii. Essex, Mr. Bosanquet to L.L. 3rd July 1803. But the clause, or rather the oath, as to rupture and fits was never abrogated.

same exemption for less than £15; men drawn for the Army of Reserve could purchase only one year's exemption from that particular ballot by payment of £20. Again, the payment of fines for exemption from the Militia gave no immunity from the Army of Reserve, though service in person or by substitute in either force gave exemption from service in the other. Also, the exemption fines of the Militia were given complete to the Deputy-Lieutenants for the purchase of substitutes; but those of the Army of Reserve were, in England, divided between the Deputy-Lieutenants and the Paymaster-General. Next, the standard for the Militia was five feet four inches until the 27th of July, when the Act 43 Geo. III. cap. 100, lowered the height required for substitutes to five feet two inches, leaving that for principals untouched; while the standard for the Army of Reserve was five feet two inches for all. Lastly, Volunteers enrolled before the 22nd of June alone were exempted as such from the Army of Reserve; a simple matter which is repeated here because it presently became complicated to the last degree. 1803

The unhappy Lieutenancies bent themselves once more to the eternal round of ballots amid ever-increasing difficulties, for the Army of Reserve Act was loathed as alike oppressive and unfair. Men who had paid £10 or £15, sometimes indeed both sums in succession, in purchasing exemption from the Militia, complained that the Government should have warned them that this penalty would not avail them against the Army of Reserve, so that they might have spent their money on a substitute. "The people," wrote the Duke of Richmond from Goodwood, ". . . have become suspicious of the magistrates. They cannot understand how a new Act can violate the engagement of the old. A ballot is a ballot with them, and when they have bought exemption from one, they cannot understand how they are liable to another. I warned Addington of this, and hoped Parliament would make some remedy."[1] It was

[1] *I.D.* vol. xxxii. L.L. Sussex, to S.S. 23rd Aug. 1803.

1803. useless for men to chafe. The question was raised more than once, but the Secretary of State was inexorable—fines paid in composition for service in the Militia were not valid as against the Army of Reserve; nor fines paid for the Army of Reserve against the Militia.[1]

If there had been a rush for substitutes before, there was now a headlong scramble. Their price, in spite of the relaxation of the rules concerning them, flew up by leaps and bounds to an extravagant height. The Secretary of State himself recognised that it was hard to expect the ranks to be filled while recruits were so dear, but he made no sign of relaxing the fines upon the parishes for men deficient. As to the Deputy-Lieutenants, they were driven in desperation to hoard the exemption-fines which were paid to them against the happy day when recruits should be cheaper, or when a lucky windfall should deliver into their hands poachers or other criminals who would be glad to serve in order to escape the gaol.[2] They suffered a sad shock when the Law-Officers of the Crown pronounced in July that, though the payment of a fine exonerated an individual from serving in person or by substitute in the Militia or Reserve, it did not exonerate the parish from fulfilling the vacancy.[3] Since the price of a substitute exceeded twice the amount of the fine, this decision practically required them, to put matters crudely, to make one sovereign purchase as much as two. But even so their cup was not yet full, for over and above three separate levies and the voluminous returns required by the first Defence Act, there fell upon them in August the heaviest blow of all, namely, the wholesale and unexpected exemption from the ballot of some hundreds of thousands of Volunteers.

[1] *W.O. Mila. Books,* S.S. to Sir A. Duckenfield, 1st July; to W. Walcot, 20th July 1803; *I.D.* vol. i. L.L. Beds. to S.S. 2nd July 1803.

[2] *Ibid.* S.W. to Messrs. Edwards and Hughes, 11th July; to Sir H. Hanley, 22nd July 1803.

[3] *Ibid.* S.W. to High-Sheriff of Cardigan, 1st Aug. 1803.

VIII

So far the subject of the Volunteers has been but lightly touched ; and it is now necessary to enter into it more deeply. They were reconstituted, it will be remembered, under the Volunteer Act of 1802, which granted to them and to the Yeomanry (who at that time were ranked as Volunteers) exemption from the Militia ballot in consideration of their attendance at five days' exercise in the year. Their allowances were also fixed at £2 a man to every Volunteer for his clothing and appointments, and £60 a year for every troop of Yeomanry which numbered at least forty rank and file. As the prospects of continued peace became more dubious, the Government, on the 31st of March 1803, invited offers from additional Volunteers, and gave an outline of the plan on which it intended to act, adding that "it must be considered with reference to a permanent system rather than to a situation of emergency," and that the extent of its application must be determined by circumstances. Finally, it directed that all offers of service should be communicated to the Secretary of State, in order that a selection might be made. As to the proposed regulations (which were presently to be slightly modified) it will suffice to say at present that they provided for paying the men for two days' exercise in every week from Lady Day to Michaelmas, and granted them exemption from the Militia ballot during their term of service. But the point that calls for notice is that a Government which talked about erecting a permanent system, and added in the same breath that "the extent of its application must be determined by circumstances," could not be considered to be clear as to its own intentions. 1803.

The new regulations remained under consideration for two months, in the course of which they were submitted to Colonel Vyse, an officer who had gained considerable experience of Volunteers in Scotland during the late war. His advice may be summed up

1803. as follows:—(1) Do not be too hard in grudging pay to officers; they throw it into a general fund to make good deficient allowances. (2) Make every corps swear to serve in any part of Great Britain in case of invasion; and (3) to obey the orders of the King and of the Generals appointed by him. (4) Form regular regiments in the great towns only;[1] encourage independent companies in the coast towns only, and possibly a few in the north, but not so as to incur the heavy and useless expense of the last war. Seventy-five corps, with 12,560 men, will be ample for Scotland; in the last war you had 228 corps with 30,000 men. You might add a few more men on the coast, but always as parts of battalions. (5) The great defect of our last Volunteers was the confused and unmilitary conditions under which they were formed. Establish one system for all for clothing, interior economy and discipline, and we shall hear no more of committees, quarrels, and insubordination. (6) Men should be required to give so many days' notice of resignation. (7) The Government should have arms ready to give to every accepted corps.

This was excellent and sound advice. Against the second article the Secretary of State wrote the words, "I prefer to trust to the spirit of the corps"; and against the third, "Very proper, but *quaere*." It will presently be seen that the Government gave much the same degree of attention to the whole of Vyse's recommendations.

Meanwhile the offers of Volunteers increased; and in June the Government at last produced and circulated their definite plan for the Volunteers.[2]

[1] Three regiments in Edinburgh; two in Glasgow; one each in Perth, Dundee, and Aberdeen.

[2] I cannot give the date of the circular, for I cannot find a sign of it in the Entry Books; but the new plan seems to have been circulated to the Scottish Lords-Lieutenant on 20th June. Other important letters were also unentered; and I have been obliged to gather their purport from the answers sent to them. Nay, so careless were the clerks, that the "June Allowances" themselves, the centre of thousands of letters and the subject of innumerable speeches, would

This plan or code of regulations was known by the name of the "June Allowances," a name which the reader must be careful to bear in mind; for he will shortly be confronted with another code under the name of the "August Allowances." Its purport was as follows:— 1803.

(1) Every man must take the oath of allegiance.

(2) Every corps that claims pay must engage to serve in any part of its Military District.

(3) Battalions of ten companies, or of 250 to 500 men, will be allowed to have an Adjutant and a Sergeant-Major on permanent pay.

(4) Companies are not to be of fewer than 50 men, or of more than 100. Four officers will be allowed to companies containing 80 or more men.

(5) Sergeants on daily pay and drummers on constant pay are to be subject to military law.

(6) In each company one officer, not above the rank of Captain, will be allowed to draw pay. If he is taken from the half-pay and has served eighteen months in the Regulars, Embodied Militia, or Fencibles, he will receive the constant pay of his rank as a Volunteer. One such officer, not on half-pay, who has served two years in the Regulars, Embodied Militia, or Fencibles, may receive constant half-pay of his rank as a Volunteer. Other officers are to receive pay for each day's exercise, as do the men. No officer is to receive pay for two commissions.

(7) The former services of the officers on constant pay must be stated in the pay-list.

(8) When Volunteers are not called out, constant pay will be allowed for one sergeant and one drummer in each company at the same rate as in the disembodied Militia. The rest of the non-commissioned officers and

have been undiscoverable had not a Lieutenant fortunately sent his own copy back to the Home Office to emphasise his views as to their meaning. Indeed, if a paper were printed at that time, the chances are that not a copy of it is to be found. The clerks appear to have kept loose copies for their own use, but only occasionally to have stuck one into the Entry Book for record. This is all of a piece with the general slovenliness of their conduct of business.

1803. men are to receive pay at the same rate as the disembodied Militia for two days in every week from the 25th of February to the 24th of October, and for one day a week from the 25th of October to the 24th of February, making in all eighty-five days' pay for effectives under arms on each day.

(9) Corps called out to suppress riots will receive pay as disembodied Militia;[1] if called out to repel invasion they will receive the same pay as the Regular Army.

(10) Clothing for infantry is to be red; for artillery blue; for rifles, green with black belts.

Clothing Allowances

	£	s.	d.	
For each Sergeant . .	£3	3	9	Once in three years.
,, Corporal . .	1	12	0	
,, Drummer . .	2	3	6	
,, Private . .	1	10	0	

For permanent non-commissioned officers the like allowance will be made annually.

Allowance for Contingencies

£25 per annum for every company of fifty men.
£5 for every ten men over.

(12) Field officers and Adjutants will be excused the horse tax for one horse.

The proposed regulations of March had added that all officers and men would be exempt from the Militia Ballot during their period of service; but this was a matter already regulated by the Volunteer Act of 1802. The June Allowances, in fact, were purely a financial matter, which incidentally tempted Volunteers to undergo training for eighty-five days in the year. For their purpose they were liberal; and, attracted by them and stimulated by the First Defence Act, the Volunteers began to come forward very rapidly. It seems, how-

[1] Sergeants, 1s. 6d.; Corporals, 1s. 2d.; Privates, 1s. a day.

ever, that early in the day Ministers became alarmed as to the effect of the exemptions of Volunteers upon the ballot; and that early in June they circulated an intimation that no further offers of Volunteers would be accepted until the ballots for the Supplementary Militia were ended.[1] Certain it is that, in spite of the Government's invitation to Volunteers to come forward, few corps were accepted in June and July,[2] and that there were loud complaints that the Government was damping the ardour of the people. However, the Levy en Masse Act was passed on the 27th of July, and circulated on the 30th, with a letter which sought with indifferent success to make matters clear. 1803.

"Under section 29 (such was the purport of the Secretary of State's circular) provision is made for the training of a certain number of men in the first instance, to avoid the delay if all training be deferred until the returns of the classes required by the Act are made. This proportion should be not less than six times the number of Militia named by the Militia Act of 1802,[3] exclusive of the Supplementary Militia quota. It is the decided opinion of Ministers that in all places where Volunteer corps can be formed, upon such conditions as the King shall approve, it would be advisable to give every encouragement for that purpose; such an arrangement being calculated to concentrate the force, in order to promote the convenience of the public, and to render it unnecessary to have recourse to the compulsory clauses of the Act. I need not point out the difficulty of issuing arms for the extensive training required

[1] I can nowhere find this Circular, but I deduce its existence and its date from a letter of L.L. Banff, to S.S. 25th June, *I.D.* vol. iii.

[2] I judge this from statements in the Commons' debates and from the Entry Book, which contains the letters as to the offers of Volunteers at this period (*H.O.M.E.B.* vol. ciii.) but it is impossible to say whether these entries are complete.

[3] That number was, for Great Britain, 51,489; therefore the number of men to be trained in the first instance under the Levy en Masse Act would be 308,934, distributed according to the quota of Militia in each county.

1803. under the Act. I recommend an appeal to the inhabitants of the country to procure a return of the arms in their possession in order that they may for a time be applied to the service of the country, and to take measures for distributing them. Twenty-five firelocks is considered enough for the training of one hundred men. The information given by these returns will aid the Government much in arranging for the distribution of arms.

"The object of the Act is to obtain such a force, in addition to that which has been already provided, as may enable any attack on the country to be frustrated, and by combining economy and vigour to continue the contest as long as may be necessary for the honour and security of the empire. This communication is made under the impression of the inexpediency of establishing a voluntary force to the extent now proposed upon the allowances already transmitted to you [*i.e.* the June Allowances], and I am persuaded that in the offers of service made to you greater proofs will be afforded of the liberality and public spirit which have been so justly excited by the inordinate ambition and avowed intentions of the enemy."

This last sentence hinted unmistakably that the June Allowances were to be discontinued for future corps of Volunteers; and a new circular of the 3rd of August set all doubts at rest. "Although in many instances the persons forming new corps have offered to put the Government to no expense, yet it could not be expected, no matter how great the public spirit of individuals, that such an arrangement should become general." And therewith were promulgated the new allowances, known thenceforth as the August Allowances, for the Volunteers accepted after the 22nd of June.

They were as follows:—

In the case of Infantry £1 a man was to be granted for clothing once in three years, and a shilling a day per man was to be given for twenty days' exercise in the year.

In the case of cavalry £120 a year, payable half-yearly, was to be allowed for every troop.[1] 1803.

This arrangement, it was added, was to be final, unless it could be so altered as to produce no increase of expense to the public. Notice, therefore, must be given to corps which had tendered their services but had not been accepted, in order that they might reconsider the matter before renewing their offer under altered conditions.

Here, then, was another vast burden of work, both difficult and complicated, laid upon the Lieutenancies, a full examination of which shall presently follow. But within a little more than a week the Billeting Act was passed which, it will be remembered, exempted all Yeomen who attended twelve days' exercise, and all Volunteers who attended twenty-four days' exercise in the year from the ballot for the Army of Reserve and for any other Additional Force that might be raised in the future. How Ministers contrived to commit this extraordinary blunder is a mystery. It is certain from sec. 8 of the Army of Reserve Act, and indeed from their own admissions, that they had no intention of granting this exemption ; and for some time they would not confess that they had granted it. But indeed they were so ignorant of the effect of their own enactments that the Secretary at War actually thought that no Volunteers, saving those whose offer of service had been accepted before the 22nd of June 1803, were exempt from service in the Militia.[2] According to one Member of Parliament, the clause which did the mischief was smuggled through the Commons after most of the country members had left London in order to drill their Yeomanry and Militia at home.[3] But the insertion of the fatal words, however surreptitious, can hardly have been unknown to Ministers. It seems

[1] This item does not appear in the circular of 3rd August, but in a later circular of 28th Sept. 1803.

[2] *W.O. Mila. Books*, S.W. to C.G.M. Argyll, 30th July 1803

[3] Sir W. Yonge's speech, 14th Dec. 1803, *H.D.* Commons.

1803. probable that they really aimed at increasing the number of days prescribed by the Volunteer Act of 1802 to qualify Volunteers for exemption from the *Militia*, and that by some mistake or conspiracy the term Army of Reserve was inserted in its place. Be that as it may, the thing was done, and the country had to take the consequences.

Meanwhile, quite apart from this particular question of exemption, it may be said that the entire nation had sprung to arms, and was anxious to form itself into Volunteer corps. Though, on the one hand, Volunteering brought with it immunity from the Militia ballot, and, on the other, the Levy en Masse Act threatened to drill every able-bodied man whether he liked it or not, there was much sound patriotic feeling in the movement. The people were zealous to defend their country, and though they decidedly preferred to do so in the way which they thought best, chiefly because it was easiest, yet they asked above all for guidance. The Secretary of State had called for more Volunteers in March, and his appeal had met with a willing response. The Lieutenants, seeing that the Government had committed itself to the policy of Volunteers, backed it with loyal energy and good-will, albeit there were not wanting men among them who, in their hearts, considered that policy fallacious. Even after the Levy en Masse Act had been passed, they abated none of their energy, since Ministers evidently wished the people to come forward of themselves without compulsion. But the Government, despite of loud murmurs, had checked the patriotic movement by delaying the acceptance of offers during the best part of two months, and seemed about to pin its faith to the ballot; and hence when it backed once more, like an unstable wind, to the voluntary principle, there was a sigh of relief and a rush to be enrolled. But then came another disappointment. The Government limited the number of Volunteers, as has been seen, by its circular of the 30th of July. Many willing men who aspired to shoulder a musket were excluded; so also were a certain number more who had apprehended the meaning of the Billeting Act; and there was a fresh cry of discontent. 1803.

By the 18th of August the War Office was so heavily inundated with offers of voluntary service that the Secretary of State on that day issued a circular to the Lieutenants suspending the compulsory training of the classes under the provisions of the 53rd section of the Levy en Masse Act, but insisting none the less upon the enrolment of men in the districts and parishes and the furnishing of the returns required by the Act. Also he made another effort, by a new circular to the Lieutenants, to keep the numbers of the Volunteers within bounds. "The inconveniences which must unavoidably attend the carrying of the Volunteer system to an unlimited extent has determined the King at present not to authorise the formation of any additional Volunteer corps to be raised in any county where the number of effectives in their corps (including the Yeomanry) shall exceed the amount of six times the Militia, exclusive of the Supplementary quota. In providing that number you will use your judgment in selecting such as shall be best suited to local considerations; but if the effective numbers of the corps recommended by you have arrived at the figure laid down above, you will postpone the communication of any further offers of service until the King determines to increase the Volunteer corps in your county."

Evidently Ministers were terrified at the monster which it had called into being; and they were not encouraged by the fresh outburst of murmurs which greeted this new attempt to keep it within reasonable limits. At this crisis the direction of the Volunteers, which, contrary to all precedent, had been so far conducted by Lord Hobart, the Secretary of State for War, was transferred to its old place, the Home Office, under Mr. Charles Yorke. That unhappy man, confronted with mountains of unanswered letters containing offers of Volunteer corps, took perhaps the only course that

1803. was open to him, and issued another circular of 31st August to settle matters once for all.

"*All* the offers are accepted," he said, "provided that they do not militate against the regulations of the Defence Act and Levy en Masse Act, or against the general rules adopted or to be adopted. The limit of six times the Militia must be preserved, but Volunteers exceeding that proportion may be attached to established corps, though without any allowance for pay, arms, or clothing, and without claim to exemption from any ballot. Further, all corps accepted since the passing of the two Acts above named must be formed with reference to the general Militia system, that is to say, companies of infantry must be at least sixty, and troops of cavalry at least forty men strong; and no infantry of fewer than three companies, or cavalry of fewer than two troops, will be reckoned a corps."

Thus the question was at last decided, so far as rules could decide it; and the country was finally committed to the maintenance of a huge amorphous mass of undisciplined men, subject to two different Acts of Parliament, two different sets of regulations, and two different spheres of service, namely the Military District and Great Britain at large; the whole of them immune from the Militia ballot under one set of conditions prescribed by the Militia Act of 1802, and from the Army of Reserve under a second set ordained by the Billeting Act of 1803.

Meanwhile for some weeks there was great uncertainty as to the true state of the law respecting exemptions. It is demonstrable that many men knew the purport of the Billeting Act long before the Lieutenants; and Yorke was bombarded with queries as to its legal bearing upon the question,[1] for in all quarters the Magistrates held different opinions, and framed their conduct of the ballot accordingly. Ministers, alive by this time to the effect of the Billeting Act, and

[1] *E.g. I.D.* vol. i. L.L. Beds. to S.S. 13th Sept.; vol. iv. Brecon, C. Morgan to S.S. 24th Oct.

greatly dismayed by it, referred its interpretation in despair to the Attorney-General, who could not but pronounce that Volunteers who fulfilled the requirements of that Act were indeed exempt from the ballot for the Army of Reserve. There was nothing for them but to give in, to circulate this unwelcome construction[1] of their own Act and submit to the consequences. It may be added that this decision was by no means received with deference in all quarters. The Lieutenant of Roxburgh announced boldly that he differed from the Law-Officers; and many magistrates of the West Riding of Yorkshire equally declared themselves unconvinced. They could not believe that the old Volunteers, who had come forward from patriotic motives, were to be put on the same footing with the new, who, as the Lieutenant put it, were only Volunteers under compulsion.[2] In counties where there had hitherto been hesitation on the part of Volunteers to present themselves, there was now great eagerness to form corps, for the sake of the exemption; and thus the Government found its scheme for the Volunteers legally defined in a form which was exactly contrary to its own intentions. 1803.

IX

The result of the withdrawal of some hundreds or thousands of men from the ballot was immediate. By December 1803 the effective Volunteers of all ranks in Great Britain were returned at 380,000, which, added to 70,000 in Ireland, made a round total of 450,000.

[1] The circular appears to have been dated the 7th of October, but the Lieutenant of Roxburgh was evidently aware of it several days earlier, so possibly it may have been circulated on an earlier date. The circular of 7th October purports to enclose two important decisions of the Law-Officers; but the Entry Clerks, with their usual intelligence, give no clue to the nature and date of the enclosures.

[2] *I.D.* vol. xi. L.L. Roxburgh, to S.S. 28th Sept. 1803; vol. xxxv. L.L. Yorks W.R. to S.S. 2nd Oct. 1803.

1803. The price of substitutes rose higher and higher, and their quality sank lower and lower as the autumn of 1803 gave place to the winter, and to the spring of 1804. Nevertheless, the figure varied greatly in different localities. In Aberdeen the cost of a substitute was £20; in Argyll and Bute it was £24; in Berwick men were hardly to be obtained on any terms. In Buckinghamshire substitutes commanded from £30 to £40; in Dorset, £25; in Middlesex, £30 to £60; in Northumberland something over £37; in Sussex, £50. Cases were also known where the figure had reached £70, £80, and £100.[1] Yet with all this the levy did not prosper. The Army of Reserve grew more and more unpopular, insomuch that even in Scotland the Militia, which all the while was of course competing with it for men, was welcomed as a refuge from it.[2] To obtain recruits at all in North Britain it was necessary to violate the law[3] and to pay them the entire bounty due to them, instead of withholding one-half until they should have joined their battalions.[4] In Staffordshire the people, who had come forward generally with enthusiasm as Volunteers, suspected the limitation of their numbers to be due to a desire to complete the Army of Reserve, and declared "that they would sooner die on the spot than submit to it."[5] Nor was the Army of Reserve distasteful only to the people at large; it was also intensely disliked by the Lieutenancies. The principal reason for this was the friction to which it gave rise with the military authorities; for not unfrequently substitutes who had been

[1] *I.D.* vol. xxxvii. V.L. Argyll and Bute, to S.S. 5th Sept. 1804; vol. xxxix. V.L. Berwick, to S.S. 11th Feb. 1804; vol. xl. L.L. Bucks, to S.S. 26th Dec. 1803; vol. xlvi. C.G.M. Dorset, to S.S. 28th Feb. 1804; vol. xxii. Vestry Clerks of Spitalfields to S.S. 13th Oct. 1803; vol. xxiii. (*ad fin*), undated, 1804; vol. xxv. C.G.M. Northumberland, to S.S. 25th Sept. 1803; vol. xxxii. L.L. Sussex, to S.S. 9th Sept. 1803. *Military Transactions*, i. 61.

[2] *I.D.* vol. xxxviii. L.L. Nairn, to S.S. 9th Feb. 1804.

[3] 42 George III. cap. 91, section 58.

[4] *I.D.* vol. xl. Mr. Donald M'Leod (Ross) to S.S. 28th Feb. 1804.

[5] *Ibid.* vol. xxix. L.L. Staffs, to S.S. 12th Sept. 1803.

passed by the medical authorities of the county were rejected by the doctors of the Army.[1] But the most fruitful source of dispute lay in the discrepancies between the county returns of the men who had been produced and the regimental returns of the men who had been received. It had been wisely arranged by the Government to draft the Army of Reserve into fifty battalions, numbered as the second battalions of as many regiments of the Line; and England, for the purposes of the Act, was divided into sixteen districts, to each of which sufficient officers were furnished to form young, sickly, or worn-out recruits into distinct Reserve battalions. Between these two separate sets of regular officers the Lieutenancies sometimes suffered severely. In innumerable cases counties were summoned to make good deficiencies in their quota upon the showing of the Inspector-General of the Reserve, and made answer by indignantly producing their own figures, and showing that no deficiency existed. 1803.

Again, Ministers had never made any secret of the fact that they hoped by means of bounties to pass most of the Army of Reserve as Volunteers into the Line; and very soon rumours were current that the officers were putting the largest clothes upon the smallest men, giving them misfitting shoes, and applying other such methods of petty tyranny in order to force them to take service at once with the Regulars.[2]

This, of course, did not promote good-will between the two parties, and sometimes an unfortunate mistake made the relations between them very bitter. In Bute the local battalion of the Army of Reserve reported one man to be wanting, and the Deputy-Lieutenants held a ballot to fill the vacancy. The lot fell upon a thrifty and industrious shepherd who had contrived to buy and breed a few sheep of his own. In despair he sold all that he had, bought a substitute for £26, and was left

[1] *E.g. I.D.* vol. xxxvii. L.L. Ayr, to S.S. 26th March 1804.
[2] *I.D.* vol. xxxii. L.L. Sussex, to S.S. 26th Sept. 1803.

1803. a ruined and broken-hearted man. Shortly afterwards it was discovered that the returns of the battalions were wrong, and that he ought not to have been ballotted at all. The Deputy-Lieutenant wrote an indignant report of the occurrence to the Secretary of State, but the mischief was done, and there was no undoing it.[1]

The difference between the accounts of the Inspector-General and the counties was generally explicable by desertion, aggravated not unfrequently by the omission or the inability of military officers to send a sufficient escort to bring the recruits in. For, as the bounties rose, so fraudulent enlistment and desertion increased, until at last, by the actual admission of Mr. Secretary Yorke,[2] the recruits gained for the Army of Reserve during the first three months of 1804 barely outbalanced the loss by deserters. Meanwhile crimping had been so general as to engage the energies of an appreciable portion of the population. Even Adjutants of Militia turned their attention to it occasionally, and doubtless made a handsome profit.[3] Deputy-Lieutenants, moreover, in despair passed men both for the Militia and the Reserve who were quite unfit for service in either ;[4] but even so they could not prevent the accumulation of enormous fines upon the parishes in their districts. Before long they abandoned the attempt altogether, and Addington himself was fain to confess that after November 1803 the inconveniences of the Act exceeded its advantages. In April 1804, to adopt the official language used by the Horse Guards, the Act died a natural death, men having ceased to come in, and the

[1] *I.D.* vol. xxxvii. Minute of D.L. of Bute, 30th July 1804, in L.L. to S.S. 26th Oct. 1804.

[2] H. D. Yorke's speech, 28th March 1804.

[3] *I.D.* vol. xxiv. O.C. Montgomery Militia to A.G. 17th May 1803.

[4] General Simcoe reported that he was training the Volunteer Artillery of the Stannaries to work the great guns at Plymouth. "They are of sufficient stature for the duty, which the Militia attached to the Artillery strikingly are not" (*I.D.* vol. xxviii. Simcoe to Warden of Stannaries, 26th Nov. 1803).

fines having reached a sum so absurdly great as to be impossible of enforcement. 1803.

By the end of 1803, the term appointed for the enlistment of the 49,880 men required by the Act, there had been raised in all 40,897 men. Of these, 4278, or over one-tenth, had deserted, 1301 had been rejected or discharged for various reasons, and 286 had died, leaving a total of 35,032 nominally effective, and a deficiency of 14,748, or fully 30 per cent. The 35,032 again were reduced to little more than 30,000 by the elimination of boys who could not be fit for service for two or three years. By the 1st of May 1804, when the Act was acknowledged to be dead, the Army of Reserve had produced a nominal total of 45,492 men, of whom 2116 had been discharged as unfit or for other causes, 589 had died, and 5561, nearly one-ninth, had deserted or were claimed as deserters by other corps, leaving 37,136 nominally effective. Of these, however, 7000 were young and undersized, and had to be drafted into garrison-battalions until they could grow up. Thus while paying for 45,000 men, the country gained the immediate services of little more than 30,000. Further analysis of the figures, fortunately rendered possible by contemporary returns, reveals another very remarkable fact. Of the entire number of men raised, only 2873 were principals, whereas the substitutes numbered 41,198 ; so that practically hardly one man in fourteen accepted personal service.[1] The Army of Reserve, therefore, can only be described as a deplorable failure.

For the Militia, unfortunately, there are no such figures to hand ; but beyond all question if they could be produced they would show much the same result. It is at least certain that in June 1804 the deficiency in the Militia of England alone amounted to 6476 men, and in that of Ireland (which had no Supplementary Militia)

[1] These figures are drawn from *Military Transactions of the British Empire, 1803-1807*, a volume compiled by the Military Secretary for the Commander-in-Chief, apparently for official circulation only, pp. 63-68.

1803. to 829. It is therefore safe to assume that the deficiency for the three kingdoms must have reached a total of fully 8000; but this was relatively much smaller than in the Army of Reserve, the proportion of men lacking being only one-twelfth as compared with one-fourth. Nevertheless the position was very far from satisfactory.

As to the Regular Army, its powers of recruiting were simply killed by the competition of the Militia and the Army of Reserve. During the last six months of 1803 there were 360 recruiting parties out, offering a bounty of £7 : 12 : 6 to men who as substitutes could gain at any time from £20 to £50. They succeeded in raising 3481 recruits, of whom 291 deserted, leaving a net total of 3190. It is true that several thousand of the Army of Reserve in due time enlisted in the Regulars for an additional bounty of eight to ten guineas,[1] which, added to that which they had already received as substitutes, made them probably the most expensive recruits that ever were obtained.[2] Had Addington sought first to fill the ranks of the Regular Army before increasing the Militia or forming the Reserve, he might have secured exactly the same men for one half of the price.

The sum of the whole of his elaborate measures, therefore, amounted to this—that he starved the Army to make a large body of Militia and Reserve, and starved the Militia and Reserve in order to raise a vast crowd of Volunteers.

X

It is now time to examine the composition and value of those Volunteers, again reminding the reader that with them is included the Yeomanry, which originally bore the designation of Volunteer Cavalry. The Government's action towards the Volunteers, so far as we have followed it, may be summarised as follows:—In 1802 they called them into existence upon their own terms

[1] Eight guineas at once and two guineas more (subject to deductions for necessaries) upon joining the first battalion. C.C.L.B. 25th Feb. 1804.

[2] See Appendix.

of service, and granted them exemption from the Militia ballot in return for five days' exercise annually, together with certain allowances. 1803.

On the 31st of March 1803 they called for more Volunteers, and proposed to give them what were afterwards known as the June Allowances.

Having called for them, they became nervous lest the exemption of a number of Volunteers should interfere with the various ballots, and left many of their offers of service unanswered.

On the 11th of June they passed the First Defence Act for general training of the people, and exempted the Volunteers from its operation.

A few days later they issued the June Allowances, which offered pay to the men for eighty-five days' exercise in the year, and required of them an agreement to serve within their Military District, in return for which pay was granted to a limited number of officers and to a permanent staff. A list of the said Military Districts was issued at the same time.[1]

[1] Scheme of Districts for Home Defence ordered by the Duke of York

District.	Contents.	G.O.C.
Southern.	Kent, Surrey, Sussex (exclusive of London).	Gen. Sir D. Dundas.
Eastern.	Norfolk, Suffolk, Cambs, Hants, Essex.	Lt.-Gen. Sir J. Craig.
London.	(Including Surrey within the bills of mortality).	Lt.-Gen. Gwyn.
South-West.	Hants, Wilts, Dorset.	Lt.-Gen. Gardiner.
Western.	Devon, Cornwall, Somerset (exclusive of Bristol, Bath, Troubridge, Uxbridge, or other places garrisoned from Bristol).	Lt.-Gen. Simcoe.
N. Western.	Cheshire, Salop, Lancs, N. Wales.	Lt.-Gen. Prince William.
Northern.	Northumberland, Cumberland, Westmoreland, Durham.	Lt.-Gen. Sir H. Dalrymple.
Yorkshire.	Yorkshire, Lincs.	Lt.-Gen. Lord Mulgrave.

1803. While circulating these allowances the Secretary of State announced that corps accepted after the 16th of June would not be exempt from the ballot for the Army of Reserve.[1]

Ministers then again became nervous as to the expense of raising Volunteers upon the June Allowances, and delayed the acceptance of offers of service.

They then passed the Levy en Masse Act on the 27th of July for the compulsory training of all able-bodied men, with a clause to suspend the operation of the measure if a sufficient proportion of Volunteers should be produced for each county, which Volunteers should be bound to serve in any part of Great Britain. A circular of the 30th of July directed that immediate training should be given to a number of men equal at least to six times the quota of the Ordinary Militia.

Next, on the 3rd of August, were produced the new regulations known as the August Allowances, making the third set of such regulations issued within twelve months, for the government of the new Volunteers to be created under the Levy en Masse Act.

Then on the 11th of August they passed two Acts, the one to cancel the rigid rule as to the proportion of Volunteers to be raised under the Levy en Masse Act; the other to grant Volunteers exemption from the ballot for the Army of Reserve, on condition that the infantry underwent twenty-four days' and the Cavalry twelve days' training within the year.

Finally, on the 31st of August Ministers accepted the

I. of Wight.	...	Maj.-Gen. Hewett.
Severn.	Glos., Worcester, Hereford, Monmouth, S. Wales.	Lt.-Gen. the Duke of Cumberland.
Home.	Middlesex, Herts, Berks.	Lt.-Gen. Lord Cathcart.
North Inland.	Derby, Notts, Staffs, Leic., Warwick, Rutland.	Lt.-Gen. Gardiner.
South Inland.	Beds., Oxon, Bucks, Northants.	Lt.-Gen. Gwynn.

[1] W.O. 6/193. Circular of 20th June 1803.

offers of all Volunteer corps, only stipulating that any men over and above the quota of six times the old Militia should be supernumeraries and not entitled to exemption of any kind. 1803.

It is hardly surprising that the Lord-Lieutenants should have been puzzled by the amazing confusion of these successive measures. "I wish," wrote the Lieutenant of Devon,[1] plaintively on the 29th of August, "that the Acts of Parliament and instructions framed upon them were clearer. The general idea is that Volunteers to any extent are to be accepted, and there is disappointment owing to the corps being refused. Refusals also spread a false notion that the danger is abated." And this is but one example out of many. Much trouble also was caused by the carelessness of the Home Office in omitting to forward copies of Acts of Parliament to the Lieutenancies, but communicating them to the newspapers. "I never heard," wrote the Vice-Lieutenant of the West Riding of Yorkshire on the 2nd of May 1804, "of the Act of 27th July 1803 for completing the Militia until yesterday, nor had another very active magistrate of this county."[2] The Lieutenant of Bedford, a peer of the realm, complained bitterly that the Acts were not forwarded to him; but he was obliged to write twice before he could obtain a copy of the Billeting Act.[3] "Your last circular," wrote the Lieutenant of Cornwall, "I read complete in the *Sun* newspaper before I received it. In the newspaper it was dated the 22nd of September; in the official copy it is dated the 28th."[4]

Added to the difficulty of ascertaining the law of the land was that of divining the wishes of the Government. Did Ministers really want Volunteers or not? This was a question which the Lieutenancies found it hard to answer, and they found it none the easier

[1] The writer's great-grandfather, the mild patience of whose protest he cannot but admire. [2] *I.D.* vol. lxvii. 2nd May 1804.

[3] *I.D.* vol. i. LL. Beds. to S.S. 13th, 30th Sept. 1803.

[4] *Ibid.* vol. viii. LL. Cornwall, to S.S. 5th Oct. 1803.

1803. because the direction of the Volunteers, as has been seen, changed hands from the War Office to the Home Office in the course of 1803. A few of the Lieutenants were opposed to the whole principle of Volunteering, but though these did not conceal their opinions, only one of them, Lord Essex in Herefordshire, frankly set his face against them until the ballots should have been held. He was at once taken to task for neglecting the Volunteers. He answered sharply enough, "Every one will offer [to volunteer] to escape the ballot. . . . The Militia are 246 men short; and the subdivison-clerks supported by the country gentlemen ballot illegally by throwing several parishes into one, so that the parishes guilty of failing to complete their quota shall not be detected. I thought that I was acting in conformity with your orders in discountenancing Volunteers until the ballots were complete, but now that I know to the contrary I will act differently. Most of the Volunteer offers here have originated with a view to meet the approach of the next General Election rather than the enemy. I shall be glad to leave the whole business to the Vice-Lieutenant."[1] On the other hand, in the county of Montgomery, where Volunteers were unknown before the passing of the Levy en Masse Act, the Lieutenant submitted no offers until he had received all that were likely to be sent in. Whereupon Mr. Yorke wrote in the margin, "Perfectly right. I wish every one had done the same."[2] No doubt it would have been more convenient if all the Lieutenants had acted upon this principle; but Ministers solely were to blame, for at the beginning they had only asked vaguely for more Volunteers, upon which the Lieutenants naturally forwarded every offer that was sent to them.

Another extraordinary mistake on the part of the Government lay in fixing the same quota for all counties, whether inland or upon the coast. The maritime counties naturally demanded, and some of them ulti-

[1] *I.D.* vol. xvi. L.L. Hereford, to S.S. 12th Oct. 1803.

[2] *Ibid.* vol. xxiv. Mr. Mytton to S.S. 5th Sept. 1803.

mately obtained, a larger allowance than the rest; but the omission to discriminate between them led to vast correspondence and to a good deal of ill-feeling. 1803.

But the most fruitful source of confusion undoubtedly lay in the existence of three different codes for the regulation of the Volunteers, and in the variety of their conditions of service, which not only gave enormous trouble to all concerned, but in case of invasion must have caused great embarrassment to the Generals in the field. Of the whole number of 342,000 effective rank and file (that is to say corporals and privates) comprised in the Volunteers of Great Britain, 207,000, or, including supernumeraries, 211,000, were more or less subject to the Levy en Masse Act and the August Allowances, and were therefore liable to serve in any part of Great Britain; 67,000 were more or less under the June Allowances, and by the positive act of the Government were liable to serve in their Military District only; and 63,000 were more or less self-supporting and subject to special terms which might extend to service all over Great Britain or might limit their sphere of action to their parish or a short radius beyond it.[1] The Government was naturally anxious to have as few little isolated corps as possible, and rightly encouraged the amalgamation of troops and companies into regiments and battalions. But the inevitable result was that within the same corps were to be found perhaps two troops on the June Allowances, and five or six on the August Allowances. The latter were, of course, very jealous of their more favoured brethren, and this inevitably gave rise to friction. Again, there arose the difficulty as to filling vacancies in the corps on the June Allowances. Were these corps to be kept up to strength or not? There could be but one answer. The men who raised them having undertaken to do so

[1] I derive these figures from a long MS. return in the Library at Windsor Castle, dated 16th Dec. 1803. I have used the modification, *more or less*, because it is often extremely difficult to understand what were the allowances granted to some of the corps.

1803. under certain conditions, it was impossible for the Government to go back upon them. Hence officers commanding corps under the June Allowances may be said to have enjoyed a peculiar kind of patronage ; and it was not unknown for the commander of a corps under the August Allowances to find that several of his men, without saying a word to him, had transferred themselves to another regiment on the June Allowances. The distinction between the two conditions was felt the more acutely because in many instances volunteers had sent in their offers of service in good time to be accepted before the 22nd of June, but, receiving no answer until after that day, were reduced to the level of men who had only become Volunteers under pressure of the Levy en Masse Act. This trick, for it cannot be dignified by a higher name, was very much resented ; and it need hardly be added that the burden of making good the shortcomings of the Government fell upon a few patriotic gentlemen. One such, who had raised two companies in Gloucestershire, counting upon the June Allowances, and had already spent £7 a man in clothing, equipping, and arming them, found himself saddled with a further expense of £100 for the purchase of substitutes for some of his men. The Duke of Atholl wrote that the pernicious results of two concurrent rates of allowance could only be averted in Perthshire by private subscriptions, which would raise the August Allowances to the level of the June Allowances. He reckoned the cost to himself and his colleagues at £10,000 annually, and added that in many instances landlords would have to pay more than their annual rental. "Had the August Allowances been the only allowances," he wrote, "we might have carried the measure into effect, though so small proportion of discipline [twenty days' exercise] would have formed little better than an armed rabble ; but to call on them [the recipients of August Allowances] for more extensive service [in any part of Great Britain] when the June Volunteers were called on for service in the district only, makes it impossible." However, the Duke called a meeting to collect subscriptions ; and by the generosity of himself and of his brother landlords the full proportion of Volunteers for the county was completed. None the less it was iniquitous that these gentlemen should have been subjected to an extraordinary tax, simply to make good the mismanagement of the Government.[1] 1803.

Another miserable complication was that no one knew whether Volunteers receiving the August Allowances were governed wholly by the Levy en Masse Act, or in part also by the Volunteer Act of 1802. Under the Volunteer Act all claims for exemption from the ballot had to be furnished by the 21st of September in every year, so that the days of exercise necessary to qualify for exemption had to be accomplished before that day. The magistrates in various parts, possibly indeed in the whole of England, very naturally and sensibly took the Volunteer Act of 1802 as their principal guide in dealing with that particular force ; and finding that few of the new corps had performed the necessary number of drills, promptly declined to allow them exemption. The case was hard, because the Government had so long delayed the acceptance of Volunteers, and the clerks, moreover, were so dilatory in giving them official recognition in the *Gazette*, that many corps, with the best of good will, could not possibly have fulfilled the necessary days of training. They went out, however, as often as they could ; and their commanders appealed to the Secretary of State to be indulgent. In Surrey the magistrates, perceiving the hardships that might be involved in the question, suspended the ballot until all doubts should be resolved by the Law-Officers, lest men who had really earned their exemption should be drawn. The Secretary of State's answer, however, was short—he could not interfere with the working of Acts of Parliament—and there arose new causes of discontent among the Volun-

[1] *I.D.* vol. xv. Gloucestershire, Capt. Bricknell to S.S. 27th Feb. 1804 ; vol. xxvii. L.L. Perth, to S.S. 14th, 27th Aug., 8th Oct. 1803.

1803. teers, and new confusion as to the enactments by which they were governed.[1]

Yet another trouble arose from the action of the Government in combining the requirements of the June with the pay of the August Allowances. The new Volunteers of course needed adjutants and sergeant-majors as much as the old, but were informed first that no pay would be allowed for a permanent staff, except in very special circumstances, in corps raised after the 3rd of August.[2] This position proving untenable, Ministers in November offered pay for an adjutant to every infantry corps of 500, and every cavalry corps of 300; for a sergeant-major to every infantry corps of 200, and every cavalry corps of 120; and both adjutant and sergeant-major to every infantry corps of 1000 and every cavalry corps of 600 effective rank and file, provided that they agreed to undergo eighty-five days' exercise in the year. This roused much indignation in the parties concerned, for whereas the corps under the June Allowances received pay for the whole of the eighty-five days, those under the August Allowances received pay for but twenty. The theory seems to have been that fifty-two out of the eighty-five drills were to be held on Sundays, on which day no man received wages; that twenty days' payment made up the fifty-two to seventy-two, and that each corps must make its own shift to eke out the remaining thirteen days, or, in other words, must be indemnified by the officers. The complaints against such treatment were bitter, especially in Scotland. "We enlisted our Volunteers for twenty days' drill," wrote Lord Dalkeith; "we cannot now call on them for sixty-five days more; and yet on that account we must lose our adjutant."[3] The Secretary of State then fell back on the excuse that twenty days' pay was enough for eighty-five days' drill of only two hours a day.

[1] *I.D.* vol. iv. Brecon, Charles Morgan of Tredegar to S.S. 24th Oct.; vol. xviii. Kent, Capt. Powis to S.S. 25th Nov.; vol. xxxi. V.L. Surrey, to S.S. 8th Dec. 1803.

[2] Circular of 28th Sept.

[3] *I.D.* vol. xi. L.L. Dumfries, to S.S. 3rd Nov. 1803.

"But this," wrote Sir John Murray, from Perthshire, "makes no allowance for time consumed in dressing and coming to parade, in these parts often six or eight miles. Moreover, two hours a day is not training enough for recruits. Men cannot be disciplined as soldiers in 170 hours, much less in 40 hours. Again, it is urged that the men have the advantage of clothing. This is no advantage. The men have only the trouble of cleaning it, and the Government pays not one-third of the cost. . . . The eighty-five days' drill was claimed in return for the use of an adjutant, as if it were a personal advantage to the Volunteers. But the Government will not get the value even of its trifling twenty shillings [twenty days' pay for one man] unless it provides proper instructors."[1] 1803.

Complaints such as this could hardly be passed over; and the Government presently receded once more, granting in January both adjutants and sergeant-majors on easier terms, and adding in February that Volunteers who attended inspections should receive pay for the same, provided such inspections did not recur more frequently than once in two months. Thus, under the pretext of anxiety for frequent musters of Volunteers, Government doled them out pay for six additional days in the year.[2] These concessions, having been wrung from Ministers against their will, were, of course, received with a growl instead of with thanks; but this was always the fate of Addington and his colleagues. Having by sheer ignorance and carelessness called the Volunteers into being on easy terms, they tried to impose harder conditions by a side wind, and were invariably beaten in the attempt.

XI

The most serious trouble of all arose out of the lack of arms. Colonel Vyse, it will be remembered, had particularly cautioned Ministers against creating

[1] *I.D.* vol. xxvii. Sir John Murray to S.S. 14th Dec. 1803.

[2] Circular of 15th Jan. 1804.

1803. corps which they could not arm; but they boldly enrolled hundreds of thousands of men on the understanding that twenty-five muskets for every hundred men would be sufficient for purposes of instruction, and that pikes would be cheerfully accepted by the remaining seventy-five. Never were the authorities more pitifully deceived. It has already been mentioned that the clerks in Downing Street were extremely casual as to the gazetting of officers; and as no corps could receive arms until gazetted, this formed an initial source of discontent. There was one case of twenty-four companies, which were offered in May, accepted in June, and still waiting to be gazetted in September.[1] But the majority of the complaints upon this head arose from actual failure in the supply of arms. Such complaints are very numerous, but the selection of a certain number will show how serious would have been the danger of an invasion, had Napoleon attempted it in the autumn of 1803. From Ayr it was reported in November that many of the Volunteer corps were still incomplete, want of arms having checked the spirit of the people.[2] The Lieutenant of Berkshire asked plaintively how he was to distribute 603 muskets among 2763 men; and one of his commanders complained in October that his men had been clothed and drilled for weeks, but that unless weapons were given to them at once they would learn nothing about them till next summer.[3] From Nairn came in September a wail that was distressing. "The situation of the North of Scotland is truly deplorable, left without arms of any description. . . . All efforts to get arms for the Volunteers so far useless. . . . Not a man in arms (though many are willing) to north of Aberdeen, except two companies at Elgin. . . . We are all at the mercy of any petty privateer."[4] From Sutherland a com-

[1] *I.D.* vol. i. V.L. Argyll, to S.S. 11th Sept. 1803.

[2] *Ibid.* vol. i. L.L. Ayr, to S.S. 9th Nov. 1803.

[3] *Ibid.* vol. ii. L.L. Berks, to S.S. 19th Sept. 1803; J. Weyland to S.S. 24th Oct. 1803.

[4] *Ibid.* vol. iii. L.L. Nairn, to S.S. 6th Sept. 1803.

mander reported late in October that he had had 1120 men enrolled in his two battalions for some months but had no weapons for them.[1] In Dumfries, at about the same time, only 106 firelocks had been supplied for 1200 men.[2] The Lieutenant of Buckinghamshire protested at the end of October that so far the county had not received a single musket or pike.[3] In Cornwall the Lieutenant, after war had been declared fifteen months, went near to lose his temper. "No new corps," he wrote, "will ever be effective unless the Ordnance supply arms. I lately applied for some, and was told that Cornwall had a thousand more than she was entitled to. If you continue to accept corps, pray order the Ordnance to arm them, or acceptance is a farce."[4] From Denbigh, towards Christmas time, the Lieutenant, having with reason lost patience, wrote likewise with unusual warmth: "I cannot get from the Ordnance a single musket, nor a word as to the price that they will allow to those who provide themselves with arms. Unless something is done soon, the Volunteer corps will disperse."[5] In Derbyshire the lack of arms was lamented as a grievous misfortune.[6] In Durham the Lieutenant took a higher tone: "If only half the Volunteer force is to be armed, and if that half is to depend on the arms issued during the last war, it will damp the spirit and energy of the people, who are already in some degree hurt and disgusted by all the changes in the arrangements for the Volunteers."[7] . . . From Flint, in July 1804, a gentleman who had offered to raise and clothe a corps if the Government would arm it, reported that he had been obliged to exceed his contract and purchase weapons as well as clothes, and would therefore be obliged by the grant of the usual 1803.

1 *I.D.* vol. vi. Sutherland, David Campbell to S.S. 21st Oct. 1803.

2 *Ibid.* vol. xi. V.L. Dumfries, to S.S. 22nd Oct. 1803.

3 *Ibid.* vol. v. L.L. Bucks, to S.S. 28th Oct. 1803.

4 *Ibid.* vol. xliv. L.L. Cornwall, to S.S. 25th Oct. 1804.

5 *Ibid.* vol. ix. L.L. Denbigh, to S.S. 24th Dec. 1803.

6 *Ibid.* vol. ix. Joshua Strutt to S.S. 17th Nov. 1803.

7 *Ibid.* vol. xii. L.L. Durham, to S.S. 10th Sept. 1803.

1803. clothing allowance.[1] The Mayor of Bristol brought forward a new difficulty. He had 1400 Volunteers who, in rotation, were finding a guard for French prisoners. There being but 500 stand of arms between the 1400, the muskets were necessarily passed from hand to hand, which led to disputes as to who should keep them clean, and to much discontent.[2] In Hampshire, a county in which every man should have been trained, several Volunteers resigned from impatience at being left without arms.[3] From Lancashire the Lieutenant, most loyal and zealous of men, week after week in vain repeated his remonstrances against the Ordnance for leaving his county unarmed.[4] In Northumberland the Duke had raised and clothed 1300 men at his own expense, asking no allowance for them but only arms and belts; yet the General commanding the district reported that the Volunteers were "likely in point of discipline to be no more than a name, as the greater number were without any arms whatever."[5] From Pembrokeshire the Lieutenant sent word in September that he had written to the Ordnance repeatedly, but had failed to obtain half the arms necessary for his Volunteers: "Their zeal is cooling," he added, "and I firmly believe that in the course of a month the greater part or the whole will go to the right about."[6] In Staffordshire, as Lord G. Leveson Gower declared in debate, not a firelock had been received up to the middle of December.[7] In Shropshire, by February 1804, only 600 arms had been obtained out of 1300 due to the county; and it was only by general patriotic exertion that 4000 out of 5000 Volunteers were provided with weapons.[8] Lastly,

1 *I.D.* vol. xiv. W. D. Shipley to L.L. 21st July 1804.

2 *Ibid.* vol. xv. Mayor of Bristol to S.S. 5th Oct. 1803.

3 *Ibid.* vol. xvi. L.L. Hants, to S.S. 4th Oct. 1803.

4 *Ibid.* vol. xix. L.L. to S.S. 10th Sept. 1803, and subsequent letters.

5 *Ibid.* vol. xxv. Sir H. Dalrymple to A.G. 21st Sept. 1803.

6 *Ibid.* vol. xxvii. L.L. Pembroke, to S.S. 26th Sept. 1803.

7 *H.D.* Commons, 13th Dec. 1803.

8 *I.D.* vol. lxii. V.L. Salop, to S.S. 22nd Feb. 1804.

from Surrey a Colonel of Volunteers wrote that his men had provided themselves with 220 muskets out of 600, and that unless the remaining 380 were at once found by the Ordnance, the corps would be broken up: "The men," he added, "have drilled for three months without arms, and are tired of it."[1] 1803.

Such are samples of the cries that assailed the War Office and the Home Office during the years 1803 and 1804; but these by no means indicate the whole of the mischief and confusion. Owing sometimes to the carelessness of Lieutenants, and sometimes to sheer foolishness at headquarters, violent local jealousies were aroused by the partial issue of arms. Staffordshire was much affronted at receiving no muskets, while Derbyshire, Leicestershire, and Warwick were fully supplied.[2] Berkshire was rent asunder and the Lieutenant much incensed by the action of the Ordnance in consigning 190 muskets direct to the Windsor Volunteers, an insignificant corps of 180 men, and that though they were only entitled to one firelock for every four men, and the distribution was supposed to be left to the Lieutenant.[3] In Shropshire, by a similar blunder, the whole proportion of the county's arms was delivered to the Shrewsbury Volunteers, the last corps which came forward to offer its services and, even so, under 600 strong. The Secretary of State, being adjured to make these Shrewsbury men disgorge their ill-gotten treasure, declined in the name of peace and quietness to interfere; whereupon the commander of another corps of 1800 men peremptorily demanded the muskets in order to keep his men in a good humour. And so the battle raged in Salop, with the general result that every one was aggrieved.[4] In Hertfordshire similar dissensions

[1] *I.D.* vol. xxxi. Letter enclosed in L.L. Surrey, to S.S. 10th Sept. 1803.

[2] *Ibid.* vol. xxix. L.L. Staffs, to S.S. 26th Dec. 1803.

[3] *Ibid.* vol. ii. L.L. Berks, to S.S. 20th Nov. 1803.

[4] *Ibid.* vol. xxviii. L.L. Salop, to S.S. 31st Oct. 1803; Mr. Kynaston Powell to S.S. 10th Nov. 1803.

1803. arose from the action of the Lieutenant himself. The Board of Ordnance sent 590 stand of arms, being the due number for a quarter of the county's Volunteers; but the Lieutenant, who was interested personally in the First Regiment, seized 480 of them for behoof of the favoured corps, and left the rest to "scramble as they could" for the remaining 110.[1]

Even this did not exhaust the troubles that arose from the Government's want of foresight in the matter of weapons. It was ordained by Act of Parliament that, to gain their exemption, Volunteers must appear at exercise "properly armed and equipped." This of course brought up the question whether such a regulation could be enforced when the Government had failed to provide arms. As usually happened, the Deputy-Lieutenants took different views in different parts of the country. In Shropshire they chose the strictly logical, though very unfair, method of exempting the officers, who of course had provided themselves with swords, and not exempting the men; a decision against which the Colonel protested with justifiable indignation. "Surely," he wrote, "arms and clothing are not necessary, besides twenty-four days' drill, to give exemption?"[2] In Plymouth a Deputy-Lieutenant likewise tried to deny the exemption, but finding that he was rousing serious agitation, and that his colleagues in other parts of the country were divided in opinion upon the subject, wrote to the Home Office to ask for instructions.[3] The answer was given in a Circular of the 23rd of November: "It is the opinion of the Law-Officers that a commandant of Volunteers cannot return as *effective* men who for want of discipline are unfit to have arms in their hands or who, even from no fault of their own, have had no opportunity of learning the use of arms. Such men, therefore, cannot be exempted."[4]

[1] *I.D.* vol. xvii. W. Baker to S.S. 24th Oct., 10th Nov. 1803.
[2] *Ibid.* vol. xxviii. Lord Kenyon to S.S. 17th Oct. 1803.
[3] *Ibid.* vol. x. Jonathan Elford to S.S. 15th Nov. 1803.
[4] Circular of S.S. to L.Ls. of counties where any officers are on

The whole question was complicated by the fact that some officers, from natural and proper unwillingness to use up the whole of the twenty days' drill without a day's instruction in the use of arms, reserved a certain number of drills against the happy moment when the long-expected weapons should be delivered. By so doing they prevented their men from earning their exemption in time; and up came a fresh crop of indignant letters to the Secretary of State.[1] 1803.

The Government feebly endeavoured to right itself by averring that pikes to any number would be furnished, if only officers would apply for them. But the Volunteers would not be content with pikes. In Scotland the people entertained not only material but sentimental objections to them; the weapon of rebel Ireland being in their judgment unfit for a loyal Scot.[2] In Flintshire the Volunteers would hardly take pikes into their hands, except on the assurance that they would be speedily exchanged for muskets.[3] The Duke of Richmond, a soldier of experience, declined to receive pikes for the Volunteers of Sussex, declaring them to be useless except in the hands of perfectly trained men and yet capable of being turned to dangerous account by a mob.[4] In Berkshire one officer concentrated his objections to the weapon into a single enthymeme. "The pikes issued by the Ordnance are eight feet long; the French ones taken last week were thirteen feet long; therefore an English regiment so armed could not attack and beat a French one."[5] Finally, in Somerset a Major of Volunteers, who disliked pikes as much as did his men, gave his company orders to leave their pikes at home when they came to drill, and being

permanent duty. The hardship was redressed, as shall presently be seen, at the first possible moment by Act of Parliament.

1 *I.D.* vol. v. L.L. Bucks, to S.S. 6th Nov. 1803.

2 *Ibid.* vol. iii. L.L. Inverness, to S.S. 10th March 1804; vol. viii. L.L. Kinross, to S.S. 16th Sept. 1803.

3 *Ibid.* vol. xiv. L.L. Flint, to S.S. 7th Nov. 1803.

4 *Ibid.* vol. xxxii. L.L. Sussex, to S.S. 23rd Aug. 1803.

5 *Ibid.* vol. ii. Sir I. Pocock to S.S. 16th Nov. 1803.

1803. rebuked by his Colonel, resigned his commission.[1] Such were the consequences of neglecting the advice, deliberately sought, of an experienced officer like Colonel Vyse.

XII

Passing from these lengthy, though preliminary, details as to the administrative difficulties which were thrown in the way of the Volunteers, let us now examine more closely their composition and their discipline. And first let us make a brief survey of Britain, noting the quarters in which the patriotic spirit was lively or the reverse.

It must be premised that among the Volunteers were certain corps in various parts of the country who, upon enrolment, expressly disclaimed their title to any exemptions whatever. They numbered in all about 7000 men,[2] of which the city of Edinburgh furnished 1162, the county of Devon 877, and the city of Westminster 508. The remaining counties and cities furnished only small contingents to this body of really self-denying men, whose public spirit is worthy of record.

Speaking generally, Scotland responded remarkably well to the call for Volunteers, the unpopularity of the Militia making this alternative service extremely welcome. In Aberdeen by the beginning of September 12,000 men had offered themselves against a quota of 3840; in Bute 598 men came forward to fill 366 places; in Berwick there were almost immediately 1350 offers to fill a quota of 930; at Haddington the figures were 1500 and 634. So too Kinross covered her quota of Volunteers three times over within August and September; Dumfries immediately offered more than twice the number required from her, and Edinburgh, by the first week in August, also had more than double her

[1] *I.D.* vol. xxx. L.L. Somerset, to S.S. 13th Nov. 1803.

[2] The return shows 6620, but it is admitted to be incomplete. *I.D.* vol. lxviii. Miscellaneous, 31st March 1804.

quota on foot and effective. In Argyll more than half the quota was already enrolled in June; Banff supplied nearly its full contingent before the introduction of the Levy en Masse Act; Elgin in the same time had furnished 480 out of the 780 assigned to her, and Inverness 2540 out of 3320. Dumbarton produced two-thirds of her men in May and June, and had small difficulty in enrolling the rest; Fife, Forfar, and Kincardine could show half, or more than half, of their respective quotas early in June. In Ayr voluntary enrolment soon exceeded the demands of the Government; though certain parishes stood aloof, and a few positively refused any service. Ross also found few men before the Levy en Masse Act compelled her to do so, and in Stirling there was less forwardness than usual, some difficulty being found in raising the allotted number before the end of October. In Linlithgow two-thirds of the quota had been enrolled before the 26th of July; and Nairn, Caithness, Peebles, Cromarty, and Sutherland had furnished their full contingent before the end of June. So it was also in Selkirk and in Roxburgh, even though the Lieutenant gave preference to the men who were less likely to be drawn for the Army of Reserve. In Clackmannan no corps were accepted until September, but on the other hand the whole contingent was self-supporting, receiving no allowance whatever from Government. Lanark added 300 Supernumeraries to the 4473 privates which were due from her. The difficulties in Perth have already been mentioned, but they did not prevent her from doing even more than her duty, half of her Volunteers having come forward in time to receive the June Allowances. Lastly, Renfrew had over four thousand offers from which to choose her quota of 2424. Altogether the record would be creditable to North Britain, were we not compelled to bear in mind that she was extremely backward in producing any Militia.[1] 1803.

[1] Returns at Windsor Castle. *I.D.* vol. i. L.L. Aberdeen, to S.S. 8th Sept.; L.L. Argyll and Bute, to S.S. 17th Aug.; L.L. Ayr,

1803. In England there was by no means the same uniform eagerness to volunteer, and in some parts there was a positive reluctance. Speaking generally, it may be said that a few counties, notably Anglesey, Middlesex, Brecon, Monmouth, Bedford, Devon, and Kent, came forward with the same enthusiasm as the best counties of Scotland. Kent, indeed, whose natural quota was just under 8000 men, wished for her own safety to raise 15,000, and actually raised 10,000. It is, however, noteworthy that the Mayor of Canterbury at first refused to call a meeting to form a Volunteer corps for that city, one citizen averring that there was no occasion to arm the people, as the Government would send soldiers enough.[1] The Cinque Ports, under the leadership of Pitt, brought forward 3500 men. Devon, whose quota was 9000, produced over 16,000; and the rest of the maritime counties, from considerations of their own security, generally obtained permission to enrol additional men. Lancashire, Norfolk, and Somerset, however, were exceptions, having failed to make up even the quota required of them. Middlesex, with London, Westminster and the Tower Hamlets, turned out about 35,000 men. For the rest, Derby, Hereford, Nottinghamshire, Radnor, Shropshire, Worcester, and the East Riding of Yorkshire handsomely brought forward more than their complement. Buckinghamshire, Cambridgeshire, Northamptonshire, Stafford, Warwick, Wiltshire, and the West Riding of York showed deficiencies more or less great; and the remainder produced their quota or thereabout.

Of the counties that failed, Cambridge seems to have been the worst, though her deficiency amounted to only 300 wanting out of 2886. Her Volunteers gave a deal of trouble; and by September 1804 the

to S.S. 9th Sept.; vol. iv. D.Ls. Berwick, to S.S. 7th Sept.; L.L. Haddington, to S.S. 23rd Sept.; vol. viii. L.L. Kinross, to S.S. 24th Aug.; vol. xii. Edinburgh returns of 9th Aug.; vol. xvii. L.L. Wigtown, to S.S. 25th Aug. 1803.

[1] *I.D.* vol. xviii. L.L. Kent, to S.S. 15th Aug. 1803.

number lacking had increased from 300 to 800 owing 1803. to the persistent refusal of the larger parishes to produce a man. It seems that the people had grown suspicious over the 58th section of the Levy en Masse Act, which ordained that the men raised under that Act could be attached to other regiments, whether of Militia or Regulars, if called out for service. The Duke of Richmond found exactly the same apprehension prevalent in Sussex, and was so nervous as to its results that he urged the Government to proclaim that the King would not enforce this particular section. In another section, the 54th, it was expressly laid down that Volunteers should not in any circumstances be placed in corps of Regulars ; but Yorke as usual chose to maintain, for as long as he dared, that this applied only to men enrolled under the Volunteer Act of 1802. The folly of leaving so important a point for a moment doubtful is obvious ; but such was the way of Addington's Ministry.[1]

In Buckinghamshire the failure in Volunteers seems to have been due mainly to lack of men, for the county had always done its duty admirably both towards Militia and Regulars, and had before June mustered 1000 Yeomanry. Moreover, the Grenvilles, who mainly controlled all local business, were most zealous in military matters. The quota of Volunteers required of it was 3594 ; and the Militia lists contained in all but 9900 names. Strangely enough, however, many of the inhabitants were troubled with ignorant fears lest the oath of allegiance required from every Volunteer should bind them to some unknown military service. Lord Grenville went in person to argue with them and to reassure them, but they would not be convinced ; wherefore, lest such an example should spread, he at once called up the peccant parishes to undergo compulsory training under the Levy en Masse Act. This

[1] *I.D.* vol. vi. L.L. Cambs, to S.S. 11th Sept.; vol. xli. C.G.M. Cambs, to S.S. 16th Sept. 1804 ; vol. xxxii. L.L. Sussex, to S.S. 23rd and 30th Aug. 1803.

1803. suspicion does not appear to have prevailed elsewhere except in the Isle of Man, where the people disliked the combination of oath and red coat as much as in Scotland. "They will be difficult to persuade of their error," wrote the Lieutenant-Governor, "and even if persuaded they will be undisciplined." The Manxmen may be pardoned for their ignorance, which was reported to be excessive; but it is extraordinary that their misgivings should have been shared by men living within twenty miles of London.[1]

In Lancashire, where the deficiency was less than 400 out of a quota of 14,600, the fault seems to have been due chiefly to the blundering of the Government in the matter of regulations and arms, for the people came forward with enthusiasm enough; and the same holds good of Staffordshire, where the deficiency amounted to over 700 on a quota of 6800. In Warwickshire the Lieutenant wrote that he could not trust arms in the hands of many men who came forward; but to show that he was not lacking in zeal, he offered to subscribe £10,000 towards the cost of arming the loyal; to which generous offer, astounding as it may appear, he received no answer.[2] In Wiltshire and Northampton no particular cause for lukewarmness of patriotism can be traced. In Norfolk excessive jealousy of the different corps among themselves may have accounted for the fact that only 6900 Volunteers were forthcoming instead of 7254. But it is difficult to say what petty agencies may have affected the levy for good or for evil. In Salop the enrolment of Volunteers was checked for a time completely by the action of some Friendly Societies, founded for the support of the sick and infirm, whose rules contained a clause ordaining the expulsion of any member from the moment when he became a soldier.[3]

[1] *I.D.* vol. v. L.L. Bucks, to S.S. 31st July, 6th Oct. 1803; vol. xxi. Lt.-Gov. of Man to S.S. 26th April 1803.

[2] *Ibid.* vol. xxxiii. L.L. Warwick, to S.S. 12th, 22nd, 25th Aug. 1803.

[3] *Ibid.* vol. xxviii. Salop, J. Kynaston Powell to S.S. 17th July 1803.

The careful publication of this clause was of course the work of mischief-makers ; and one of the Deputy-Lieutenants drafted a short bill to declare such rules of such Societies to be null and void. But it would need a very long bill to guard against all the contrivances imaginable by men who wish to shirk their duty towards their country. 1803.

I pass next to the composition of the Volunteer corps. This of course varied greatly according to locality. When powerful magnates, such as the Duke of Northumberland or the Duke of Bedford, enrolled their tenants into one or more corps and provided them with everything but arms, the procedure was simple. The great man summoned his people, and called upon all who were able and willing to take service with him for the King, under command of himself or of one of his family. Such a lead was readily followed, feudal feeling and the example of the landlord being sufficiently strong to rally every able-bodied man on the estate to the ranks. Lesser magnates in like fashion formed their tenants into troops, companies, and squadrons, and sometimes (but by no means always) amalgamated them under the command of one of themselves into regiments or battalions. From the relative position of officers and privates in these corps, there was comparatively little difficulty in enforcing discipline. In the first place the men were often of superior station and intelligence. In the second every one of them wished to stand well with his landlord ; and even if the landlord refrained from using the enormous powers which he then enjoyed over his tenant, yet expulsion and liability to be ballotted as a Militiaman, meaning as they did not only personal inconvenience but social degradation, were sufficient deterrents from insubordination.

But in cases where no individual's station marked him out from among his fellows as the natural leader, and most notably in the towns, the proceedings were uniformly as follows :—A meeting of the citizens or parishioners was summoned, an individual was called to the chair, and

1803. after a solemn preamble setting forth the ambition and the vices of the hated Bonaparte, a series of resolutions was passed that an Association for the defence of the locality should be formed, that subscriptions should be invited, and that a committee should be organised for the general direction of its affairs. Then followed the rules of the Association, which included the conditions of service and the regulations for internal economy and discipline. The Committee did not necessarily include none but officers of the corps. On the contrary, it consisted commonly of the largest subscribers who, with sound commercial instinct, claimed an influence proportioned to their contribution. It was the great ambition of every Association to be, if possible, self-supporting, to the end that it might be self-controlled. In fact the Associations were, or aspired to be, simply clubs formed for purposes of defence, on the principles of equality that govern social clubs ; that is to say, that the Committee was elected ; that the officers also were either elected or chosen by the Committee; and that the general proceedings of the Committee, together with any matters of extraordinary importance, were subjected to the criticism of General Meetings, ordinary and extraordinary.

There were, of course, cases, notably among the metropolitan corps, where the system worked well. Such corps were composed of men, indeed of gentlemen, to whom self-suppression for a common object came as an instinct, and who thought it no shame, but rather a proud duty, to yield obedience to their fellows. The rules of such corps, and indeed of many other corps besides them, were exceedingly drastic ; the need for vesting all power of discipline in the commanding officer was generally recognised ; and there was always sufficient moral support in the mass of the regiment to enable him to enforce the rules without hesitation.

A few samples of such rules will not be out of place. Among those of the Monmouthshire Cavalry, subject to the Duke of Beaufort, it was enacted that no member of the troop should leave it unless he produced a substitute, on pain of a fine of twenty guineas; that no horse should measure less than fourteen hands two inches; and that no horse once approved should be exchanged, except for a better, under penalty of a fine of one guinea.[1] In the Isle of Ely Association it was laid down that the members should be householders; that officers should be recommended by the Association to the Lord-Lieutenant; that the majority should be entitled to reject any proposed member; and that the Government should supply arms only.[2] The regulations of the Gravesend Rifle Corps provided that every private and non-commissioned officer should subscribe five shillings a quarter, and every officer half a guinea a quarter, the officers and non-commissioned officers being elected by ballot of the members.[3] In Clapham the Association resolved to form two companies of infantry and one or more of cavalry; the officers and men to serve without pay and the whole to be governed by a military committee of twenty, elected by the members. Zachary Macaulay commanded one of the companies, and doubtless exercised it on Clapham Common under the eyes of his marvellous little boy Tom, who at three years old was probably ready with historical parallels for the transformation of so staid a citizen into a soldier. The Battersea Association was formed on much the same lines, the Committee supplying uniforms out of a general subscription of the parish.[4] But the variations of rules and terms of service could be indefinitely multiplied, the Government having taken no precautions before the passing of the Levy en Masse Act to secure uniformity. 1803.

But if associations of enlightened gentlemen and corps of tenants commanded by landlords were comparatively successful in securing discipline and

1 *I.D.* vol. iv. L.L. Brecon and Monmouth, to S.S. 2nd Jan. 1804.
2 *Ibid.* vol. vi. Cambridge, Owen Gray to S.S. 30th July 1803.
3 *Ibid.* vol. xviii. Kent, Regulations dated 24th July 1803.
4 *Ibid.* vol. xxxi. Surrey, 21st July and 1st Aug. 1803.

1803. efficiency, such was not the case when the direction of affairs lay in the hands of the great middle class, which, with all its merits and all its virtues, seems unable to crush down its imperious instinct to give nothing without expecting something in return. Under its guidance the associations broke down in all directions, and there was not only insubordination but occasionally sheer chaos.

To understand the story thoroughly it is necessary briefly to mention a further proceeding of the Government towards the Volunteers in 1803, after its decision to accept the whole of the corps that had been offered. Its first step was, in the circumstances, eminently wise and prudent. Napoleon's preparations, though as a matter of fact hopelessly backward and misdirected, were reported to be far advanced; and there was reason to fear that the local forces in the maritime counties might at any time during the winter be called into the field. Preference had rightly been given to these counties in the distribution of arms; and early in October Ministers determined to invite such corps in England as were ready and willing to come out on permanent pay and duty within their own counties and districts. The defence of Newcastle in particular was recommended for special attention, and the Lieutenant was asked to ascertain if any of the corps within reasonable distance of that city were prepared to assemble there, relieving each other successively either in fractions or as complete battalions after a fortnight's duty. "The King," added the Circular, "can *invite* the Volunteers to do so; he cannot *compel* them except in case of invasion, or appearance of invasion on the coast."[1] The response to the invitation was for the most part hearty; and in the winter of 1803 the Volunteers had a chance of showing their quality.

The signs of indiscipline in that year were relatively unimportant, though they brought into glaring relief the defects of the Government's measures. Thus, under the

[1] Circular to L.Ls. 12th Oct. 1803.

Levy en Masse Act, provision had been made for fining men who neglected to attend their drills, but none for imprisoning them in default of payment. The result was that early in the day a Volunteer in Hampshire attended the first day's drill, for which his Commanding Officer had provided a dinner, and refused to come out again. He was fined to the extent of thirty-six shillings, but, having no property, snapped his fingers at the penalty and remained master of the situation.[1] The Lieutenant of Gloucestershire was confronted with exactly the same difficulty, and complained that men with no property to distrain upon were uncontrollable. "A force," he said, "which depends upon the good-humour of several hundred illiterate persons cannot last long."[2] The other cases recorded in 1803 seem to have arisen out of the changes which distinguished the system initiated in 1802 from that which obtained between 1794 and 1801. In Devon during the month of July a battalion refused to work, except in separate companies under sergeants of their own election, as in the last war. They repented very speedily, for the Lieutenant disbanded them on the spot, and swept every man into the ballot for the Army of Reserve; but this salutary example was of course unknown except in the immediate district, and insubordination was not always so well-timed as to bring on itself immediate punishment.[3] In another case, in Herefordshire, it was the officers who showed a mutinous spirit; a number of subalterns protesting very discourteously to the Vice-Lieutenant against the action of the Commanding Officer who had recommended a stranger to be his Major, instead of allowing promotion to go by seniority within the battalion. The real grievance was that the Colonel had hitherto consulted his officers before making any such appointments, and on this occasion had omitted to do so. The Vice-Lieutenant, instead of ordering the 1803.

1 *I.D.* vol. viii. Cornwall (misplaced letter), Lawrence Reynolds to V.L. Hants, 13th Nov. 1803.

2 *Ibid.* vol. l. L.L. Gloucester, to S.S. 15th Jan. 1804.

3 *Ibid.* vol. x. L.L. Devon, to S.S. 16th July 1803.

1803. subalterns to withdraw their letter, under pain of instant dismissal, forwarded it to the Secretary of State, who likewise contented himself with rebuking the writers severely. Thereupon twelve officers of the corps resigned on the spot, and doubtless made the county ring with the fame of their spirited behaviour.[1] In yet another case a sergeant of Volunteers refused to collect the fines imposed on privates by the rules of the corps, abused his officers, and even threatened them with his pike. He was brought up before a Justice and fined five shillings in pursuance of the Act; after which he calmly sent in his kit and retired into private life.[2] "Discipline will be injured if every discontented man can thus discharge himself," commented the writer of this memorandum; and his opinion was shared by many other officers.

There was, indeed, a sharp controversy as to this same right of Volunteers to quit the service at their pleasure before the conclusion of peace, which, until decided, led to much trouble. The question was one which had not been anticipated by Ministers, otherwise they would undoubtedly have settled it by Act of Parliament, and settled it, moreover, in the negative. They referred it, however, to the Law-Officers of the Crown, Spencer Perceval and Manners-Sutton, who decided against the right of resignation. "If," said Perceval afterwards in the House of Commons, "Volunteers enter into an engagement, as undoubtedly they do, they ought not to be able to renounce it at all times except at the period of actual invasion."[3] This, on the face of it, appeared to be common sense; and the opinion was at once circulated[4] to the Lieutenants without a doubt that it would be final. But a champion of the right of resignation arose in the person of Thomas Erskine, the future Chancellor, who being at the time Colonel of the Law

[1] *I.D.* vol. l. V.L. Hereford, to S.S. 28th Jan.; Colonel J. Matthews to S.S. 6th April 1804.

[2] *Ibid.* vol. xviii. Kent, Memo. of 27th Dec. 1803.

[3] *H.D.* Perceval's speech, 8th Feb. 1804.

[4] Circular of 7th Oct. 1803.

Association Volunteers, or "Devil's Own," immediately took the field against the Law-Officers, and in a public letter to the newspapers upheld precisely the opposite contention. This letter, with marvellous rapidity, made its way all over England, and put new heart into the insubordinate. In Devon it caused great agitation; and in two different corps men who under their regimental rules had been summoned for absenting themselves from exercise, pleaded that they meant to resign. In Yorkshire likewise Erskine's flowery speeches and letters were read with avidity, so pleased were the Volunteers to find yet one more opening for the evasion of discipline.[1] Meanwhile, however, the Secretary of State's faith in the Law-Officers was beginning to totter; and he actually wrote to one of the Devonian commandants that he had better allow all men who did not choose to stay in his corps to go about their business. "If there are not Volunteers enough, the classes will be called up," he added, doubtless wishing in vain that he had never allowed the nation to be trained to arms at all except under the Levy en Masse Act. But it was too late. The question was presently brought before the Court of King's Bench, which decided that Volunteers had undoubtedly the right in law to resign whenever they chose, though not to the prejudice of regimental regulations to the contrary. 1803.

In Norfolk the effect of this decision was startling. Men sent in their kits and arms from all quarters, without taking the trouble to obtain a proper discharge; and the officers, to check the evil, begged that the seceders might be called out under the Levy en Masse Act.[2] But the mischief was by no means confined to displays of this kind. Such a defeat of Government by a popular hero of Erskine's type was in principle extremely bad for discipline; for with all his ability as an advocate,

[1] *I.D.* vol. xlv. Devon, Lord Rolle to S.S. 24th Jan.; Lt.-Gen. Simcoe to S.S., 4th Feb. 1804; vol. lxvii. V.L. Yorks, to S.S. 3rd Feb. 1804.

[2] *Ibid.* vol. lviii. Norfolk, P. L. Powell to S.S. 24th March 1804.

1803. he was compounded chiefly of vanity and egoism.[1] The triumph of such a man upon such a question was the worst possible example for self-governing corps; and in the winter and spring of 1803-4 there was a succession of very discreditable incidents.

The St. Pancras Volunteer Association was governed by a "Military Committee" with undefined powers, the said Committee consisting of three officers and twelve privates, with a private for president. An inferior mechanic and a disreputable attorney, by frequenting night clubs and public-houses in company with the lowest class of privates, obtained election as officers, and therewith demanded for the Committee the control of the subscriptions, which by law were vested in the Commanding Officer. The Attorney-General, being consulted upon the point, declared that beyond all question the control of the subscriptions lay with the Commanding Officer, and that the legality of the Military Committee was very doubtful. Upon this, without consulting the Colonel, the malcontents summoned a general meeting of the corps, and after a scene of scandalous indeceny persuaded forty-five members to sign a protest denying, in the face of the law, that the funds were vested in the Colonel. The case was examined by the Deputy-Lieutenants, who recommended the expulsion of the offenders, but blamed the Colonel also for his unconciliatory bearing. On receipt of this report the Secretary of State wrote a letter annulling the appointment of the Military Committee, and the rules as to election of officers by the corps. This letter the Colonel read on parade, and at the close called upon the five ringleaders to fall out. Several voices from the ranks answered, "One and all, one and all," and the Colonel, after manœuvring the regiment for an hour,

[1] As a Colonel of Volunteers he was helpless without a card to recall to him his words of command, and very inefficient with one. But Lord Ellenborough, afterwards Lord Chief Justice, even with the aid of chalked marks upon his boots, could never remember to step off with the appointed foot. Campbell's *Lives of the Chancellors*, vi. 547.

left the dismissal of the ringleaders to the Adjutant. Both parties then appealed with much mutual recrimination to the Lord-Lieutenant and the Secretary of State; to which the Lieutenant, being a sensible man, replied by recommending that the corps should be disbanded.[1] 1803-4

The Royal Southwark Volunteers, commanded by Tierney, the politician, distinguished itself in somewhat similar fashion. The Colonel had rejected a sergeant chosen by the men of one company in favour of a candidate selected by himself; and against this the company handed in resolutions of protest, as also against his appointment of an officer without first consulting them. Tierney at once paraded the company and ordered it to deliver up its arms, which the men did without a murmur, being ignorant of the meaning of subordination rather than insubordinate.[2]

In another London corps, the North Britons, a corporal refused to be silent on parade, or to obey an officer who bade him hold his tongue, on the ground that the officer in question belonged to a different company. The corporal then addressed the following letter to his Commanding Officer:—

> SIR—I am desired by several privates in my company to acquaint you it is their determination to withdraw themselves unless you immediately order Leake[3] to resign. I think he ought to bless his stars I did not bayonet him—but, damn him, I have done with him—Yours, etc. P. WOOD.

And the Commanding Officer, instead of turning Mr. Wood out of the corps and taking measures to have him drawn by the ballot, reported the case to the Secretary of State in utter helplessness and despair.[4]

[1] *I.D.* vol. lvi. Middlesex, Report of 5th Jan.; C.O. St. Pancras Vol. to S.S. 30th Jan.; L.L. Middlesex, to S.S. 30th Jan.; C.O. St. Pancras Vol. to R. Pole-Carew, 19th March 1804.

[2] *Ibid.* vol. lvi. Tierney to S.S. 10th Jan. 1804.

[3] I take Leake to have been the officer who ordered the writer of the letter to be silent.

[4] *I.D.* vol. lvi. Lt.-Col. Alex. Davison to S.S. Jan. 27th.

1803-4. In Lambeth there was a Loyal Lambeth Corps, wherein the right of electing officers was supposed to be vested in such members as had clothed and equipped themselves. The original officers had been nominated by a Civil Committee, whose members, no doubt, had given liberal subscriptions; but the Commanding Officer presently appointed a Military Committee, consisting of officers, non-commissioned officers and privates, for the regulation of military, as distinguished from financial, affairs. A vacancy for a Lieutenant occurred, and the Civil Committee recommended several persons for election. The corps, ignoring the recommendations, elected a man not mentioned by the Civil Committee, whose name was then submitted, without any details of the circumstances, to the Lord-Lieutenant. Five ensigns, feeling themselves aggrieved, thereupon addressed a remonstrance to both committees through the Commanding Officer, who, after expostulating with them in vain, laid the letter before the Military Committee, which decided against them. The ensigns then threatened to appeal to the parish, when the Commanding Officer invoked the Lieutenant's authority to prohibit publication of the appeal; and the whole body of the officers was appointed a court to inquire into the matter. Unfortunately, I have been unable to trace the further career of this interesting corps.[1]

Later in the same year a company of Camberwell Volunteers, with the connivance of their officers, held a mutinous and disorderly meeting, subversive of all discipline. It was at once disbanded by the Vice-Lieutenant, when the men offered themselves to a Southwark corps and were readily accepted.[2]

But such occurrences were by no means confined to London and its vicinity. Major-General Jeffery Amherst, after thirty years' service in the Army, in an evil moment for himself, yielded to patriotic enthusiasm and took command, as Major, of the Evesham Volun-

[1] *I.D.* vol. lxiv. V.L. Surrey, to S.S. 26th Jan. 1804.
[2] *Ibid.* vol. lxiv. V.L. Surrey, to S.S. 11th Aug. 1804.

teers. Unfortunately there was another old soldier in the corps, a very remarkable man. He had begun life as a private in the cavalry, had been employed in the recruiting service, and had made sufficient profit out of it to purchase a commission, which he had finally laid down in order to keep a pot-house at Evesham. Owing to his military experience he was appointed an officer in Amherst's corps, and his first quarrel with the latter arose from the fact that Amherst forbade him to parade his men in front of the pot-house's door, thereby depriving him of the profits of selling ale to them. He then insulted the Adjutant, a veteran of fifty-two years' service, during exercise, and challenged him to a duel while in the execution of his duty. Upon this the officers sent a deputation to him to ask him to resign; but he took one of them, the son of a shoemaker, into his councils, and the two between them contrived to excite a mutiny of the corps on parade. The affair caused such disturbance and scandal that the Magistrates took it up, and appealed to the Lieutenant to dismiss this precious pair; whereupon the culprits went to the Justices with tears in their eyes, and promised not to interfere further with the corps if the matter were allowed to drop. However, they made false representations of their conduct to the Home Office, and managed to extract from the Under-Secretary a letter which spoke of the "honourable motives which induced them to resign." This they published in Evesham, of course filling the inhabitants with disgust, and reducing poor Amherst to speechless indignation. No better example could be found than this to show the essential defects of the Volunteer system.[1] 1803-4.

In Somerset a private of the Loyal Bath Volunteers appeared on parade in liquor, and fell to quarrelling with the officer of another company. He was ordered by the Colonel to apologise to the officer, and as he

[1] *I.D.* vol. lxvi. Worcester, Major-Gen. Amherst to S.S. 5th Jan. 1804.

1803-4. refused to do so he was dismissed. Next day the privates of his company met, and after duly debating the conduct of the Commanding Officer, passed, with nine dissentients, resolutions that they could not attend another muster until their comrade was reinstated, and that it was ungentlemanlike for officers of one company to interfere with men of another. These resolutions they handed to their Captain to be laid before the Colonel, together with an expression of their confidence in the said Captain. That individual, who, though fully cognisant of what was going forward, had not moved a finger to prevent it, thereupon approached the Colonel; and he, good, easy man, offered to refer the affair to a General Committee of the regiment, though he delayed to do so for some hours, in the hope that matters would right themselves spontaneously. On the following day, however, the men who had held the meeting printed and published a full account of the proceedings, announcing at the close that no alternative remained to them but to resign. The entire city of Bath, at that time by no means the most orderly in the kingdom, was stirred to its foundations; and the Lieutenant, for reasons best known to himself, referred the matter to the Secretary of State. That functionary, more in sorrow than anger, rebuked the original offender, who then apologised to the officer. The men who had held the meeting also apologised; and, in fact, there seems to have been a carnival of apology, without, however, any remarkable benefit to the discipline of the Bath Volunteers.[1]

In the East Riding of Yorkshire the officers of the Derwent Dale Volunteers resigned in a body, their grievance being that their Commanding Officer never convened them for consultation upon any subject relating to the regiment. So well satisfied were they as to the legitimacy of their complaint that they urged it without concealment in a letter to the Lord-Lieutenant, and were somewhat taken aback when he disbanded the

[1] *I.D.* Somerset, vol. lxiii. Statement of 21st Aug. O.C. Bath Volunteers to L.L. 8th Sept. 1803.

regiment "without regret, owing to their unmilitary behaviour."[1] 1803-4.

In Gloucester two companies of Volunteers were formed at Wotton-under-Edge, under the direction of a Committee which undertook to provide, not for its finances, but for its support and for making the necessary regulations. The Committee consisted of a Magistrate, who was chairman, two clothiers, a doctor (none of them Volunteers), and the officers of the corps; and the chairman was the person who had recommended the officers for appointment by the Lord-Lieutenant. One day on parade a lieutenant addressed some contemptuous words to an ensign, who replied by challenging him to mortal combat. The Committee took the matter up, and recommended to the Lieutenant the dismissal of the ensign, who was duly gazetted out. The non-commissioned officers thereupon drew up an address to the General commanding the district, protesting against the ensign's dismissal as highly arbitrary and contrary to the rules of the corps. It is noteworthy that of 108 signatories to this document, 37 were unable to write their names. The case is curious as an example of a Volunteer corps appealing to a military chief against the action of its own Committee. But in truth they would appeal to any one in order to get their own way.[2]

In Cambridgeshire there was an extremely interesting corps, in which one company fell at variance with the Colonel because he objected to their drinking in the ranks when at drill. The Colonel appealed to the officers of the company, who declined to intervene, saying that the practice was usual; and one of the men, having finished his draught, stripped off his coat, rolled up his sleeves, and doubling his fists challenged his Colonel to fight him. Meanwhile another officer came forward to remonstrate with the ensign of the erring

[1] *I.D.* vol. xciii. L.L. Yorks, E.R. to S.S. 29th Sept., 5th Oct. 1805.

[2] *Ibid.* vol. l. L.L. to S.S. 3rd Jan.; Richard Nelmes to L.L. 6th April 1804.

1803-4. company, whereupon the ensign brandished his sword in the intruder's face, and retired with twenty of his men to a cask of ale hard by, from whence, after further refreshment, they marched off the ground. A court of inquiry was held, when it appeared that the ensign and five of the ringleaders were drunk on this occasion ; indeed, one of them, bent upon maintaining his character, was drunk when he came before the court. The chief offenders were dismissed, but to no purpose, for the company only repeated its misconduct a few weeks later, and was then disbanded.[1]

In Cheshire there was trouble with the Nantwich troop of Volunteer Cavalry, which refused to go out for ten days' training or for eighty-five days' drill in the year.[2] In Yorkshire the Wakefield Volunteers declined to obey an officer not of their own election, and nominated a Committee of officers and privates to give such directions as the privates thought proper ; but they came to their senses after the dismissal of their leaders, and submitted to officers of the Lieutenant's appointment.[3] At Ripon there were scandals in a Volunteer corps which occupied the pens of the clerks at the Home Office for months. Even in Scotland there was one corps at Falkirk which joined issue with the Lord-Lieutenant over the right to elect its own officers, and threatened to resign unless indulged with its own way. The Lieutenant commanded them to parade without arms, ordered in another corps with muskets loaded with ball cartridge, and resolved to disband them on the spot unless they repented. The General, however, deprecated any display of force and contrived to bring the regiment to reason ; the entire trouble being due to a few turbulent men who were disarmed and dismissed on parade.[4]

[1] *I.D.* vol. xli. M. Brackenbury to L.L. Cambs, 12th April ; L.L. Cambs, to S.S. 4th May 1804.

[2] *Ibid.* vol. xlii. Cheshire, L.L. to S.S. 18th Feb. 1804.

[3] *Ibid.* vol. lxvii. Yorks W.R. V.L. to S.S. 19th Jan. 1804.

[4] *Ibid.* vol. xliii. L.L. Stirling, to S.S. 2nd Feb. 1804.

The first call upon Volunteers for permanent duty led also to considerable insubordination, and fortunately to one very salutary example. In Cambridgeshire the appeal for this service was a failure. Few of the commanding officers took the trouble to answer at all; only four thought that their men would be willing to come out, and of the four one doubted the success of embodying his corps outside the limits of his parish. The company at Little Swaffham could not even refuse to go on permanent duty without riotous and disorderly conduct; and the West Wrathing company declined either to drill at home or to march out to drill elsewhere. Both were disbanded; and by September 1804 Cambridge had increased the number lacking to her quota of Volunteers from 300 to 800.[1] In Caermarthen one regiment mutinied while on permanent duty, but the fact was not reported by the Commanding Officer, and would not have been known at headquarters had not some of the officers favoured the Secretary of State with a criticism on the judgment of a court of inquiry upon some of their fellows.[2] In Dorset two companies marched to Dorchester for permanent duty, but declined, in spite of remonstrances and a strong feeling against them, to proceed to Weymouth. The Lieutenant was weak enough to write to the Secretary of State for orders, instead of disbanding them with ignominy in their county town, but in due time they were sent about their business.[3] 1803-4.

In Devon the Sidmouth Artillery Volunteers came out with others on permanent duty, and were warned that while so engaged they were subject to the same discipline as the Army. One man appeared on parade an hour late, asked his officer for leave of absence, and abused him violently on being refused. The officer ordered some men to take charge of him, but they

[1] *I.D.* vol. xli. C.G.M. Cambs, to S.S. 15th April, 16th Sept.; L.L. to S.S. 13th, 23rd May 1804.

[2] *Ibid.* vol. lxxi. Maj.-Gen. Gascoigne to S.S. 23rd July 1805.

[3] *Ibid.* vol. xlvi. L.L. Dorset, to S.S. 7th, 12th May 1804.

1803-4. declined, one of them saying that he knew the rules of the Volunteers and that "he would be damned if he would take the prisoner to the guard-room." The officer thereupon seized the first offender by the collar and dragged him off, fighting furiously all the way, while the second mutineer harangued the populace and tried to stir up a riot. Matters became serious; the local magistrates were feeble; and it was at last necessary to send for an escort of the Army of Reserve to bring in the prisoners. But now the case was taken up by stronger hands. The two men were tried by regimental court-martial and sentenced, the one to 150 lashes, the other to 100 lashes, and both to be drummed out. The Commanding Officer rightly and wisely reduced the punishment to thirty lashes and twenty lashes, but the drumming out was performed with all due ceremony; and the effect was good. "The Sidmouth company," wrote General Simcoe, "considering all circumstances—the village politics, the tea-table interferences, the want of energy in the magistrates—have behaved tolerably well. Thirteen resignations have taken place (out of a full strength of 269); and two of these wished to withdraw their resignations but were not allowed."[1]

It may be asked whether it were not an indignity to resort to the lash in the case of the Volunteers. The answer is that, with the exception of some of the corps from the larger towns, the ranks were filled chiefly with ordinary labouring men, that is to say, with the same class as supplied the rank and file of the Army. There are no statistics to show actually that this was so, but there are casual allusions which prove that it was true of Buckinghamshire, Cambridgeshire, Cornwall, Denbigh, Gloucestershire, Middlesex, Norfolk, Radnor, Stafford, Sussex, and Yorkshire in England, and of Lanark and Ross in Scotland, so that it would be reasonable to conclude that it was not otherwise in

[1] *I.D.* vol. xlv. Lt.-Gen. Simcoe to S.S. 23rd March, 12th April; L.L. Devon, to S.S. 27th March 1804.

the remaining counties.[1] It was evidently not originally 1803-4. contemplated that this class would fill the ranks of the Volunteers, otherwise the Government would have provided other punishment than fines for breaches of discipline. Under a Levy en Masse they would, of course, all have been enrolled; and it was almost certainly a mistake for Ministers ever to have placed them in the state of Volunteers, especially under the August Allowances. In the first place, as has been seen, they were too poor to afford a day's drill without pay; and yet if their corps was to be provided with an efficient staff, they were required to exercise on fifty-two Sundays and thirty-three week-days for the wages of £1. Some entertained earnest and conscientious objections to drill on Sundays, which made their trial the severer. Nor was this their only hardship. Masters in some cases refused to hire servants who belonged to Volunteer corps, or deducted part of their wages when they went to drill. A case is recorded of a Volunteer, enrolled with his employer's knowledge and under no special agreement as to wages on that account, who at the end of the year found that twelve shillings out of his annual wage of five pounds had been stopped by his master for twelve and a half days' attendance at exercise.[2] Lastly, there was the extremely troublesome complication

[1] *I.D.* vol. v. L.L. Bucks, to S.S. Oct. 1803; vol. xli. Sir J. Mackenzie (Ross) to S.S. 17th March 1804; vol. vi. L.L. Cambs, to S.S. 11th Sept. 1803; vol. xliv. F. Gregor to L.L. Cornwall, 14th Jan. 1804; vol. xliv. Denbigh, Rich. Willding to S.S. 2nd July 1804; vol. l. L.L. Glos. to S.S. 15th Jan. 1804; vol. xxiii. Vestry Clerks of Spitalfields to S.S. 13th Oct. 1803; vol. lviii. L.L. Norfolk, to S.S. 2nd Oct. 1804; vol. lxi. enclosed in L.L. Radnor, to S.S. 9th June 1804; vol. xxix. Magistrates of Lichfield to S.S. 19th Nov. 1803; vol. xvii. Lanark, J. Geddes to S.S. 17th Dec. 1803; vol. xxxii. L.L. Sussex, to S.S. 14th Nov. 1803; vol. xxxv. Yorks W.R., Thomas Plumer to W.O. 12th Nov. 1803.

[2] *I.D.* vol. xxxv. Tho. Plumer to W.O. 12th Nov. 1803; vol. xliv. Denbigh, Rich. Willding to S.S. 2nd July 1804. The salary of £5 a year is called a low wage by the writer. The case occurred within the Lieutenancy of Denbigh and Merioneth. The employer was evidently a farmer, so that probably the man received board and lodging as well as the £5 a year.

1803-4. that agricultural labourers of a great many counties both in England and in Scotland changed their master annually at Michaelmas or Martinmas, shifting into new parishes and consequently taking service in new Volunteer corps, or at any rate in different companies of the same corps. As Parliament met in November it was necessary to prepare the returns of the Volunteers for the estimates and for the perusal of the House immediately before this annual change; and hence the returns were never more than approximately, if even approximately, correct.

As regards the officers of the Volunteers, the reader will have gained some idea already from certain of the instances of indiscipline. Taken as a body they were probably not very efficient, though of course there were exceptions. It is worthy of remark that many officers of high rank in the Army gave their services willingly to their local corps. The case of General Amherst has already been cited; and again, there were in Sussex alone Lieutenant-General Whyte, who had held an independent command over nearly ten thousand men on active service, Lord Gage, Colonels Newton and Crosbie, and the Duke of Richmond. This advantage, however, was not without its drawbacks. The Government early in 1804 appointed inspecting field-officers from the half-pay list to every county for the Volunteers, and, as these held the rank of Lieutenant-Colonel only, there was some discontent among such men as those above named at being placed under the orders of an officer of inferior rank. The Commander-in-Chief, however, set his foot at once and firmly upon any complaints of this kind. "While you are in the Volunteer service," he wrote to Colonel Crosbie, "you cannot avail yourself of your Army rank, not even if your corps is on permanent duty and serving with other corps."[1]

Occasionally an officer of the Regulars would give

[1] *I.D.* vol. xxxii. L.L. Sussex, to S.S. 3rd Oct. 1803; vol. lxv. Sussex, D.A.G. to Col. Crosbie, 5th April 1804.

enormous time and trouble gratuitously to the improvement of the Volunteers in the neighbourhood of his quarters;[1] but for the most part corps were dependent on such few half-pay officers as they could collect under the regulations, and upon their adjutants. Good adjutants, again, were not very easy to procure, as is usually the case in time of war; and the best of whom record remains was a man of fifty-two years' service. He had passed through the whole of the American War as a private in the 10th Foot, with many wounds; he had then served as sergeant-major for between twenty and thirty years in the same regiment, had finally received a commission, and after yet another ten years as an officer, had retired, only to emerge, still possessing the vigour and activity of youth, to be the soul and the mainstay of a Volunteer corps.[2] Such men, however, were rare. In many parts of Wales adjutants were especially difficult to find, for unless they could speak Welsh they were useless.[3] Indeed officers of any kind were so scarce in some counties of the Principality that the Lieutenant of Denbigh declared it to be impossible to find enough for the Volunteers unless the clergy received commissions. With this view he submitted the names of three reverend gentlemen for a single gazette, having first received the sanction of their diocesan; and was greatly disappointed when their services were not accepted. In Rutland also the Lord-Lieutenant urged that a parson should be posted Lieutenant, as every single gentleman in the country was already absorbed by some corps or another.[4] But the Secretary of State set his face on principle against the drawing of a red coat over a cassock, and the Church, as far as the Volunteers were concerned, remained restricted to spiritual warfare.

1803-4.

1 *I.D.* vol. v. L.L. Bucks, to S.S. 28th Oct. 1803.

2 *Ibid.* vol. lxvi. Maj.-Gen. Amherst to S.S. 11th Feb. 1804.

3 *Ibid.* vol. lv. L.L. Montgomery, to S.S. 8th March 1804.

4 *Ibid.* vol. ix. L.L. Denbigh, to S.S. 20th Nov. 1803; vol. xxvii. L.L. Rutland, to S.S. 17th Oct. 1803.

1803-4. In Scotland, too, there was a dearth of officers, chiefly owing to lack of wealthy men. In Ross the Volunteers numbered under 1700 rank and file, but the Commandants found it impossible to get men to lead them. A few came forward at first under the idea that the menace of invasion would at once be realised, and that the repulse of the French would leave them free to go home; but prolonged service they could not afford, so they either resigned, or left their names as a favour on the list and declined to attend any drills. It was not surprising, for many of them depended on their own industry for a living.[1] In Banff, a county that has never lacked military enterprise, the Lieutenant begged that the officers should receive as many days' pay as the men, for there were few who could afford to buy a uniform or serve without compensation.[2]

Nor were such difficulties wholly unknown in England, though they presented themselves in a different form. It was rare for an officer openly to solicit pay; but one Commandant had the courage to ask that it should be given during permanent duty, and put forward very good reasons for the request. "Government allows twenty days' pay for the men," he said, "but we, the officers, make it up to eighty-four days', besides the expense of £3 a man for clothing."[3] There lay the heart of the matter. The Government might boast of their economy in limiting the mass of the Volunteers to the August Allowances, but as a matter of fact the whole of them received the June Allowances by the generosity of their officers or of other private individuals. Even so, from want of money, innumerable corps collapsed or were stifled in their birth. First, those that had aspired to be self-supporting found the burden heavier than they could bear, and

[1] *I.D.* vol. vi. Donald M'Leod (Ross) to S.S. 11th April; O.C. 1st Ross Volunteers to Donald M'Leod, 5th Sept. 1804.

[2] *Ibid.* vol. iii. L.L. Banff, to S.S. 15th April 1803.

[3] *Ibid.* vol. xxiv. Lt.-Col. Robert Harvey (Norwich Vols.) to S.S. 19th Dec. 1803.

either broke down entirely or begged for the August Allowances. From that instant their ultimate disappearance was only a question of time. Subscriptions were forthcoming in the first moments of excitement and enthusiasm, but after a short time the excitement palled and the enthusiasm waned. Moreover, expenses tended to increase rather than the contrary. The regulation that all infantry should be clothed in scarlet naturally caused such a demand for scarlet cloth that the price rose appreciably.[1] Again, the extravagance of a few wealthy corps set an example of gorgeous raiment for the men, and in particular for the bandsmen, which regimental emulation and masculine vanity soon conspired to render infectious. Many a subscription-list was squandered in absurdly expensive clothes and head-dresses; and the exultation of the Volunteers in their plumes and trappings is, after a century's interval, positively humiliating to contemplate. Scores — I believe that I might say hundreds — of Volunteer officers all over England and Scotland called in the painter's aid to immortalise their "regimentals" and their martial bearing.[2] Every one of the London corps, whether by its own act or by the enterprise of some print-seller, obtained commemoration at the hands of some limner of fashion-plates, and has been visible in the windows of print-shops ever since. The likeness even of Pitt himself, whose scorn of frippery was hardly exceeded by his deep love of his country, was tendered to the public in the full uniform of the Cinque Ports Volunteers, mounted on a prancing charger and flourishing a sword; while for pendant there was offered a similar presentation of the vain and ridiculous Erskine. 1803-4.

All this was very well for a few months—in London and a few more rich towns for even longer—but then

[1] *I.D.* vol. ix. L.L. Denbigh, to S.S. 16th Aug. 1803.

[2] I speak as a collector, for several years past, of engraved portraits of distinguished officers of the Army. To such a collector the portraits of the illustrious obscure, many of them of great merit as works of art, are little short of a curse.

1803-4. the subscriptions were exhausted, and the civil subscribers, having done their duty as they thought by their first contributions, buttoned up their pockets and would give no more. Further, the more zealous the Volunteers, the more rapidly of course was their raiment worn out. "Eighty-five days' drill and twenty-one days' permanent duty have reduced the clothing allowed to my corps by Government to rags," wrote an officer of a Welsh corps; "the Captains will subscribe their contingent money, if the Government will help."[1] But if the Government helped one corps, it must help all; and the answer to the above application could only be in the negative. Thence followed as a natural consequence the humouring by their superiors of rich officers, so as to keep them in their corps at any cost, and of poorer officers in consideration of the sacrifices that they had made; while a general tenderness on the part of the Government towards indiscipline at large in the Volunteers evoked from Windham in the House of Commons the statement that the Cabinet was afraid of them. And this was perfectly true. How could Ministers not be afraid of a vast body of men, many of them voters, whom they had practically invited to serve their country in the way which they thought best and easiest for themselves, and at the expense of the most patriotic individuals among them? The entire force naturally claimed the indulgence that was due only to the unselfish minority among them. The subscribers as naturally demanded some share in the control of the levies which they had helped to raise and equip; and the State's rightful hold upon the Volunteers in the matter of discipline was lost.

Nor was anything gained economically. The expense of the Volunteers to the country, as it appeared on the estimates and returns, might seem relatively small; but this was only because the balance was defrayed by private subscription. Windham in

[1] *I.D.* vol. xlix. Glamorgan, Rowley Lascelles to S.S. 9th July 1804.

1806 reckoned that the Volunteers had cost in three and a half years five millions from the public purse, and at least as much more from individual contributions. This entire sum of ten millions of course came out of the pockets of the nation, and impoverished it by that amount, whether it was gathered in the form of taxation or of a patriotic gift. The burden of expense was unwisely and inequitably laid upon the willing who made shift to bear it; but no part of the outlay was thereby saved. The only difference was that the country, by leaving its defence in great measure to private enterprise, renounced even such proportion of control as was due to it in return for a grant of public funds. 1803-4.

Incidentally this relaxation of the Government's hold upon the Volunteers led also to a false system of training. Being left to themselves, these amateur soldiers, of course, aped their professional brethren; and hours were zealously devoted to the classical eighteen manœuvres of David Dundas and the stiff formality of the Prussian system. All this was utterly useless. General Money, a retired officer who had fought in command of troops of Revolutionary France in 1792 and had written one of the best books extant upon the work of Light Infantry, trained and armed three companies of Volunteers as sharpshooters. This, it must be remarked, must have cost him an appreciable sum, for the Government while countenancing by its regulations the formation of Rifle corps, would issue no rifles, nor grant more than the contract price of muskets for corps that provided rifles for themselves.[1] "You cannot make men equal to regular troops in twenty-four days' drill," wrote Money, "but you can make them good sharpshooters in ten days; whereas long, tedious drills weary the peasantry."[2] The plea fell upon deaf ears. In Parliament, as shall presently be seen, a soldier who later won immortality in the command of the Light

[1] *I.D.* vol. xxxiv. Yorks N.R., Lt.-Col. Morritt to S.S. 14th Oct. 1803.

[2] *Ibid.* vol. lviii. Money to L.L. Norfolk, 12th Aug. 1804.

1803-4. Division, Robert Craufurd, delivered a longer sermon upon the same text, but to no purpose. Of what profit was it to wear a red coat except in emulation of His Majesty's Guards? So the training of the Volunteers from the first took a wrong direction, and kept it to the end.

For the rest it must be added to the credit of the Volunteers that, with few exceptions, they came out with alacrity for permanent duty. Lord Moira, one of the best and ablest officers in the Army, declared himself ready to meet any enemy in the field with those of Scotland; and the corps in and about Edinburgh, having gathered into their ranks every old soldier that they could find, were undoubtedly not merely superior but good. It may not be inappropriate to recall that Mr. Walter Scott, Sheriff-Depute of Selkirk, was an enthusiastic officer in the Midlothian Yeomanry, not altogether to the satisfaction of the Lieutenant of Selkirk, who could count upon but one Deputy to help him with the business of the Lieutenancy.[1] From Devon also General Simcoe announced that he had over 2000 Volunteers fit for immediate service; and there were encouraging reports from inspecting officers in other quarters also. But the flaw in these flattering stories was that in few cases had the men full confidence in the ability of their officers; and in still fewer was there any real foundation of discipline. The Lieutenant of Sussex, a soldier of high rank, lamented greatly that the first class under the Levy en Masse Act had not been called out and exercised. "It would be sooner trained than the Volunteers," he said, "and we should have law to govern our proceedings instead of their endless pretensions."[2] On the other hand, the Lieutenant of the West Riding of Yorkshire averred that he should be nervous of enforcing the Levy en Masse Act in his district. "No persons of respectability, rank, and weight will submit to take commissions under the

[1] *I.D.* vol. xlvi. L.L. Selkirk, to S.S. 24th Aug. 1804.
[2] *Ibid.* vol. xxxii. L.L. Sussex, to S.S. 23rd Aug. 1803.

Act. I assure you that herein I report the opinion of every considerable man in the county."[1] There was no other complaint of this kind of the Levy en Masse Act; and it is probable that, if put to the test, Lord Fitzwilliam and his deputies would have been as zealous in enforcing it as their neighbours in other counties. But the really amazing thing is that after nine years of war, from 1793 to 1802, after many threatened invasions of England and one actual invasion of Ireland, the wisdom of Ministers and of Parliament should have been unable to produce an Act which could be accepted heartily by the whole country to govern the training of its population for defence. The task, it must be abundantly confessed, was no easy one; but after review of the proceedings of Addington's Ministry it can hardly be said, I think, that they shone in the preparation of England for war. Still it must be remembered that Addington was preceded by Pitt, and was working more or less under his protection; and that it was Pitt and no other who, under some unhappy inspiration, originated the whole of the Volunteer system, and started it definitely and irretrievably in the wrong direction.

1803-4.

[1] *I.D.* vol. xxxv. L.L. Yorks W.R. to S.S. 13th Aug. 1803.

CHAPTER III

I

1803. WITH all their imperfections on their heads—with a Regular Army starving for want of recruits, a Reserve already damned as an expensive failure, a Militia swollen to large numbers on paper, but with ranks unfilled and impossible to fill, and an enormous Volunteer force, unregulated, undisciplined, unorganised, but irrepressible—Addington and his colleagues met Parliament on the 22nd of November 1803. On the 2nd of December the Army Estimates were introduced, showing an establishment of 141,000 Regular troops (including the Army of Reserve) and 110,000 embodied Militia at home, and 61,000 Regular troops in the Colonies and India. The number actually effective at home was 69,000 Regulars, 26,000 Army of Reserve, and 80,000 Militia, Artillery not included. There was a brief preliminary debate on the 12th of December, wherein Pitt declared that according to the original intention, meaning, no doubt, according to his original plan, the Army of Reserve was to have been raised by each county in strict proportion to its population, and no substitutes were to have been received except from the county concerned or from those immediately adjacent to it. Possibly his design was to insinuate that under his own management the Act would have been differently administered. Possibly, too, it might have been; but the results would have been much the same. The true
1804. defect in the Act lay in the admission of substitutes at all; and it was futile for Pitt to argue that his bantling

had been maltreated, when it had been conceived in fallacy, brought forth in weakness, and was foredoomed by constitutional debility to an early grave. 1804.

But the great battle of the session, as may be imagined, was fought over the Volunteers. In order to extricate Ministers from the thousand difficulties in which haste, feebleness, and carelessness had involved them, Yorke, on the 13th of December, introduced, in the first place, a Volunteer Exemption Bill, a simple measure which was designed to set all doubts upon exemption at rest, and to enable Commanding Officers to certify that men had undergone training without arms in cases where no arms had been issued. This was passed on the 20th of December 1803 (44 Geo. III. cap. 18); and Yorke shortly afterwards presented a more important Bill to consolidate all existing Acts concerning the Volunteers. This was, in fact, an effort to correct the many blunders of the past session, and as such was likely to enjoy a stormy career.

As a first step it was proposed that the number of days' exercise required to exempt Volunteers from the Militia ballot should be raised from five to twenty-four, so as to place exemption from the Militia and the Army of Reserve upon the same footing. This was at once opposed as a breach of faith, and Addington was fain to plead that the new regulation would not come into force until May, so that Volunteers who disliked it would have plenty of time to resign.

An attempt was also made to override by enactment the decision of the Court of King's Bench as to the right of Volunteers to resign, when Perceval, as has been seen, upheld his own contention against that right, while Erskine vindicated the judgment of the court. Fox summed up the action of Ministers on the question in a single sentence. "First," he said, "it was intended that the Volunteers *might* resign; then the Attorney-General said that they *could not* resign; then the Court of King's Bench said that they *could* resign; and now Ministers bring in a Bill to say that they *can* resign,

1804. and insert a provision which renders it impossible for many to resign."[1] Against Fox and Erskine united the Ministry could make little fight, and the clause containing the obnoxious provision was withdrawn.

The third and most important novelty introduced into the Bill was a declaration that Volunteers should no longer be allowed to elect their own officers; and this proposition was warmly combated. Whitbread, a shrewd, sensible man and Colonel of a Volunteer battalion at Bedford, defended the practice of electing officers, provided that their names were submitted to the King through the Lieutenant for approval. "Had I offered my services as private in my Volunteers," he said, "I own that I should be very unwilling to serve under any officer appointed by the Crown to command me without my own consent." Sheridan warned Ministers against interference with the right as a breach of faith, and Fox adjured the Volunteers not to allow themselves to be bullied.[2] The question was compromised by making all future rules of corps subject to disallowance by the King. From this point to the general question of discipline the transition was easy; and since most of the members were officers of Volunteer corps, there were few who had not stories to tell or suggestions to put forward. Yorke considered that discipline was sufficiently safeguarded by giving Commanding Officers power to discharge men, and so to make them liable to the ballot, and by using the machinery of the Levy en Masse Act to call up disorderly or irregular men for training.[3] Pitt, full of his experience as Colonel of the Cinque Ports Volunteers, actually moved to omit as unnecessary the clause empowering commandants to discharge men; but Yorke, who knew the ways of Volunteer Committees better than Pitt, insisted upon it, because the regulations or many corps forbade the dismissal of any man without

[1] *H.D.* Commons, 19th March 1804.
[2] *Ibid.* 8th Feb., 27th Feb. 1804.
[3] *Ibid.* 8th Feb. 1804.

consent of the majority of the members.[1] On the other hand, it was argued that it was dangerous to give a commandant authority to subject a man to the ballot and to the probable expense of finding a substitute, without any appeal; but none the less the clause was carried as it stood. 1804.

The question of fines for irregular attendance or misconduct was also brought forward; but the Attorney-General was shy, as he said, of proceeding too far with a compulsory system for the Volunteers; and, though Pitt took a different view, a great many members seem to have held with Perceval. One member, Mr. Giles, had from the first maintained that Volunteers might discipline themselves, but that Parliament had no right to impose discipline.[2] Yorke condemned the enforcement of attendance and discipline by fines and imprisonment as "inconsistent with the Volunteer system;"[3] and Whitbread said roundly that any attempt to enforce fines with severity would cause many Volunteers to run away.[4]

In truth, the more the question of the Volunteers was debated, the more obvious it became that, whether their military value were great or small, they were extremely expensive and utterly unmanageable. No one knew how to draft a Bill which could control them; and if any one knew how to draft it, no one knew how to carry it. Addington and his colleagues shuffled and shifted their ground upon every point with pitiable weakness, trying always to obtain some mastery of the huge creature that they had called into existence; but invariably they failed, and were always not undeservedly chastised by biting comments from Fox and Windham. By the 19th of March 1804 the Bill had been committed and recommitted four times; twenty-four new clauses had been added; nearly all the original clauses had been altered and amended; and yet it was as far from passing as ever.

[1] *H.D.* Commons, 6th March 1804. [2] *Ibid.* 13th Dec. 1803.
[3] *Ibid.* 2nd March 1804. [4] *Ibid.* 19th March 1804.

1804. There were suspicions in more than one quarter that the whole principle of Volunteers was wrong; and even Pitt, in course of the debates, betrayed some misgiving as to their usefulness. He admitted that the Volunteer system had been pushed to a far wider extent than had been at first foreseen, and that he looked with great concern upon its imperfections; but he vowed none the less that he believed in it.[1] He admitted further that there should be permanence and consistency in a defensive force, which should render it equal not only to the present but to all future dangers; and added that in his opinion the principles upon which the Volunteer system had been founded were perfectly right. "But," he continued, "it is impossible to trust continually to the operation of the Volunteer spirit. When the danger is past they may doubt the necessity of future exertions. It then becomes the duty of Parliament to do that for the country which spontaneous zeal cannot do. . . . If the Volunteer system fails, we can fall back on the National Defence Act."[2]

It is difficult to see why, when a permanent defensive force was wanted, Pitt should have approved the expenditure of enormous sums in creating one which was avowedly built upon ephemeral sentiment. "Zeal is in its nature a very transitory feeling," said Windham, "and a permanent Volunteer system is almost a contradiction in terms." Whitbread put the case more strongly still. The Volunteers, as he truly said, were in daily danger of being dissolved. The dismissal of a corps was the only remedy for a difference between it and the Government. Moreover, every corps that he knew of was more or less in debt; and the calls for a second subscription would only collect from the liberal that which should be exacted from all. "We have gone to enormous expense in drawing men from the Militia to the Regulars [from 1799 to 1801]; we have gone to enormous expense in raising an Army of

[1] *H.D.* Commons, 27th Feb. [2] *Ibid.* 29th Feb. 1804.

Reserve, and finally we fall back on the Volunteer system, which is the most expensive of all."[1] 1804.

But by far the most clear-sighted man in either House was the soldier, Robert Craufurd. Being imbued with the foolish notion that it was his business to treat his audience to all the paraphernalia of exordium, peroration, and so forth, he spoke at enormous length, and hence received little attention. From the first he declared that the Volunteer system was a mistake from beginning to end, wrong in its constitution, in the defrayal of its cost, in its committees of management, in its training, in the use to be made of it, even in its clothing. The system of private contribution was wrong. The country ought to bear the entire expense of the Volunteers, and would thus do away with the necessity for committees which were constantly coming into collision with Government. The training was wrong. The Prussian system of drill was ill-adapted for fighting in England, and would be a mistake for the whole Army if the troops were to be employed in England only. The whole of the first class under the Levy en Masse Act ought to be called up, dressed in an uniform coat, and trained principally to marksmanship and to withdraw at the word of command from shelter. The clothing was wrong. It was an error to dress Volunteers in red, for, if they retired, the Regular troops might think that their comrades of the Line had been defeated, and would be disheartened, whereas the enemy would be encouraged. It was wrong also to cheapen military titles. Lastly, it was a fatal defect that among the Volunteers it was impossible to enforce discipline. "If you try to enact regulations, you are told, not that they are unjust or just, but that they are not agreeable to the Volunteers. So delicate a machine is unfit for war."[2]

The unhappy Volunteer Consolidation Bill dragged on its weary way through both Houses until the middle of April without making any great progress; but mean-

[1] *H.D.* Commons, 8th Feb. 1804.

[2] *Ibid.* 27th Feb., 22nd March 1804.

1804. while the repeated remonstrances of Craufurd, Windham, and others against the neglect of the Regular Army and the want of an offensive force had borne fruit, and on the 29th of March Yorke unfolded a fresh bundle of proposals. The Army of Reserve Act, as he was fain to confess, had ceased to produce any recruits. He proposed therefore, first, to suspend it for a year, and to limit the bounty in such counties as had not yet provided their quota to ten guineas; secondly, to bring 10,000 Militia over from Ireland in order to set free as many Regular troops; thirdly, to make good the loss to Ireland by augmenting the Irish Militia from 15,000 to 28,000 men. Castlereagh, who supported the measure, added that this would be the cheapest way of accomplishing what was needed, since Irish Militiamen could be obtained for a bounty of four guineas, whereas the price of substitutes in England ranged from forty to fifty guineas.[1] The Bills were accordingly brought in, the one to enable 10,000 Irish Militia to volunteer for service in England; a second for raising the additional Militiamen by beat of drum and without local expense to the counties, the bounty of four guineas being fixed by the Treasury; and, lastly, a bill to suspend the Army of Reserve Act.

Even so the Government's resources were not quite exhausted. They now proposed to increase the "disposable" force of the country, that is to say, the force that could be spared to strike outside England, from 10,000 to 25,000 men. This they hoped to do by levying new regiments on the old system of raising men for rank; but no officer was to gain more than one step; the step was not to be granted at all unless the men were produced within six months; and the prescribed bounty was not to be exceeded under penalty of a court-martial. This experiment, it must be added, was tried, and resulted in the raising of second battalions to the 78th and 79th Highlanders, and of four new battalions in Ireland, three of which became

[1] *H.D.* 29th March 1804.

new regiments of the Line;[1] but a contract given to two officers to raise 5000 men for levy money of thirteen guineas a head was a complete failure.[2] 1804.

During the early months of 1804 the incompetence of Addington and his colleagues became so apparent that on the 23rd of April, in a general debate on the defence of the country, Pitt turned upon them with the strongest censure. "No one measure for public defence can they truly be said to have originated," he declared, "whereas several they have enfeebled and retarded." On the 25th, in Committee on the Army of Reserve Suspension Bill, Pitt reviewed the entire policy of the Government, and explained that which he proposed to substitute for it. The formation of new Regular regiments he condemned as impossible; but he advocated in their place the reduction of the Militia in England from 70,000 to 48,000 men, the augmentation of the Army of Reserve by ballot to 60,000 or 70,000 men, and its maintenance at that figure so that there might be drawn from it annually 14,000 to 15,000 men for the Regular Army. To render the ballot effective and to disarm subscription-clubs he proposed that ballotted men should be able to purchase exemption for a moderate fixed sum, and if they served in person, should receive that sum as bounty; that substitutes should be found by the parish and not by the individual and taken from the hundred and not from the market towns; that the bounty should be limited and that the magistrates should see that the limit was not exceeded; and that, if the substitutes could not be found in the hundred, the bounty-money should be handed to the Colonels of the county-regiments to obtain a recruit for that amount and no more. He reckoned that thus the Army of Reserve would offer always the larger bounty, and

[1] The remaining battalion was drafted into the 87th Foot. *C.J.* vol. lxi. p. 630.

[2] S.C.L.B. 30th April 1804. The officer was a certain Colonel French, who was mixed up in the scandals of Mrs. Clarke. He produced only 154 men by 31st Jan. 1805.

1804. by drawing its recruits from the locality would leave the market towns open without competition to the Regulars.[1]

Such initiative in suggestion, added to so much careful and explicit detail, showed pretty clearly that Pitt expected very shortly to take the reins of Government into his own hands. The scheme, however, did not pass without criticism. Yorke declared that it was hopeless to think of drawing substitutes only from the same hundred as the ballotted men, and impracticable to expect to put down subscription-clubs; while Fox, an acknowledged authority on such matters, averred that "he had never heard of an Act which laid down that five men must not subscribe £5 apiece to provide a substitute for the one among them that might be ballotted, but must toss up which of them must pay £25."[2] But the House was more eager to condemn Yorke's measures than to consider those of Pitt, and the majority in Addington's favour was so small that on the following day he resigned office.

Owing to difficulties which need not detain us here, fully three weeks passed before Pitt was able to form a new Administration, wherein Lord Camden held the office of Secretary for War and the Colonies. Hence Pitt was unable until the 5th of June to bring forward the Bill which embodied his new and mature scheme for raising men. The objects which he set before himself were good and statesmanlike, namely, first, to put an end to the competition for recruits between the Regular Army, the Militia, and the other forces engaged for home-service only; secondly, to abolish the obstacles in the way of establishing a Permanent Additional Force as a standing foundation for the recruiting of the Army. As a first step he proposed to repeal the Army of Reserve Act and reduce the establishment of the Militia to its original figure of 40,000 men for England and 8000 for Scotland. He then proposed to merge the quota of the Army of Reserve

[1] *H.D.* Pitt, 25th April 1804. [2] *Ibid.* 25th April 1804.

and of the Supplementary Militia into one, making a total force of 79,000 men.[1] As fast as this number was diminished by the enlistment of its members into the Regular Army, the counties were to be called upon to fill the vacancies, with the proviso that in no one year should the number of men to be so raised exceed one-sixth of the entire force. In plain words, he proposed to devise machinery for establishing a Permanent Reserve of 79,000 men for the Army, and for making good any drains upon it to the extent, at most, of 13,000 men annually, over and above any recruits that might be obtained for regiments by ordinary and voluntary enlistment. As an encouragement to the counties to favour this measure he proposed, if the men were produced, to remit all fines incurred by them for deficiencies under the Army of Reserve Act. 1804.

Had the Army of Reserve and the Supplementary Militia stood at their full strength at this time, there would have been no occasion to put the new Bill into force until casualties had occurred; but, as has been told, both were seriously below their establishment, and to increase them to the appointed figure it was necessary to raise at once little short of 20,000 men.[2] In addition to this it was necessary that at least 11,000 men should be levied annually to replace those who should have volunteered from the Army of Reserve into the Regular Army, the first instalment falling due on 1st October 1805. Altogether, therefore, the scheme required 31,000 men to be supplied within the succeeding fifteen months.

How was this number to be obtained? The ballot had broken down, having produced, thanks to the admission of substitutes, an indifferent lot of men and a gigantic rise in bounties. The first step, therefore, was

[1] Army of Reserve of United Kingdom, 49,880; Supplementary Militia of Great Britain (Ireland had no Supplementary Militia), 29,071. Total, 78,951.

[2] Deficiencies in the Army of Reserve, 12,477; in the Militia, 7305. Total, 19,782.

1804 to reduce bounties; and Pitt hoped to achieve this end by putting an end to the ballot and throwing upon the parochial officers the responsibility for producing the quota of men assigned to their parishes. He proposed to empower them to give a bounty, which was not, under penalties, to exceed three-fourths of the bounty offered to recruits for the Regular Army, and to take an appointed share of it for their own encouragement. On the other hand, they would be forbidden to accept men who resided more than twenty miles away from the parish, if in the same county, or more than ten miles distant if in another county. If they failed to produce their men, the parish was to be fined £20 for every man deficient of the quota, and was therewith to be quit of all further trouble. Effective Volunteers and Yeomanry were to be exempted from the rates levied for payment of these fines. The money thus collected was to be paid into the general recruiting fund of the kingdom; and the Commanding Officer of the regiment concerned was then to fill the vacancy by ordinary recruiting, paying the same bounty as that offered by the parish and no more. Finally, the men were to be enlisted for home service only, and for five years or until six months after the cessation of war; and the bounties proposed were as follows:—For the Regular Army, £16 : 16s.; for the Reserve, under the new Bill, £12 : 12s.; to the Reservists upon enlisting in the Regular Army, £10 : 10s. The fee granted to the parish officers for each recruit was to be £1 : 1s. The men when raised were to be formed into second battalions to the Regular Army, promotion of officers being interchangeable between the two battalions, so that the attachment between officers and men might encourage enlistment for general service.

Such was the plan proposed by Pitt in his introductory speech, and such it remained in substance when the Bill, on the 27th of June, became an Act. Not, however, that it passed uncriticised. Windham, while approving the reduction of the Militia and the abolition of the ballot, declared himself sceptical as to the soundness of the scheme, and prophesied that if parish officers produced any men at all they would buy them from the crimps. Other members predicted that the Bill might produce money but would never produce men, and that the fines would be equivalent to a double land-tax on landed proprietors; for which reasons they deprecated the disuse of the ballot. One member, Mr. Elliot, very pertinently pointed out that to offer a man £16 : 16s. to enlist directly into the Line, and £23 : 2s. to enter the Line through the new force, was on the face of it an absurdity. But most conspicuous among the objectors was Robert Craufurd, speaking as usual at extravagant length, who opposed the measure without reserve or compromise. The Bill, as he urged with unanswerable force, held out no inducements to recruits, increased the competition between the Line and the Militia, and was sufficiently drastic to irritate the parishes though not enough so to produce men. He advocated compulsory training for all men between certain years of age, but not as an embodied force; and then there would be an end of enlisting men for service at home and bribing them to serve abroad. His remedies for the Regular Army were (1) substitution of limited service for service for life; (2) liberal provision for retired soldiers; (3) abolition of military service in the West Indies for the regiments of the Line. 1804.

The arguments of the opponents of the Bill were thrown away. Pitt thought that he had made a master-stroke by turning the parish-officers into recruiting sergeants, and would listen to no prophecies of evil. Upon one point—that of keeping a Reserve to feed the ranks of the Army, and feeding that Reserve by a steady annual supply of recruits—he felt most rightly that his views were sound; and in respect of other opinions he showed strong sense and an open mind by declaring his readiness to accept short service for the Army if it could safely be introduced. But to contemplate the possible failure of his scheme he utterly refused. Perhaps with declining health, with the knowledge

1804. that the followers both of Fox and Grenville were against him, and the consciousness that they were subjecting him to more powerful and damaging criticism than he had ever encountered, he felt it imperative to assert his will. Be that as it may, the Bill became law, and by a melancholy fate was practically the last of the great statesman's important legislative achievements.

Its provisions may be summarised as follows. The Act itself was known as the Permanent Additional Force Act (44 Geo. III. England, cap. 56 ; Scotland, cap. 66 ; Ireland, cap. 74) ; and the first section provided for raising 58,235 men in England ; 10,666 men in Scotland ; and 10,000 in Ireland (sec. 1). The men already raised under the Army of Reserve Act were to be accepted towards the fulfilment of these quotas. Returns were to be made in each county of the men deficient of the full quota under the Army of Reserve Act, and that number was to be forthwith raised as part of the force required under the present Act (sec. 2). Ample facilities were given for comparison of the returns of deficiencies presented by the counties and by the Inspector-General of the Army of Reserve, and for the adjustment of differences between them (secs. 3-9). The Militia of Great Britain was to be reduced to its original quota under the Militia Act of 1802 (sec. 10), and, in cases where the Militia exceeded that strength, no further ballot was to be held until this number had been reduced as aforesaid (sec. 11). In counties where the Militia was below its quota, the deficiency was to be raised as part of the Additional Force under the Act (sec. 11), unless the deficiency fell short of the quota of 1802 ; in which case the numbers short of the quota were first to be made good (sec. 12). For the year beginning on 1st October 1804, and ending on 1st October 1805, and for each succeeding year, a maximum of 9000 men in England, of 1800 men in Scotland, and of 4000 men in Ireland (14,800 in all) was to be raised to fill the vacancies of men who had enlisted in the

Regular Army from the Additional Force (sec. 15). 1804.
Parish-officers were authorised to obtain men, and were to be entitled to a share of bounty for every man produced (sec. 20), provided such men had resided for thirty days in the parish or in some other parish not more than ten miles distant from it in the same county, and provided that the parish-officers brought a certificate of the recruit's residence to the magistrate on attesting him; the penalty for refusing to bring such certificate being a fine of £1 to £5 (sec. 21). The levying of rates and raising of subscriptions to induce persons to enlist was forbidden, and the penalty for offering more than the prescribed bounty was a fine of £20 (sec. 22). The bounty was not to exceed three-fourths of the bounty given for the Regular Army; it was to be paid out of the Imperial Treasury; and it was to be accepted in lieu of all payments and allowances prescribed by the Army of Reserve Act (sec. 24). Parishes failing to produce men within one month after notice given (in the first instance, within six weeks after the passing of the Act) were to be fined £20 for every man deficient, after which the Commanding Officer of the corps concerned was to be at liberty to enlist recruits to the number deficient, for the bounty named in section 24 and no more (sec. 26). The men were to be enlisted for five years or until six months after the signing of peace, and were to swear that they were not lame, ruptured, or subject to fits (sec. 28). If a parish paid its fine for any man deficient, but managed to produce a man before a recruit had been enlisted by the Commanding Officer, three-fourths of the fine were to be remitted (sec. 33). Rates levied for payment for fines were to be separated from the poor rates. Effective Yeomen and Volunteers and Militiamen serving by person or substitute were exempted from such rates, if the property on which they were assessed for poor rates did not exceed the annual value of £20.

The most noticeable point in the Act, apart from the dispensation with the ballot, was the shifting of the

1804. expense of bounties from the parochial funds to the Imperial Treasury, thus marking a temporary advance in the more equitable distribution of the expense of recruiting the Army.

II

A few weeks before this Act, Pitt's administration passed also the Volunteer Consolidation Act (44 Geo. III. cap. 54; 5th June 1804), which in its final shape contained the following provisions. First, the Volunteer Act of 1802, the Billeting Act of 1803, and the Exemption Act recently passed, were repealed. The King was empowered to continue the services of accepted corps and accept the offers of new corps (sec. 1). Volunteers entitled to exemption under the repealed Acts were to have the benefit of them until the 1st of July 1804 (sec. 2). Effective Volunteers were also to be exempt from the ballot for the Militia and for any additional force; though such corps as had disclaimed exemption were to be held to their bargain (sec. 4); and an effective member was defined to be one who in the cavalry attended four days and in the infantry eight days of exercise every three months (sec. 5). Men belonging to corps to which arms and accoutrements had not been issued were equally entitled to the exemption if they duly attended muster and exercise (sec. 6). Men on leave of absence were permitted to do the whole of their drills within four months (sec. 7), or in two successive periods of four months each (sec. 8). It is to be noted that effective men enrolled in the Yeomanry or Volunteers were by the new Act not exempted from the ballot, but from service in the Militia and Army of Reserve, their names being kept on the ballot-list so that they might be called up at once if discharged from the Volunteers (sec. 17); and the like exemption was guaranteed to them after the signature of peace if they continued to serve as effective Volunteers throughout the war (sec. 18). Infantry corps voluntarily assembling for permanent duty were subjected to the Mutiny Act and Articles of War (sec. 23); but not corps of Yeomanry cavalry (sec. 24). Officers of Yeomanry and Volunteers were to rank with those of the Militia and Regular Army as the youngest of their respective grades (sec. 26). Commanding Officers were authorised to discharge men for misconduct, though not to the prejudice of any rules, made by the corps, which had received the King's approval, and subject always to the King's pleasure (sec. 27). Commandants were further empowered to disallow the day on which a man misbehaved as a day of attendance, or to disallow his day's pay, unless the case were otherwise provided for by the rules of the corps (sec. 28). They could also order a man into custody for misbehaviour for so long as the corps might remain under arms on the occasion (sec. 29). The right of resignation was affirmed conditionally upon a man giving fourteen days' notice, delivering up his arms, and paying all fines due from him (secs. 30, 31). Upon resignation a man became liable to serve in the Militia or any Additional Force; and the Commanding Officer was required to certify his discharge to the Clerk of the General Meeting of the Lieutenancy (sec. 32). Persons aggrieved by the refusal of the Commanding Officer to accept their resignation might appeal to two Deputy-Lieutenants, whose decision was to be final (sec. 33). The clause in the Levy en Masse Act allowing 2s. 6d. a day to be paid to persons employed to instruct Volunteers was repealed (sec. 34). On being called up for active service two guineas were to be paid to the Captains for each man, and when called out for permanent duty, one guinea; for which sums the Captain was required to account to the men (sec. 36). Another guinea was to be allowed them on return from active service (sec. 39). Finally, no future rules and regulations of Volunteer corps were to be binding unless submitted to the Secretary of State and not disallowed by the King (sec. 56); and the right was reserved to the King of annulling any rules which might

1804. have been made in the past or should be made in the future (sec. 57).

The passing of the Act was of very solid advantage, for it gave at any rate some powers of discipline to Commanding Officers, and assured all ranks of pay during permanent duty. The only misfortune was that it should have come so late, when indiscipline had already become deeply ingrained in many corps. It was also shameful to enforce by enactment the disclaimer of exemption given by the 7000 patriotic men at the opening of the war. They might at least have been left at liberty to continue their offer gratuitously. But this was practically the only blemish in the Act, and a few additional regulations tended to heighten the improvement brought thereby. The first step in 1804 was to appoint and station field-officers to inspect the Volunteers.[1] The next was to arrange for the mobilisation of the Volunteers themselves. Orders had been issued on the 31st of October 1803 for the removal of all cattle and so forth, or, as it was called, for "driving the country" upon the enemy's approach or landing; but these were contested by the Duke of Richmond in Sussex, who declared the plan to be impracticable;[2] and as Sir John Moore agreed with this opinion, it may be accepted with confidence that the Duke was right. Incidentally, however, the order had led to thoroughly careful registration of horses and vehicles; and the Duke of York took advantage of this to suggest that one light cart for every company should be set apart and marked for regimental transport,[3] and that waggons also should be set apart, marked and provided with seats for the conveyance of men from the remoter districts to London, the expense being borne by the Imperial Treasury.[4] Later on, in August, an improved disposition of the

[1] Circular of 12th Jan. 1804.

[2] *I.D.* vol. xxxii. L.L. Sussex, to S.S. 3rd Nov. 1803.

[3] Of course the phrase "regimental transport" was unknown in those days; but I use it for convenience.

[4] Circular of 16th and 19th Jan. and 10th Feb. 1804.

Volunteer Force was made by the War Office, for the speedier concentration of the Volunteers upon any threatened point, and for that purpose a muster of the regimental waggons was ordered.[1] But then arose a difficulty. The farmers of the West Riding of Yorkshire refused to produce their waggons for a muster: they were ready enough to give them up if wanted, but muster them they would not.[2] Their reason is not stated, but was probably not unconnected with the Department of Excise; and though no similar objections seem to have been urged by other counties, the example was likely to spread among folk so suspicious as British farmers. 1804.

Some further pecuniary concessions had also been made to the Volunteers. A day's pay, over and above the twenty days' pay allowed annually by the August Allowances, was promised to every non-commissioned officer and private present at an inspection of his corps by a General Officer or Inspecting Field-Officer, provided that such inspections did not recur more frequently than once in two months.[3] A grant of pay for one sergeant to every company on the August Allowances was also conceded,[4] as also a further sum for hiring or obtaining safe depôts for arms. At about the same time were issued, in anticipation of the Volunteer Act of 1804, further regulations to encourage all corps, whether of maritime or inland counties, to go on permanent pay and duty for periods of not more than a month or less than ten days. But here, as usual,

[1] Circular of 11th and 17th Aug. 1804. This Circular of 11th August is not in the Circular Book, but may be found in *I.D.* vol. lxviii. Miscellaneous. It was arranged to take troops by post-carriage for the last four stages to London, the stations fixed upon for the purpose being Guildford, Andover, Marlborough, Bedford, Banbury, Daventry, Northampton, Kettering, Stilton, and Cambridge. It was reckoned that the waggons would carry the troops forty miles a day for three days; and the proprietors were directed to send three days' forage with them.

[2] *I.D.* vol. lxvii. L.L. Yorks W.R. to S.S. 22nd Aug. 1804.

[3] Circular, 10th Feb. 1804.

[4] Circular, 19th March 1804.

1804. Addington and his colleagues contrived to import confusion into their orders. In a circular of the 5th of March they promised an advance of a guinea, which was known as the marching-guinea, to all men who would come out on permanent pay and duty as aforesaid. In a second circular of 12th April they engaged to give also ten days' additional pay to all men under the August Allowances who within the next two months would do so many additional days' exercise without leaving their homes; but denied them the marching-guinea. Men under the June Allowances, on the other hand, were to receive no special pay when on permanent duty, as the days taken up thereby were to be reckoned among the eighty-five for which they received pay annually; but they were to receive the marching-guinea. It appears, further, that yet more regulations were issued, which I have been unable to discover, reducing the extreme term of permanent duty to three weeks, but still holding out the reward of the marching-guinea. Then came a series of painful disillusions. The Haddington Volunteers went out for permanent duty for fourteen days, and received only fourteen shillings instead of the twenty-one which they had expected. Some of the Durham Volunteers went out and received pay, but could obtain no guinea. In Glamorganshire a corps under the June Allowances went out, claimed its guinea, and was refused because it had agreed to serve in its Military District only, and not in any part of Great Britain. All of these cases occurred before the passing of the new Volunteer Act of 1804, and were partly due to the old confusion between June and August Allowances; but they did not fail (and they were by no means solitary instances) to rouse bitter discontent.[1]

The new Act, however, set doubts upon these points at rest, and in September the Government gave still further encouragement to the training of Volun-

[1] *I.D.* vol. xxxviii. Lord Haddington to S.S. 5th June 1804; vol. xlvii. L.L. Durham, to S.S. 6th Feb. 1804; vol. xlix. R. Lascelles (Glamorgan) to S.S. 18th Jan. 1804.

teers by offering ten days' pay to all who would go out 1804.
for ten days of additional exercise during the following six months.[1] Under such stimulus and with the experience of continuous service the Volunteers improved rapidly during 1804. The number of men who came out for permanent duty between the 1st of November 1803 and the 5th of March 1804 was just over 80,000 of all ranks; and as these belonged to the maritime counties only, the figure is creditable to them. In June Pitt announced that the number had been swelled to between 100,000 and 150,000.[2] In fact, the men enjoyed permanent duty. The unmarried only were by preference taken for it, and their reunions were sometimes so festive that critics were found who denounced them as demoralising to the population. No doubt permanent duty had its drawbacks; but no one who has witnessed the salutary change wrought in country lads by even a week of continuous training can doubt that those drawbacks were far outweighed by the advantages.

Meanwhile arrangements had also been made for forming the Yeomanry and Volunteers into brigades, the proportion being as follows:—

Eastern District . .	2	brigades of cavalry;	4	brigades of infantry.		
Southern District .	1	"	"	3	"	"
South-Western District	1	"	"	4	"	"
South Inland District .	1	"	"	4	"	"
London . . .	1	"	"	7	"	"
Home . . .	0	"	"	6	"	"

Further, every effort was made to group small isolated corps into regiments and battalions, not always with success, owing to the bitterness of local jealousies. Norfolk and Suffolk gave particular trouble in this matter; and indeed it was from Suffolk that there came the only protest against the new system of brigades, Lord Rous declaiming vigorously against the Suffolk Yeomanry being brigaded under a regular officer,

[1] Circular of 24th September 1804.
[2] *H.D.* 18th June 1804.

1804. General Money, if called out to repel actual invasion. Lord Rous, it may be observed, was not himself an officer of Yeomanry at this time, though he had been so during the last war. Moreover, though Suffolk supported thirteen troops of Yeomanry, these were so jealous of each other that they were not even regimented. Lastly, Money, though a retired General of considerable reputation, had given enormous pains to the Volunteers, and actually commanded a regiment of Norfolk Yeomanry. However, the General of the District, Sir James Craig, was obliged to come forward, smooth the ruffled feathers of the incensed magnate, and point out ostentatiously to Money, who had been guilty of no more than announcing the organisation of the brigade in orders, that his command as a brigadier was strictly limited to the event of active service, and that great caution must be employed in proclaiming such facts, as the Volunteer's obedience was only voluntary.[1]

Thus, at every turn, the old difficulty recurred. The Volunteers had undoubtedly improved greatly under permanent duty, but large numbers of them were still utterly useless. In Norfolk, in May 1804, the Inspector could report only three corps out of thirty-three to be fit for service; and the Lord-Lieutenant, himself a General, was obliged to confirm his judgment.[2] This was a maritime county, which had enjoyed for eight months the privilege of sending men on permanent duty; and the condition of the Volunteers in inland counties can hardly have been as good. Moreover, such improvements as there were had been bought only by enhanced expenditure, by doles of pay for this, allowances for that, bounties or marching-guineas for the other. And though the men might be steady on parade and proficient at their manual exercise, their officers remained always a weak point; nor was this weakness likely to be strengthened while their jealousies

[1] *I.D.* vol. lxiv. Suffolk Mil. Sec. to Mr. King (with enclosure), 4th Aug. 1804.

[2] *Ibid.* vol. lviii. L.L. Norfolk, to S.S. 1st May, 17th June 1804.

forbade them to work together under a competent instructor. The tone of the entire force was parochial, or at best provincial, never national. Its commanders clamoured for non-commissioned officers from the King's Regular regiments, for these were their inferiors, or at most their equals; but Volunteer officers thought themselves hardly used when the Colonels of the Line declared, very truly, that their sergeants and corporals could not be spared from their legitimate work. Yet they revolted from guidance by the King's Regular officers, who knew nothing of their local importance and judged them simply by their fitness or unfitness for their work. It must be remembered also that they were wholly under the protection—one cannot call it the control—of the Home Office; the War Office and Horse Guards having no part in them. General Tarleton, commanding the Severn District, complained to the Commander-in-Chief that he could not get a Yeoman in his district to travel for him five miles with an official order. After ten days' delay he received a "cold, phlegmatic answer" from the Adjutant-General that he had nothing to do with the Volunteers. The reply was strictly true, nor could have any other have been returned. Had the Adjutant-General infused any warmth into his letter, he would doubtless have added that he thanked Heaven that he had nothing to do with the Volunteers, seeing that their obedience was voluntary. When on permanent duty, which it must be remembered was not compulsory, or called out to repel invasion, the Volunteers were indeed bound under military law to obey the King's Generals, but at other times they could and did snap their fingers at them, and indeed very often at every other authority. Well might Craufurd exclaim that so delicate a machine was unfit for war. 1804.

III

So the winter of 1804 drew on, and the Government's attention became fixed chiefly on Pitt's Per-

1804. manent Additional Force Act. Passed on the 25th of June, it allowed a fortnight's grace to the parish officers to master its contents, and one month more for the raising of the allotted number of men, so that, according to the wording of the law, Ministers expected the first batch of 20,000 men to be raised by the 9th of August. On the 23rd of August they issued a circular to the Lords-Lieutenant asking what measures they were taking to execute the Act and with what success, repeating the request on the 30th of August. Answers came in slowly, but were uniformly the same. Hardly a man could be obtained ; the area of recruiting was too much restricted ; the bounties were too low ; the reward to parish officers was too small. The Lieutenant of Norfolk added that recruiting was much hampered by the number of young labouring men serving in the Volunteers. It made little difference what reasons were assigned. The parish officers, after perusal of the Act, had made up their minds that it was hopeless to obtain recruits under such conditions, and that the Government only wanted fines in lieu of men ; so they christened the measure "The Twenty Pound Act," and resigned themselves to the inevitable payment. The Government, therefore, issued another circular on the 25th of September, pointing out that, after all, only the men deficient of the Army of Reserve and Supplementary Militia were required for the present, and that the limit of time would be extended to the 15th of November, after which the officers of the Regular Army would receive orders to raise recruits, and the fine of £20 upon the parishes would be rigorously enforced. This produced no greater result than an exceedingly sharp answer from Inverness to the effect that, from a county where some districts were two hundred miles distant from the county town, the Secretary of State was expecting impossibilities.[1]

The Government then sent round another circular, of the 17th of October, conceived in terms of bland insinuation. Would it not help the levy if the

[1] *I.D.* vol. xxxviii. L.L. Inverness, to S.S. 4th Oct. 1804.

churchwardens and overseers of every parish were 1804.
informed that they would receive a guinea, free of all deductions, for every man produced, and that for every man so found no expense or burden would be laid upon the parish, whereas for every recruit raised by the Colonels of regiments a fine would be imposed? "It is conceived," continued the circular, "that by such a comparative statement it will be made manifest to the inhabitants how materially they will consult their own advantage by providing the men required of them by the 15th of November." Then at last there was some little sign of movement in the counties; and it was high time, for by the 1st of November only 778 recruits had been raised out of the 19,782 which were required, and of these 95 had deserted. The amelioration was not such as to prevent violent attacks upon the measure
when Parliament met in January 1805. Returns were 1805.
called for, and on the 15th of February a motion was brought forward in the Lords for the repeal of the Act as a total failure. Lord Hawkesbury defended it, alleging that practically it had not come into force until November 1804, and that during the past fortnight it had produced 300 recruits a week, at which rate it would bring in 11,000 in the year. Upon this very inconclusive assurance the House rejected the motion for repeal; but a week later (21st February) the attack was renewed in the Commons by far more powerful advocates. Windham led the way with a detailed criticism of all past measures of recruiting, and pointed out that such men as had been raised had been produced chiefly by crimps who, in spite of the professed limitation of the bounty, received in practice both the fines from the parish and the sums allotted to tempt recruits, making a total of £34 for every man. He contended that the Army could be maintained by voluntary enlistment if it were made attractive enough; and to that end he advocated short or (as it was then called) limited service, the abolition of drafting, special regulations of service in the West Indies, abolition of flogging except for certain

1805. specified crimes, and increase of the private soldier's privileges in default of increase of his pay.

Canning was put forward to answer Windham, which he did with no great effect; and on the 6th of March 1805 Sheridan moved the repeal of the Act. Pitt, in its defence, declared, like Hawkesbury, that the measure had not begun to work until the middle of November, and that it was too early yet to judge of its failure or success. Whitbread, however, pointed out that the actual raising of men had begun in the first week of September, and Castlereagh, on behalf of the Government, was obliged to admit that this was true.[1] Sheridan's motion was lost by a majority of 140, but the situation was serious, and Pitt knew it. He had already caused another circular[2] to be sent to the Lords-Lieutenant with fresh explanations and threats for the parish officers; but the House was anxious to look into matters for itself, and ordered returns to be made of the special rates levied for fines under the Act and of the bounties paid to parish officers. These would suffice to show that the Act was a failure so far as raising recruits was concerned; and the country was not inclined to be lenient to failures.

The great need of England was a compact and sufficient force of Regular troops which could be employed over sea in offensive operations. The casualties from deaths, discharges, and desertions at home during 1804, and abroad during the first nine months of that year, amounted to 16,400; the recruits gained during 1804 numbered but 13,400.[3] Lord Grenville indeed stated in the House of Lords[4] that the Regular Infantry, which on 1st January 1804 had numbered 105,886, had sunk by 1st January 1805 to 105,033, showing a net decrease of 853 in a single year. Moreover, it was not a question whether Ministers could abstain from sending more forces abroad even if they wished to avoid it. In

[1] *H.D.* 6th March 1805. [2] 18th Feb. 1805.
[3] *C.J.* Returns in Appendix 15 to vol. lx.
[4] *H.D.* 8th March 1805.

the same month of March the French fleet had appeared in the Caribbean Sea, threatening raids upon the British West Indies; there was an unpleasant little campaign going none too favourably in Ceylon; and in India the Mahratta war, so brilliantly opened by Lake and Wellesley, was beginning to assume a disagreeable aspect. Also there were signs that Russia, Prussia, and Austria would shortly incline to renew the contest against France, and it would be necessary for England to produce a military force as well as subsidies. Ordinary recruiting was practically at a standstill, the number of men obtained both in 1803 and in 1804 being far less than in 1800; and that though the bounty had been swelled more than twofold between 1803 and 1804. The Commander-in-Chief gave orders for the enlistment of boys, since men could not be obtained; but it was perfectly clear that some other method must be found for filling the ranks of the Regular Army. Pitt, therefore, notwithstanding the fair promise which he professed to detect in his Permanent Additional Force Act, was fain to supersede it, for the time at any rate, by an old-fashioned expedient. 1805.

On the 31st of March, therefore, he brought in a Bill to enable the excess of the British Militia over the established quota, or, in other words, the Supplementary Militia, to enlist in the Regular Army. There were, he said, 68,000 Militia embodied in Great Britain at the moment. Of this number he proposed to set aside 34,000 as the nucleus of an ultimate quota of 51,000; and to take what he wanted—17,000 men was the number named by him—from the remaining 34,000, restoring the balance to the establishment. With a few sarcasms the Bill was allowed to pass, and became law on the 10th of April (45 Geo. III. cap. 31).

Its main provisions were as follows. The King was empowered to appoint Regular Regiments and divisions of the Marines into which Militiamen might enlist (sec. 1), the number of men enlisting being restricted in every regiment of Militia to the excess over the ordinary

1805. quota, or, in other words, to the actual strength of the Supplementary Militia in each county. Not more than one non-commissioned officer for every twenty men was to be accepted (sec. 2). The Commanding Officer of every Militia regiment was empowered to ascertain how many of his men were ready to enlist, and if their number equalled four-fifths of the full quota permitted to enlist, then these could be handed over to the Regulars at once, and no more could be claimed (sec. 3). (The object of this last provision seems to have been to reward Colonels who stimulated their men to enlist, by taking fewer men away from them.) Again the Commanding Officers of the Militia might set apart any number not exceeding one-half of the original quota of a regiment, complete with non-commissioned officers, and forbid them to be enlisted (sec. 4). (This was doubtless intended as a sop to reconcile the officers to the weakening of their battalions.) Commanding Officers were also empowered to refuse to discharge any Militiaman upon due cause shown (sec. 16); no drummer, musician, clerk, or armourer could be enlisted without their consent (sec. 14); no men could be enlisted at all unless duly discharged by Commanding Officers from their regiments (sec. 10); and enlistment of men not duly discharged was strictly forbidden (sec. 17). The men enlisted were not to be under 5 feet 4 inches in height, nor above thirty-five years of age (sec. 5). If four-fifths of the allotted quota were not ready to enlist, the Commanding Officer was to read out to the battalion the terms of enlistment and explain them, and on the next day call on the men to come forward. If more than the appointed number offered themselves, they were to be reduced to the required number by ballot (sec. 6). If less than the appointed number came forward, the Commanding Officer was to open a book in which for ten days men might cause their names to be inscribed. At the close of the ten days the terms were to be again explained and the names of the men enlisted forwarded to the Clerk of the General Meeting. If the number of enlistments still fell short of the appointed tale, the process was repeated for another ten days, after which all further effort was to be abandoned (sec. 7). The recruits were allowed to choose their own regiments, were entitled to a bounty of ten guineas (sec. 10), and were not to be drafted from their chosen corps without their own consent (sec. 20). Non-commissioned officers retained their rank upon enlisting into the Line, though they might be reduced to the ranks for misconduct; but no sergeant or corporal could enlist as such into the Artillery (sec. 13). 1805.

Under this Act 10,696 Militiamen[1] passed into the Regular Army between the 10th of April and the 26th of June, four-fifths of them into the Infantry, and about one-tenth (to the huge indignation of many Regular officers) into the Marines. It is noticeable that neither Middlesex nor Surrey contributed a man to these figures; and that Kent with two battalions of Militia supplied but eleven men. Assuming that these Militiamen received, one with another, £20 to serve as substitutes, their net cost to the country in bounties before they could be finally bribed to enter the Regular Army amounted to some £330,000. Had they been enlisted directly in 1803 they would have been obtained for one half of that sum. However, by these means, and by contributions from the Army of Reserve, the effective strength of the Regular Army, infantry and cavalry, rose from 152,000 on the 1st of May to 159,000 on the 1st of June; and in view of the steady ripening of the Coalition of Russia, Austria, and Prussia against France, Pitt decided to take the offensive.

IV

It was characteristic of the man that he could not bring himself to direct the whole of his available force

[1] But another return in *W. O. Mila. E.B.*, dated 5th June, gives the figure at 170 sergeants, 236 corporals, 10,755 men. Total, 11,161.

1805. against any one point. Past experience might have warned him against frittering away his troops in small detachments ; but even before he came back to office he had foreshadowed a division of his forces between the north of Germany and the south of Italy ;[1] and to these expeditions was now added a third to the Cape of Good Hope.

The first of these armaments was that designed for the Mediterranean, which seems to have been under consideration as early as February, and was actually despatched in April, before the drafting of the Militiamen into the Line. It consisted of rather fewer than 5000 men under Sir James Craig, and was destined primarily for the protection of Sicily, but secondarily to join the Russians in operations for the defence of Naples, to occupy Alexandria, to defend Sardinia, or even to capture Minorca. Napoleon's comment upon it was as follows : "The celebrated secret expedition entered Lisbon on the 7th of May and left it on the 10th. Whither is it bound ? That's the problem. My opinion is that the only reasonable thing it can do is to capture the Cape or reinforce Jamaica or the Windward Islands. If it is destined for Malta [its actual destination in the first instance] all the better. Nothing can better prove the folly (*ineptie*) of the English Cabinet ; for these combined continental movements founded on a few thousand men are pygmy combinations. If therefore you find that the expedition is gone to Malta, you may rub your hands (*rejouissez vous*), for the English will have deprived themselves of 6000 (*sic*) men and of a certain number of ships."[2] This force in the Mediterranean, it may be added, did little profitable work from the beginning to the end of the war. The one of its achievements which is remembered is the battle of

[1] Stanhope's *Life of Pitt*, iv. 223-224.

[2] *Corres. de Napoléon*, 8787. Robert Craufurd's criticism in the House of Commons was precisely to the same effect—Craig's force was larger than was wanted for defensive purposes and too small to take the offensive.

Maida in 1806, a brilliant action which might have been turned to great account had not both the General and the Admiral concerned been shallow impostors. 1805.

The expedition to the Cape had been originally designed to reinforce the West Indies, in consequence of Villeneuve's abortive raid on the Windward Islands. It was not ready until the end of May; and meanwhile Nelson's pursuit of the French Admiral made the despatch of a force to the Antilles unnecessary. At the end of July, therefore, its destination was altered to the Cape of Good Hope. It numbered rather more than 6000 men under Sir David Baird; and, reaching the Cape after a very tedious passage, compelled the Dutch to yield up the Colony on the 18th of January 1806. This object accomplished, Baird was persuaded by the Commodore, Sir Home Popham, to lend him a battalion for an absurd expedition to Buenos Ayres, which, as shall presently be seen, entangled England, much against the wishes of the Government, in unprofitable operations in that quarter.

Meanwhile during the spring and summer of 1805 England awaited Napoleon's attack with breathless suspense. Towards the end of June confidence in the security of the British Isles seems to have been pretty firmly established; but Robert Craufurd warned the Commons that the danger was not yet passed. The enemy, he said, might draw off our naval force to the West Indies, and, hurrying back to Europe, gain temporary command of the Channel, capture the anchorage of the Downs, and bring their army over. Mr. Bragge, the Secretary at War, answered this by a smile, whereupon Craufurd retorted that the plan had actually been proposed by the Marquis de Bouillé to Count de Grasse in 1781, before the battle of the Saints. It is curious that Craufurd should actually have divined Napoleon's intentions.[1] Once indeed, on the night of the 15th of August, when some burning rapestraw was mistaken for a beacon, a false alarm was

[1] *H.D.* Commons, 28th June 1805.

1805. given, and all the forces in Derbyshire and the West Riding of York at once got under arms. The behaviour of the Volunteers generally on this occasion was most praiseworthy. The Rotherham infantry in particular, a battalion nearly six hundred strong, was at its appointed rendezvous, with all its waggons and every man present, within twelve hours, having made a march of twenty-two miles.[1] But Napoleon was never really in a condition to execute his project. He had started on the wrong lines by constructing a flotilla of vessels which were designed to be both fighting ships and transports, but answered the purpose of neither. The difficulty of bringing these small craft to the ports of the Channel in the face of the British cruisers was very formidable, and even when assembled there they could not, despite of much money spent on improving the harbours, put to sea in less than two tides. The distribution of the troops among these boats was indeed settled upon paper, but except on paper it was absurd. The great man's orders to his fleets had also been faulty ; and as a matter of fact he never had more than 90,000 troops ready for immediate embarkation. Upon the failure of his fleets to clear the Channel, therefore, he broke up his camp at Boulogne and marched on the 28th of August for the Danube, covering his failure by a number of letters wherein he laid the blame for all shortcomings upon his Admirals.

Shortly afterwards Austria and Russia declared war upon France. On the 21st of October Napoleon gained his first signal success against the Austrians at Ulm ; and having captured Vienna, marched into Moravia to combat the Russians and the remnant of the Austrians which lay at Austerlitz. The issue of the struggle depended upon the part that should be played by Prussia ; and a special embassy was sent from London to Berlin urging King Frederick William to throw in his lot with the Allies and to crush Napoleon once for

[1] *I.D.* vol. lxxv. Lt.-Col. Jebb (Derby) to S.S. 4th Sept.; vol. xcii. Yorks W.R., B. Frank to S.S. 17th, 19th, 28th Aug. 1805.

all. The King of Sweden, whose hatred of the Emperor of the French amounted to a mania, had assembled a few troops in Pomerania. Hanover, though occupied by French troops, had shown strong attachment to her lawful sovereign; and it was imagined that, even if Prussia held aloof, the Swedes, together with a corps of Russians recently disembarked from the Baltic, might, with the aid of yet another corps from England, operate on the north-eastern frontier of Holland, and make a powerful diversion against the French in Moravia. 1805.

The corps from England, thanks to the blunders of Addington and Pitt, was not likely to be a very formidable one; but it chanced that at this time the Government had the good fortune to meet with a windfall. Immediately upon the declaration of war in 1803 the French had invaded Hanover and compelled, under a convention, the disbandment of the Hanoverian army. Burning with shame and indignation, both officers and men sought to pass over to England in order to form themselves anew into regiments and fight for their sovereign. The scheme was eagerly encouraged by King George; and in August 1803 authority was given for the formation of a King's German Regiment, which by November had expanded into a King's German Legion. The corps grew apace, so that by the end of December 1804 it had grown to two regiments of cavalry, five batteries of artillery, and six battalions of infantry; and within a year the six battalions had been increased to nine. And these were no mere mercenaries like the Hessians whom England had hired in the eighteenth century. They were not only excellent soldiers under excellent officers, but spirited, patriotic men, devotedly loyal to their King, and thirsting to avenge the humiliation thrust upon them by a pusillanimous commander in 1803.

Thus it was that Pitt, besides his detachments to the Mediterranean, was actually able to send a small expedition to Germany in the winter of 1805. A first

1805. division of 11,000 men sailed in November from the Downs to Cuxhaven under General Don, and took post on the Lower Weser, the Russians having already stationed themselves higher up the river; and in December Lord Cathcart, following with the rest of the force, found himself, by January 1806, in command of over 26,000 men, without counting nearly 3000, who had been wrecked or driven back by a storm. In all, therefore, Pitt had sent out some 30,000 troops, 16,000 of them British, to North Germany, but unfortunately too late. On the 2nd of December the battle of Austerlitz was fought, which put an end to all hopes of a diversion in favour of Moravia. Prussia, by a fatal error, had kept herself aloof from the struggle; and the Tsar, by a still more fatal error, after the defeat of Austerlitz, put his troops in North Germany under the command of the King of Prussia. Strong hints reached Cathcart from Berlin that he would do well to leave the country, and in February 1806 he re-embarked his whole force for England. Prussia must be held mainly responsible for this fiasco; and yet it should be observed that if Cathcart's troops had been sent to reinforce Craig, they would have retained their power to act with effect whatever the issue of Austerlitz.

However, the troops were at least intact; and if the Permanent Additional Force Act had fulfilled Pitt's hopes, there would have been fair prospect of really telling operations in 1806. But nothing could galvanise that unhappy measure into life. After a year of disappointment Ministers sent another circular, on the 16th of September, to the Lords-Lieutenant, requesting full details of their proceedings with regard to the execution of the Act, and offering a new scale of rewards for recruits. The reward for recruiting parties for the Regular Army was raised from £3 : 3s. to £5 : 12s. for every approved recruit. £4 : 4s. also was offered for every man enlisted for the Permanent Reserve by order of the Commanding Officers of Regular battalions; and £4 : 4s. in lieu of £1 : 1s. to parish officers, of which £1 : 1s. was to be paid to the actual bringer of the recruit.[1] The object herein was stated to be that parish-officers should be able to offer to all persons who enlisted men for them the same sum as was appointed by the King's regulations for the Regular Army, namely £2 : 12 : 6. The liberality and advantages of this plan, as of former plans, were dwelt upon at excessive length, and the terror of the fine upon the parish was exhibited for the tenth time in naked and painful contrast to the temptations of the bounty. Nothing, however, could stir the apathy of the parochial officers; wherefore, after a preliminary call for returns from the 1805.

[1] SCALE OF DISTRIBUTION OF REWARDS FOR RECRUITS

Bounties to the Recruit.		For Recruits raised by Militia Officers and Regiments.	For Recruits raised by Parish Officers.
On attesting	in money	£4 4 0	
On approval by recruiting officer	" "		£4 4 0
	in necessaries	0 12 0	0 12 0
On final approval	in money	5 14 0	5 14 0
	in necessaries	2 2 0	2 2 0
Total to recruits themselves		£12 12 0	£12 12 0
Bounties to Recruiting Parties.			
To the recruiting officer on approval by the receiving officer or headquarters of regiment		0 16 0*	
To the party on final approval		0 15 6*	
To the bringer of a recruit (whether of the party or not) on intermediate approval		2 12 6	
To the party receiving a final approval			1 1 0
To parish officers (who will pay the bringer at their discretion) on intermediate approval			3 3 0
Total levy money		£16 16 0	£16 16 0

* Not allowed for recruits raised at headquarters of regiments, but one shilling in lieu for attesting.

Men volunteering for general service on being approved at regimental headquarters will receive bounty of . . £9 9 0

Bringers of such volunteers will receive £1 1 0

1805. peccant parishes, Government proceeded to analysis of their contents. It then appeared that of all the men obtained under the Act, three-fifths had been produced by ten counties, and two-fifths by eighty-one remaining counties of the United Kingdom; and, further, that five-sixths of the whole had been supplied by twenty counties, while among the rest, twenty-five actually had not furnished a man.[1] The reasons put forward to account for this failure of the Act were various; though all the Lieutenants concurred in the opinion that the parish-officers, from ignorance and negligence, had made but indifferent recruiting agents.

But some few of the Lieutenants gave details which were the reverse of reassuring. From Perth it was reported that the bounty offered was too low—a complaint echoed by practically every county—that no liberal provision was made for the families of the Permanent Additional Force, as had been made for the Militia and for the Army of Reserve, that there was want of individual interest in the levy, and that there was a great demand for labour by manufacturers.[2] The Lieutenant of Edinburgh explained that, among other discouragements, men had not been allowed to select their own regiments.[3] Caithness pleaded exhaustion owing to the numbers of recruits taken for the new battalions of the Seventy-eighth and Seventy-ninth.[4] The Lieutenant of Caermarthen reminded the Government that in the American War a battalion had been raised in his county and had been sent to Goree, from which not a private returned home, and added that in Merthyr-Tydvil there were to be found not only high wages, but total impunity for all deserters, no man daring to execute the King's warrant therein.[5] In other counties, again, there was conclusive evidence of evasion

1 Circular to Ls.L. 31st Dec. 1805.
2 *I.D.* vol. lxxxvi. L.L. Perth, to S.S. 19th Nov. 1805.
3 *Ibid.* vol. lxxvi. L.L. Edinburgh, to S.S. 1st Oct. 1805.
4 *Ibid.* vol. lxxi. L.L. Caithness, to S.S. 9th Oct. 1805.
5 *Ibid.* vol. lxxi. L.L. Caermarthen, to S.S. 22nd Oct. 1805.

on the part of the authorities. In Cornwall the magistrates assessed the penalties due from the parishes for failing to produce recruits, but professed themselves unable to find any authority in the Act for enforcing those penalties.[1] In Hampshire the parish officers, after calculating their probable losses by desertion, decided to raise no men but to pay their fines, as the lesser of two evils.[2] In London also the parish officers, finding that they were outbidden by recruiting parties for the Regular Army, made up their minds to pay their fines without more ado, hinting at the same time that the crimps were purposely starving the market.[3] It is, however, clear that there was no general combination of crimps throughout the kingdom, for the county of Anglesey appears to have offered £20 a head for recruits to one of the fraternity at Manchester;[4] and indeed Robert Craufurd said openly in the House of Commons that out of 4000 men raised under the Act by June 1805, 2292 had been obtained by payments to crimps.[5] 1805-6.

Altogether the reports were not encouraging, but Pitt would not yet give up his favourite scheme; and on the 31st of December a last circular was sent to the Lords-Lieutenant announcing that intelligent military officers would be sent round to all the parishes to relieve the Deputy-Lieutenants of the irksome duty of instructing the parochial authorities as to the execution of the Act; and asking that a competent civilian might be chosen in each county to accompany and assist them. Such, however, was the disgust inspired by the Act that even this innocent request was ill received in some quarters. The Lieutenant of Berkshire replied that no man in the county, whose assistance was worth having, would give cordial help in the matter; and the Lieutenant of Sussex observed curtly that as the failure of

1 *I.D.* vol. xcv. L.L. Cornwall, to S.S. 27th Feb. 1806.
2 *Ibid.* vol. xcviii. L.L. Hants, to S.S. 4th Jan. 1806.
3 *Ibid.* vol. c. L.L. Middlesex, to S.S. 1st Oct. 1806.
4 *Ibid.* vol. lxxii. C.G.M. Carnarvon, to S.S. 6th Nov. 1805.
5 *H.D.* Commons, 28th June 1805.

1805-6. the Permanent Additional Force Act in his county was due to scarcity of men, the despatch of a military officer would only be a useless expense.[1]

This, however, was the expiring struggle of the unfortunate measure, which, none the less, the authorities at the Horse Guards pronounced to be the most valuable that had ever been produced. For in the first place it connected the Army with the country, and in the second permanently established second battalions for all the regiments of the Line that were serving abroad.[2] Then on the 23rd of January Pitt died, and his administration gave place to the "Ministry of all the Talents" under the presidency of Lord Grenville. The war department was entrusted to Windham, the great advocate of short service and the uncompromising enemy of the Volunteers, who entered upon his new functions on the 5th of February 1806. Thus it was evident that great changes of military policy would certainly ensue; and it will be well, therefore, to review the situation at the moment.

V

In the first place, all immediate danger of invasion had been banished by the total defeat of the French and Spanish fleets at Trafalgar on the 21st of October 1805. But, on the other hand, the European Coalition had been broken up. Austria, heavily defeated at Ulm and Austerlitz, withdrew from the struggle immediately after the latter action, and on the 26th of December agreed to the humiliating Treaty of Pressburg. The Tsar, though mightily discouraged, was determined to fight in Polish territory, having been excluded from that of Austria under an armistice preliminary to the Treaty. But as the disaster of Ulm had caused the hasty withdrawal of the Austrians from Upper Italy,

[1] *I.D.* vol. xciv. L.L. Berks, to S.S. 8th Jan. 1806; vol. cii. L.L. Sussex, to S.S. 3rd Jan. 1806.

[2] *Military Transactions*, Supplement, pp. 3-4.

so that of Austerlitz had forced the Tsar to recall from Naples the small corps with which Craig had hoped to co-operate; and the detachment under Craig's orders was obliged therefore to stand on the defensive in Sicily. All offensive movements in the Mediterranean, on this account, were for the present paralysed. It depended mainly upon the attitude of Prussia whether an effective field for offensive operations could be found in Northern Europe, though in point of fact no better sphere could have been selected than that of Italy, which lay perfectly open and ready. 1806.

The effective strength of the Army on the 17th of March 1806 was, including artillery, 192,372; of which 165,790 were engaged for general service, and the rest for home service only.[1] The cavalry at this time consisted, over and above the Blues and Life Guards, of thirty-two regiments of Dragoon Guards and Dragoons, to which must be added five regiments of the King's German Legion.

The infantry counted three regiments (seven battalions) of Guards, one hundred numbered regiments of the Line, three Garrison Battalions,[2] nine Veteran Battalions, six independent corps specially formed for garrisons in West Africa, New South Wales, and Canada, and the Royal Staff Corps. The above were all European troops, and to them may be added nine foreign battalions, besides the ten battalions of the King's German Legion.

There were, further, eight West India Regiments and four independent West Indian companies.

The artillery numbered 17,927 of all ranks, over

[1] These figures are from Castlereagh's speech of 3rd April. I use them because they include the artillery; but they do not tally with the official returns in *Military Transactions*, and I do not think that the omission of the artillery in the latter accounts for the difference. The returns show a grand total of 185,701, of which 167,701 engaged for general service.

[2] These had been made up of the sixteen Reserve battalions, consisting of boys and worn-out old men recruited for the Army of Reserve.

1806. and above five recently created batteries of the King's German Legion.

Of the cavalry five regiments only were abroad, four out of the five being in India. The remainder were all at home, the King's German Legion being among them.

Of the Infantry fifty British battalions, over and above all foreign and provincial corps, were quartered in the West Indies, in Canada, the Mediterranean, the Cape, and Ceylon. Twenty more were in India. Of the foreign corps one battalion was in India, and the remainder in the Mediterranean. The British troops abroad were, generally speaking, the best in the Army; and their effective strength on the 17th of March 1806 was 67,033, or 24,910 short of establishment.

In the United Kingdom there were, besides the Guards, 106 Regular battalions and corps, from which, however, must be deducted eleven Garrison and Veteran Battalions, as well as sixty-three feeble second battalions recently formed out of the Army of Reserve and the Permanent Additional Force. These last were still very weak and raw, and for the most part were not bound to serve out of the British Isles. In all, from the beginning of the war up to March 1806, 23,370 men had volunteered into the Regular Army from the Army of Reserve and the Permanent Additional Force, and 14,271 from the Militia; and during the years 1803, 1804, and 1805, 23,860 recruits had been raised by ordinary recruiting, making a total of 60,000 Regular troops of less than three years' service.[1] On the other hand there could be set against these, six mature and three young battalions of the King's German Legion.

Altogether the Regular force at home, British and foreign, numbered 22,501 cavalry, and 60,241 infantry, recruited for general service; and 18,002 infantry

[1] Returns in *C.J.* Appendix 12 to vol. lxi. The last return (p. 630) gives the number of men raised for unlimited service, without specifying whether they were raised by ordinary recruiting or not, but I gather from other evidence that the list there given refers to ordinary recruiting only.

recruited for service at home only; making in all 100,744, or, including artillery, 110,000 men. The cavalry was 8820, and the infantry of all kinds 22,501 short of establishment. Besides these there were 75,152 effective Militia, or 8000 deficient of the establishment, and 350,000 nominally effective Volunteers. Hence, if means could be provided for making good the wastage of war, it may be said that England at the beginning of 1806 possessed a striking force of from 40,000 to 50,000 men; for by withdrawing some of Craig's battalions from Sicily and Malta, or, better still, by adding 40,000 men from England to them in the Mediterranean, not far short of 50,000 men might have been put into the field. 1806.

It was to the problem of keeping the ranks of the Army filled by some permanent system that Windham addressed himself. Hitherto he had been merely a bitter critic of the methods of Addington and Pitt, and, so far as destructive criticism went, he had a good case, for both ballot and parochial recruiting as enforced by his predecessors had failed with ignominy. But he had also adumbrated the principles which should govern his own action if he should be called upon to take their place, and upon his accession to office he did not shrink from putting his ideas into force. "We have made it our first object to make an Army," he said in the House of Commons on the 3rd of April. "Hitherto measures have been taken to create not an Army but a substitute for an Army. . . . An Army must be made by force or by choice. Compulsory service on every ballotted man would not be borne; therefore force must be abandoned for choice; and choice so far has been stimulated by bounties. But bounties mean that the pay and condition of the soldier are not the trade-value of his service; and our recruiting service can never rest on a proper basis until the necessity for bounties has ceased. Men receive no premium for other callings; they pay one. The Army therefore must be made an eligible calling or voluntary enlistment fails."

1806. After this preamble he discussed the means of making it an eligible calling. High pay, though the only certain method of ensuring his object, he rejected as economically impossible; but there remained encouragements, rewards, and short service. As to encouragements, the dignity of the Service had been impaired by the Volunteers, but there was still the resource of a generous provision for aged and disabled soldiers. As to rewards, he considered that they had been too much neglected in favour of rigorous discipline which drove men to desertion; and to enforce this point he reminded the House that of 13,000 men raised under Pitt's Additional Force Act 2800 had deserted. Apart from this, however, looking to the unpopularity of service in the West Indies, he advocated an additional allowance to men serving in the Colonies. But the reform upon which he relied above all others was short service, which both he and Robert Craufurd had already frequently pressed upon the Government. To this end he proposed that men should be enlisted first for seven years, such being the usual term of apprenticeship, and should enjoy the usual privilege on discharge of exercising their trade wherever they wished. If at the close of his first term a man was ready to re-engage for a second period of seven years, he was to receive extra pay of sixpence a week and be entitled after fourteen years' service to a pension for life. If he re-engaged for a third term his extra pay was to be raised to one shilling a week, and at the end of twenty-one years' service he was to be assured of a full Chelsea pension of one shilling a day. Incidentally Windham proposed to increase the whole of the Chelsea allowances, so that the first class of pension should be worth a shilling a day, the second ninepence, and the third sixpence. The grand difficulty, namely that of men whose service expired abroad in time of war, he proposed to face boldly by enacting that Commanding Officers should be empowered to retain them for six months beyond their term and for no longer, at the end of which period they were to be entitled to their discharge and to a free passage home. As to the existing Army, the intention was to discharge no man until he had completed his twenty-one years, but to grant the additional sixpence a week to all who had served more than seven and less than fourteen years, and the additional shilling to all who had served more than fourteen and less than twenty-one years. 1806.

The scheme was a bold one, but it came as less of a surprise than might have been expected, for the Duke of York had circulated a sketch of it, with some modifications, in June 1804, to fourteen General Officers, seven of whom could be reckoned the most distinguished men in the Army. Their replies differed very greatly. General Hewett, the Inspector-General of Recruiting, strongly opposed it, alleging the difficulty and expense of supplying foreign garrisons and preferring the system, favoured by Pitt, of establishing a Permanent Reserve of 70,000 men, of whom 20,000 might be induced to volunteer annually into the Line. General Fox, the brother of Charles James, on the other hand, seconded the proposal, opining that desertion would be less frequent and the service less unpopular if men returned to their friends young and well, instead of reappearing only as worn-out cripples at Chelsea and Kilmainham. He did not fear any injury to discipline, believing that the soldier, being better contented, would be more subordinate. Incidentally he mentioned that very cruel and severe punishments had been disused from about 1775 until about 1798, when they had reappeared and seemed likely to increase.

Lord Harrington confessed that he had been opposed to short service, but had been converted to it by the practice in the East India Company's Army and the French Army. Sir David Dundas, upon the whole, favoured short service, but would not allow men to be discharged in time of war; and Lord Cornwallis took much the same view. General Whitelocke, who had enjoyed considerable experience of recruiting, was decidedly for the change. Sir James Pulteney, a quaint

1806. but shrewd old soldier of great experience, thought that short service would undoubtedly be better in time of peace, but not in the field. Lord Mulgrave advocated short service upon every account, and particularly for the likelihood that it would attract a better class of man ; and Lord Moira, probably the only man in the Army who was of the calibre of Moore and Wellesley, summed up uncompromisingly in its favour. So also did Sir James Craig, though he did not think that it would solve the problem of keeping the ranks full in time of war. Lord Chatham, who, when he took the trouble, could both think and write, reviewed the proposal thoughtfully, and decided against it as likely to be prohibitive in regard to expense and prejudicial alike to *esprit de corps* and to discipline, especially in the matter of non-commissioned officers. Sir John Moore condemned the proposal utterly, anticipating much evil and no good from it. "If," he said, "limited service and enormous bounties could tempt men to enlist, would the Army of Reserve and the Permanent Additional Force be incomplete now ?" No change (such was his conclusion) in terms of enlistment would obtain men who could not be got without it. Nevertheless he admitted that compulsory service, if enforced, should be limited as to time. Finally, the veteran Lord Grey thought that short service might answer as a temporary expedient, but was convinced that it would not produce as good soldiers as service for life.[1]

Windham in summing up these opinions said that seven out of the fourteen answers were in favour of the reform, six against it, and one doubtful. In the House of Commons Colonel Thomas Graham, the future Lord Lynedoch, spoke with approval of it ; but the most striking testimony was adduced by Lord de Blaquière, who stated that in 1759 he had helped to raise the 17th Light Dragoons, and, finding no law to prevent him, had enlisted the men for three years. In 1762 he re-enlisted

[1] These opinions were printed in *Military Transactions*, Supplement to vol. i.

the whole of them, except two, for a bounty of two guineas, and finally re-enlisted them a third time in 1775 before they went out to America, where, as he said, they fought like lions.[1] 1806.

It was, however, necessary as part of Windham's scheme that Pitt's Additional Force Act should be repealed, and it was over this issue that the dead statesman's friends rallied to the fight. Castlereagh declared that the Act was only just beginning to be understood, that during the first ten weeks it had produced 300 men a week, and was furnishing men at the rate of 16,000 a year, though not yet enforced in more than half of the counties.[2] Generals Pulteney and Tarleton also defended it ; but Fox declared it to be miserably bad. "Where I live," he said, "it has never been acted on, within five miles of the Commander-in-Chief. It was absurd and impracticable, and therefore not executed." He added, with not unfair sarcasm, that it had taken its own framers eighteen months to understand it and put it into operation.[3] Wilberforce adverted to its total failure in the North and West Ridings of York, where not a man had been raised. A Mr. Hawthorne averred that the men had only been obtained by crimps and through flagrant breaches of the law, and that the circular to the Lords-Lieutenant of the 31st of December to all intent sanctioned both practices. Castlereagh tried hard to stem the torrent by adducing the case of Leicestershire, which, he maintained, had raised two hundred men at a much cheaper rate than those of the Army of Reserve. Mr. Babington, himself from Leicestershire, thereupon explained that these two hundred men were undersized boys who had been purchased from recruiting officers at five guineas a head. In fact there was no good defence

[1] *H.D.* Commons, 17th April 1806.

[2] Perceval (*H.D.* 18th April) gave the following figures. The Additional Force Act had produced

258 men a week, equal to 13,200 men a year, in last 15 weeks
277 " " " 14,600 " " " 10 "
356 " " " 18,000 " " " 5 "

[3] *H.D.* Commons, 3rd April 1806.

1806. to be made out for the unfortunate Act, and its repeal, together with that of the Army of Reserve Act, was carried with little real difficulty.[1] The fines paid or due by parishes for men deficient of their quota were also refunded, or remitted by the repealing of the Act; and this was a sensible measure, for they amounted in all to £1,800,000,[2] a sum which could never have been collected. Thus then Windham abjured all the expedients hitherto tried for the recruiting of the Army, and fell back upon voluntary enlistment alone, backed by short service.

The discussion upon this important subject found its place on the second reading of the Mutiny Act, but there was little worth noting in the debate. Windham dwelt upon three principal points only. The first was positive, namely, the benefit to the Army of attracting, as he trusted, a better class of recruit. The second and third were negative. He maintained that the loss of men discharged would not be serious; and that, judging by the experience of the East India Company's Army, it would not be a formidable inconvenience. Finally, the first term of service was fixed at seven years for the infantry, ten years for the cavalry, and twelve for the artillery, provided that the King should for so long require the recruits' services; to which Commanding Officers on any foreign station could add six months and no more, at their discretion, and the King could add three years by proclamation; the latter period, however, to determine in any case within six months of the signature of a definite treaty of peace. Further, men of less than eighteen years of age were not to begin to reckon their term of service until they were eighteen (46 Geo. III. c. 66, Schedules A, B).

The final regulations in amplification of the Act were not issued until 7th October 1806, when the terms were fixed as follows:—

Infantry could engage and re-engage for three

[1] 46 Geo. III. c. 51, 23rd May 1806.

[2] *Military Transactions*, Supplement, p. 11.

distinct periods, each of seven years; cavalry for three distinct periods of ten years, seven years, and seven years; artillery for three periods of twelve years, five years, and five years. No man could re-enlist until within twelve months of the end of his first period of service, or until within two years of the expiration of his second period. No man could re-enlist into another regiment until completely discharged from the first. The period of service could be extended for six months by the Commanding Officer of any colony or station abroad, and by the King, in respect of all men serving either at home or abroad, until six months after the signature of a definite treaty of peace, provided that such extension of service should in no case exceed three years. Men concluding their last period of service could not be called upon to serve for more than six months after its expiration. No man could be drafted to another regiment without his own consent. Every two years of service in the East or West Indies were to count as three. Every man who had earned his discharge was entitled to a free passage home, and to marching-money to carry him from the place of discharge to his own dwelling. The pay of corporals and privates in the cavalry was to be raised by one penny a day upon their re-engagement for a second term, and again for a third term of service. The pension to all ranks of non-commissioned officers and to privates after completion of their second term was fivepence a day. At the conclusion of the third term sergeants could retire on 1s. to 1s. 10d.; corporals on 1s. to 1s. 6d.; and privates on 1s. a day. If they served beyond their third period, they were entitled to an extra halfpenny a day.

1806.

However, in case the supply of recruits thus obtainable should fail, or, as Windham put it, because "a custom had grown up for Irish Militiamen to enter the Line," an Act was passed to enable Volunteers from the Irish Militia to enlist in the Army (46 Geo. III. c. 124, 21st July 1806). Hereby the King was empowered to allow Volunteers from the Militia to enlist in the Line

1806. during twenty days in each year after the 24th of July (secs. 1, 2). The proportion was not to exceed fifteen men for every company annually (sec. 7), and if a greater number offered themselves, the Commanding Officer might select among them which he would let go and which he would retain (sec. 9). The establishment of the Irish Militia being at the time 26,480, this source of recruiting, if the full number of men volunteered, would bring in close upon 4000 men annually.

Next Windham dealt with the Militia, which he declared to be our true army for home defence, and for that service equal to any part of our force. The one change which he purposed to institute was to continue the suspension of the ballot, and to rely upon a limited bounty to produce sufficient recruits. An Act was therefore passed (46 Geo. III. cap. 91, 16th July 1806) for the return of corrected lists of persons liable to serve in the Militia, and to suspend the ballot for two years. This enacted simply that new lists should be made out (secs. 1-5); and that as the Militia still exceeded the original quota fixed by the Act of 1802, the ballot should be suspended for two years (sec. 6). But powers were reserved to the King to cause deficiencies in that original quota to be made good by the ballot at any time (sec. 7).

VI

Finally, Windham attacked the great question of the Volunteers; and here he was absolutely uncompromising. He admitted that, when the Levy en Masse Act was passed, the difficulty of enforcing it had made him favour a voluntary system. But it would have been a very different system to that which was actually adopted. He would have scattered depôts of arms and schools of instruction all over the country, and trained the mass of the people simply to fire and hit their mark. This would have been far cheaper than the existing arrangement, which was exceedingly expensive, and moreover locked up recruits who might have been brought into the Regulars. He would have encouraged the Volunteer Associations to arm and discipline themselves at their own expense ; but the mass of the people he would have had loosely trained, so as to make useful recruits for the Regular Army. Another matter also needed to be set right, namely, section 26 of the Volunteer Consolidation Act, which gave rank to officers of Volunteers and Yeomanry next to those of Militia or the Regular Army of the same grade. This cheapening of military rank had caused great discontent. Craufurd, it must be mentioned, in a previous debate had adduced the case of a retailer of tarts and cheesecakes, who, being a Colonel of Volunteers, was authorised to give orders to Lieutenant-Colonels commanding Regular battalions. "Such a man," he said, "might be very superior to such officers in civil life, but not in military ; and yet if a General of a brigade were killed in action, the command of the brigade might devolve upon the vendor of pastry."[1] All such nonsense as this Windham intended to bring summarily to an end by enacting that in no case should an officer of the Yeomanry or Volunteers take rank above field-officers of the Regulars or Militia. An Act of one section (46 Geo. III. cap. 125) to this effect was accordingly passed on the 21st of July. 1806.

There remained the problem of reducing the expense of the Volunteers, a problem which needed to be faced at once, for the private subscriptions were nearly exhausted, and it was plain most of the corps must lean wholly upon the Government in a little while. Windham admitted that the reduction must be gradual ; and therefore proposed to begin by diminishing their allowances, cutting off their pay and granting them privileges in return. This would, of course, lead to a curtailment of their numbers, but even if a Volunteer corps were disbanded the men remained. First, therefore, he would reduce the eighty-five days' training in the year to twenty-six, and lessen the pecuniary grants to the

[1] *H.D.* Commons, 28th June 1805, Craufurd's speech.

1806. Yeomanry by reducing the pay of the officers, and the allowances both for drill sergeants and for permanent duty. As to the Volunteers he would give them clothing for the current year, but would not promise it for the following year. The principle upon which he meant to work was that Volunteers should not exist except at their own expense. No men who accepted more than arms and accoutrements from the Government were worthy of the name of Volunteers; and nothing in future was to exempt a man from national training unless he became such a Volunteer.

Next, as to the national training itself, it must be enforced by compulsion, but by as light compulsion as possible; and he therefore proposed that men should undergo it without leaving their homes, and that discipline should be as mild as might be. But obviously all could not be trained at once, and there must be selection. For this purpose he would divide the able-bodied men into three classes, and choose from them by ballot 200,000 men to be trained annually for twenty-six days, receiving pay of one shilling a day. If a certain proportion of men voluntarily offered themselves for training, the ballot might be so far diminished; and if a sufficient number came forward he would be prepared to accept it in lieu of the full quota prescribed by law. The training itself he proposed to conduct by means of detachments of Militia and of the Regulars nominally attached to the counties. In particular he would take advantage of the officers appointed to the skeleton second-battalions raised under the Army of Reserve Act, who, at great expense to the country, had been placed on full pay from the half-pay list or removed from their proper duty some time before a recruit had been levied, and had stood "waiting and gaping for their men like oysters at ebb-tide."[1] All of these provisions and regulations for the present, however, would apply to England only; for in Scotland the people were more military and the Volunteers more

[1] *H.D.* Commons, 3rd April 1806.

efficient, while the Militia laws also were of more recent introduction. 1806.

It was not to be supposed that changes so drastic would pass unchallenged in a House full of Volunteer field-officers, and yet the opposition was very moderate. Castlereagh protested that the new Training Act would be a breach of the engagement given, that the Levy en Masse Act should not be enforced if a certain quota of Volunteers were produced by the counties;[1] but this contention, though perfectly just, carried little weight. Perceval, on the 22nd of April, initiated a debate in defence of the Volunteers, but gained little by it, and when the Training Bill was actually introduced it was received for the most part in no carping spirit. General Pulteney, in his shrewd way, went to the heart of the matter by observing that much as he admired the Volunteers, he would no more trust to voluntary services for the defence of a nation than to voluntary contributions for the support of its finances.[2] In fact, despite a few vehement protestants to the contrary, the House appeared to favour some form of compulsory training. The one doubtful point was, how should that training be carried out; and this Windham left far too much to chance. Indeed he provoked a roar of laughter by insisting upon the wisdom of a provision that the parish constable should be present at all drills to enforce the instruction given by the sergeant.[3]

However, on the 16th of July the Training Act became law, being confined to England only (46 Geo. III. cap. 90). It began by repealing the First Defence Act and the Levy en Masse Act (sec. 1), and committing the execution of the present Act to the Lieutenancies of counties (secs. 2, 3). Upon the return of the lists of persons liable to serve in the Militia, the Privy Council was to apportion among the counties 200,000 men to be trained, which portions were to be redistributed by the Lieutenancies among

[1] *H.D.* Commons, 3rd April 1806.

[2] *Ibid.* 24th June 1806.

[3] *Ibid.* 27th June 1806.

1806. the hundreds and parishes, as in the case of the Militia (sec. 4). Persons exempt from the Militia were not to be exempt from the present Act, except schoolmasters and practising doctors (secs. 5, 6). In making their apportionment the Lieutenancies were to take account of the number of effective Yeomen and Volunteers who were exempted from training under the present Act, as also of persons exempted from the Militia but not from training under the present Act (sec. 7). The King could order the whole or any part of the number apportioned to be ballotted, enrolled, and trained; but if persons voluntarily offered themselves for training, then only the number deficient of the quota was to be ballotted (sec. 9). The manner of ballotting was prescribed by sec. 12; wherein it was ordained that the proceedings should not begin before 10 A.M., nor be prolonged beyond 6 P.M. Appeals against the ballot were to be heard by Deputy-Lieutenants (sec. 13). The year of training was appointed to begin on the 1st of November, and to last till the 1st of the following November (sec. 14). Persons trained for one year were not liable to be ballotted again for two years (sec. 15). Exemption for one year could be bought by payment of a fine of £10 or, in the case of persons with incomes of less than £100 a year, of £5 (sec. 16). Permanent exemption was granted to ballotted persons who entered Volunteer corps, so long as they remained efficient (sec. 18). Quakers and United Brethren were exempted by annual payment of a sum ranging from £1 to £7 : 10s. at the discretion of the magistrate (sec. 20); and infirm persons could be exempted free of charge by two Deputy-Lieutenants, or one Deputy and one magistrate, upon a medical certificate (sec. 23). The King could order persons to be trained, and fix the time and place for the purpose; but Sundays were not to be days of exercise, and no man could be called out for more than twenty-four days in the year, nor to a greater distance than five miles from his home (secs. 25, 26). Men who voluntarily offered to undergo training for any additional days might be regularly paid for them at the King's pleasure, up to the number of twenty-four days, with or without the addition of a bounty of 10s. at the close of the training (sec. 111). One constable in every parish was to attend exercise, on pain of a fine of £1 for every day's absence, and could be rewarded with a sum not exceeding £5 (sec. 28). The custody of arms and accoutrements was left to the Lieutenancy (sec. 30). The King was empowered to appoint Generals and officers and non-commissioned officers for the command and training of the men ; to embody the enrolled men on threat of invasion, and to place the men enrolled in the current or preceding year either in existing regiments or new corps, to be led out into any part of Great Britain ; and the men while embodied were subjected to the Mutiny Act and Articles of War (secs. 33-35). All men so called out were to take the oath of allegiance ; but could not be compelled to serve out of Great Britain (secs. 36, 37). The King was further empowered to give provisional orders for embodiment, and the Lieutenants to appoint signal and alarm stations. Men not appearing pursuant to order and signal were to be treated as deserters (secs. 38-40). Men and officers when embodied were to receive the same pay as the Regulars, and to be entitled to Chelsea pensions (sec. 42). An allowance of two guineas was to be given to each man for necessaries upon embodiment, and a further allowance of one guinea to enable him to return home after defeat of the enemy (secs. 43-44). Parishes refusing to ballot men under this Act were subject to a fine of £5 for every man deficient of their quota (sec. 50), but the Act did not extend to the City of London (sec. 49). Finally, all persons enrolled under the Act were subject to the regulations (sec. 22) laid down on the Schedule thereto, viz.:— 1806.

All persons trained under the Act were to receive pay for twenty-four days at 1s. a day.

All persons were to attend drill, obey the orders of officers and sergeants, and take due care of their arms,

1806. under penalty of a fine, elaborately graduated to suit variations of income, for non-attendance. In cases of misconduct the offender was to be delivered by the officer or sergeant to the parish constable, and to be brought by the constable before a magistrate, who was empowered to fine him to the extent of 10s., with two days' imprisonment in default of fines not exceeding 5s., and of five days' for fines not exceeding £1. Finally, Deputy-Lieutenants were empowered to offer rewards (to be defrayed out of fines) for skill in marksmanship. Otherwise all fines under sec. 59 were to be applied to the expense of training within the county.

Parliament rose on the 28th of July, after a momentous session; but Windham had already begun his reforms among the Volunteers. On the 9th of June he issued a circular to the effect that the allowance of £120 per troop of Yeomanry for contingent expenses would be discontinued after the 24th, and that £2 per annum for every non-commissioned officer and man would be substituted. A month later, on the 17th of July, he circulated, in the form of letters to the Secretary at War, the revised regulations for the pay and allowances of the Volunteers and Yeomanry at large; whereby in effect he swept away the June Allowances altogether.[1] To cavalry under the June Allowances he granted £3 a man for clothing, and £2 a man for all other expenses, and an adjutant for corps of three troops of forty rank and file and upwards. To cavalry under the August Allowances he gave £2 a man for all expenses, an adjutant to corps over 300 strong, and a sergeant-major to corps of over 120 and under 300 men. The infantry he appears to have placed uniformly under the August Allowances; and to corps raised after the 24th

[1] As usual the Clerks at the Home Office inserted no printed copies of the enclosures which are the essence of the circular. It is certain that Windham intended to put all the Volunteers on the August Allowances (*H.D.* 22nd April 1806, vol. vi. p. 850), but apparently he was induced to relent so far as the cavalry was concerned. The new rules as to cavalry I found in *I.D. Miscell.* July 1806.

of July 1806 he refused to give any allowance whatever. 1806.

Not unnaturally there was loud and dismal outcry. Multitudes of corps succumbed, or disbanded themselves in indignation, to the number altogether of over 11,000 men; and many counties vented their wrath by passing votes of confidence in the Volunteers, and lamenting their unhappy destruction. Windham remained unmoved, for this was no more than he expected. The Training Act, however, proved to be a more difficult experiment than he had looked for. His first step, on the 15th of September, was to send a circular to the Lords-Lieutenant saying that he proposed to station detachments of certain regiments in every county to assist in the training of the population and to collect recruits, and desiring to know if the regiments which he had selected would be acceptable, or whether any county would prefer some other or others. This as a preliminary step was sensible, but meanwhile all further arrangements were suspended while the new lists of men liable to the Militia ballot were being made out. This business took much time; and in spite of repeated reminders,[1] the lists were not ready until the end of the year, so that it was February 1807 before copies of the Act were circulated to the counties, and directions given for the apportionment of the quotas. The royal warrant for holding the ballots under the Act followed on the 17th of February, and Windham declared in Parliament that, if necessary, it would be enforced in the spring. But in the middle of March the Ministry of all the Talents resigned; and Castlereagh, Windham's ablest critic, succeeded him as Minister for War and the Colonies.

VII

Before going further it will be well to summarise once again the position of England and of Europe. In 1807.

[1] Circulars of 2nd Aug., 19th Sept. 1806.

1807. the first place, there had arrived in October the news that Sir Home Popham's absurd filibustering expedition to the River Plate had been for the moment successful, and that Colonel Beresford with his solitary battalion had taken possession of Buenos Ayres. The nation thereupon went mad with delight, and insisted on sending more troops to hold the new capture, not knowing that upon the 12th of August the Spaniards, remarking the weakness of Beresford's force, had attacked him and taken him and every one of his men prisoners. Sir David Baird, on hearing of the first success, had at once sent 2000 men from the Cape, and these arrived in the River Plate on the 12th of October, when, finding Buenos Ayres in the enemies' power, they ensconced themselves in a smaller town on the coast. About 3400 men were sent from England to the same destination under Sir Samuel Auchmuty as soon as they could be embarked, and a second detachment of 4300 men, under Craufurd, sailed on the 11th of November for the coast of Chili, under incredibly foolish orders from Windham, but was presently followed by new directions that it should join the rest of the troops upon the River Plate. In addition to this, Turkey's inclination to join with France caused the Government early in March 1807 to detach 5000 men to occupy Egypt.

In Europe, Prussia had at last drawn the sword against France, and had been utterly crushed at the battle of Jena on the 14th of October 1806; and on the 21st of November Napoleon had issued the Berlin Decrees, declaring the British Isles to be in a state of blockade, and interdicting all commerce with them. This was the decisive step in Napoleon's new policy of endeavouring to starve out Great Britain by closing all outlets for her trade. Russia, however, still resisted the French arms, and at Eylau inflicted a check, which was not far removed from a defeat, upon the redoubtable Emperor himself, bringing him for the moment to a standstill. There was therefore good hope that England might intervene in conjunction with Sweden to some effect by landing a force in North Germany, provided that she would send one of respectable size. The detachment of 7500 men to South America, and of 5000 to Egypt, was therefore a great misfortune. 1807.

The Army Estimates, when introduced into Parliament, provided for an establishment of 279,602 Regular troops, including all veteran and garrison battalions, all British and Colonial corps, and all foreign corps at home and abroad; besides 108,384 embodied Militia, and about 360,000 Volunteers.[1] The new system initiated by Windham seemed at first sight to be a great success. Between 20th October 1806 and 15th January 1807, 2155 recruits had been raised against 1208 in the corresponding period of 1805-6; and men engaged only for service at home had showed decidedly greater willingness to enlist into the Line under the new conditions. In two of the Reserve battalions alone nearly 600 men had exchanged home service for general service within six months; the weekly average of ordinary recruits had risen from 214 to 509, and desertions had decreased from 1 in 157 to 1 in 268 men enlisted.[2]

Altogether things seemed to be extremely satisfactory, and yet they by no means came up to the requirements of the military authorities. On the 15th of February the Commander-in-Chief submitted a memorandum in which he declared that ordinary recruiting was quite inadequate to produce an army sufficient for England's various needs. Already the demands upon the Regular Forces were so great that the defence of the country depended chiefly upon the Militia, which consequently required to be kept in a high state of discipline, and must be stationed on the coast, to the great inconvenience of officers. It was therefore imperative, first, to provide a large "disposable" force; secondly, to institute a defensive force from which the former

[1] The Secretary at War gave the number of the Volunteers at 363,400. *H.D.* Commons, 12th Jan. 1807.

[2] *H.D.* Speeches of Windham and Sir J. Doyle, 12th Jan., and of Windham, 12th March 1807.

1807. could be recruited, experience having shown that men who had once embraced a military life were generally willing to extend their service without limit; and, thirdly, to form a more extended Militia, which might obviate all the objections to the present system and to the Volunteers. The Commander-in-Chief therefore recommended that the Infantry of the Line should consist of its existing 101 regiments, and that each of them should consist of two battalions, 1000 strong apiece, the first battalion enlisted for general and the second for home service. Each of these regiments should be allotted and attached to one of the counties of the United Kingdom. The second battalions should be raised and kept complete by ballot for seven years, their service being limited to the British and Channel Islands, but with liberty to enlist for general service in the first battalions. The deficiencies in the second battalions only should be filled by the ballot.

As to the Militia, it should be increased from 84,000 to 150,000, either by ballot or exemption,[1] formed into battalions which should be officered by county gentlemen, and which should not be liable to be moved from their counties except in case of invasion or internal commotion. The battalions should be called out for one month's training in the year; the companies should be further exercised once a week or once a fortnight in their parishes, and there should be an inspecting field-officer to each four or five thousand men to superintend their discipline, and to take command of them in the event of their marching out of their counties.

The cavalry, artillery, Guards, and Sixtieth Rifles[2] would be able to maintain themselves by ordinary recruiting.

The cost of the new plan, for pay and clothing for the Regular Infantry and Militia, would be £9,799,000;

[1] I use the exact words of the memorandum, but I do not know what "by ballot or exemption" means.

[2] The Sixtieth, it must be repeated, was practically a foreign corps.

against £9,699,000, which was the cost of the Regular Infantry, Militia, and Volunteers at the time.[1] 1807.

It was probably the production of this scheme which made Windham pause before proceeding further with the enforcement of the National Training Act; but in March all power passed out of his hands, as we have seen, into those of Castlereagh. Most likely this was a great stroke of good fortune, for Castlereagh, notwithstanding the lamentable failure (to be presently narrated) of Walcheren, was on the whole the ablest Minister who has ever presided at the War Office. Immediately upon installing himself he ascertained the number of Regular soldiers with the colours, which was returned to him at 93,677 rank and file serving abroad, 88,857 serving at home, and 76,433 Militia, exclusive in every case of Artillery. Of the force at home 33,622[2] rank and file were fit for active service, namely, 23,596 infantry and 10,026 cavalry, leaving 131,768 rank and file for home defence. Of the 33,622 he reckoned that 2000 must be held in readiness as reinforcements for the East Indies, and 5000 for South America; and he therefore thought it imprudent to hazard more than 10,000 or 12,000 men for Continental diversions unless the French should be driven back, in which case the number could be extensively reinforced. Meanwhile he proposed to provide immediately and to keep in readiness transports for that number.

As to the Training Act, he judged its execution, as regards actual training, to be impracticable, and recommended that it should proceed no further than ballot and enrolment. Meanwhile the zeal and discipline of the Volunteers must be revived, in order to restore them to their former condition of order and efficiency, which had rapidly declined under Grenville's administration; and a flattering appeal must be made to them in the

[1] *Military Transactions*, Supplementary Volume.

[2] To arrive at the full strength it is necessary to add one-eighth for officers and non-commissioned officers above the rank of corporal. One may therefore call it 38,000 men, to which at least 2000 artillery could have been added.

1807. King's name to rouse them to new exertions. In a future session he hoped to replace this "fleeting and inapplicable mass" by a Sedentary Militia; but this for the present was impossible, as the ballots for filling vacancies in the Militia were already beginning.[1]

It is plain that the Commander-in-Chief's memorandum had sunk deeply into Castlereagh's mind, and that, in his heart, he was as strongly opposed to the Volunteers as Windham himself. However, for the present he felt constrained to humour them, and as a first step issued a circular on the 27th of April announcing that Windham's allowances would be granted to all Volunteer corps whether raised after the 24th of July or not, and that other matters concerning the Volunteers were under consideration. This last phrase was coupled with an expression of sanguine hope that the measure would encourage Commanding Officers to make their regiments efficient and prevent the gradual decline of the movement. Beyond doubt this and the employment of Volunteer sergeants as recruiting officers, with an allowance of five guineas, did infuse new life temporarily into the "fleeting and inapplicable mass"; though the course of events showed more and more the fatal error that Addington had made in neglecting the Regular Army for the sake of the Volunteers.

But the matter of real urgency was the need for augmenting the Regular Army, and to this end Castlereagh could at first sight suggest but two methods "without involving the Government in Parliamentary difficulties"; namely to complete the Irish Militia, which was 6000 below strength, so as to draw the annual 15 per cent of its men into the Line after the 1st of July, and to employ Volunteer sergeants all over the United Kingdom as recruiting officers. A fortnight's further study, however, convinced him that some more effectual means must be discovered; and he found himself reduced to one of two alternatives, either to draw more men from the Militia, or to extort them if possible from the

[1] Castlereagh, *Desp.* viii. 46-51.

parishes by means of fines, as in the case of the Army of Reserve Act. The latter expedient had so recently failed that he could not hesitate to recommend the former; and he therefore inclined to call for 20,000 men from the Militia of Great Britain, and so to regulate the process of volunteering from that force as to shorten as far as possible the period of drunkenness and disorder which invariably accompanied it. Lastly, in order to avoid a ballot if possible, he suggested that £10 should be given to the Colonels of Militia for every man taken from them, to be applied by them to the purpose of obtaining voluntary recruits. 1807.

But now bad news began to flow in from all quarters with dismal iteration. First came that of the mutiny at Vellore, which, though happily quelled by the amazing gallantry and readiness of a single officer, called for the immediate despatch to India of 4000 men. Then came the story of the disgraceful failure in Egypt, accompanied by what was, in the circumstances, deplorable waste of lives. Then Lord Hutchinson wrote from the Russian headquarters pleading earnestly for a diversion in the Baltic; and the King of Sweden pressed as earnestly for a force to co-operate with him and with the remnant of the Prussian Army to save Stralsund. For the French had begun to move again, always with success in spite of Eylau. Dantzig surrendered to them on the 24th of May; and Stralsund was one of the few ports left open to British merchandise on the Continent. The case was so urgent that the Cabinet resolved to send at once such men as could be spared; and on the 9th of June Lord Cathcart received orders to take command of about 28,000 British and Germans, and to proceed with a first division of about 8000 Germans to Stralsund, as soon as transports could be procured for them.

The despatch of this detachment caused Castlereagh deep searchings of heart. He reckoned that it would leave the British Isles with but 21,290 trustworthy infantry, including the Guards, for home defence; the second battalions, formed from the Army of Reserve

1807. and nominally nearly 29,000 strong, being too poor to be relied on for service in the field. Ordinary recruiting could not be counted on at best to produce more than 16,000 men a year, which was about the figure of the casualties in each of the two years last past. The Army was therefore stationary. The second battalions were valuable as recruiting depôts, but no more. There were fifty-six of them, complete in officers but with only 200 men apiece. The cost of the recruits which they gathered worked out altogether at £73 a head. They kept 16,000 men, enlisted for general service, in idleness because these could only be transferred to the first battalions of their own regiments; in fact, unless they were at once filled up by 20,000 men from the Militia, they could never answer their double purpose of feeding their first battalions and furnishing an efficient force for home defence. The deficiencies in the Militia consequent upon so heavy a draft could only be made good by the ballot, more especially as the five years' service of some 6000 principals would expire at the beginning of 1808.[1]

Such, then, was the conclusion to which Castlereagh had been driven by the end of May, and to this he rigidly adhered in spite of much private advice to the contrary. For, as the summer progressed, the situation became more and more serious. Cathcart, pursuant to his orders, sailed for Stralsund with his German troops, and arrived there on the 16th of July; but meanwhile not only had the Russians been utterly defeated at Friedland on the 14th of June, but the Tsar had thrown himself into the arms of Napoleon by the conclusion of the Treaty of Tilsit on the 7th of July. Thereby not only was England left without a friend in Europe except hapless Sweden, governed by a half-demented King; but she was threatened with the forcible closing of the ports of Sweden, Denmark, and Portugal against her, and with the active hostility of all three countries. Thus with the Danish fleet at his command Napoleon might hope to renew his plans of invasion.

[1] Castlereagh's *Desp.* pp. 53-66.

The peril was very great. It seemed certain that England must be driven back once more to the defensive, and must undergo yet another term of the miserable anxieties of 1803 and 1804. Fortunately some inkling of the secret agreement between Napoleon and the Tsar reached the British Cabinet, which determined it to forestall France in her designs upon Denmark. On the 19th of July a powerful fleet was ordered to proceed to the Baltic, and Cathcart was directed to bring his German troops back from Stralsund to Elsinore, where the British part of his force would meet him. With an army completed to 28,000 men he was then to demand the surrender of the Danish fleet, and, if it were refused, to besiege and capture Copenhagen. 1807.

Three days after this momentous decision, and while the country was still quaking over a fresh alarm of invasion, Castlereagh unfolded his plans to a newly-elected Parliament. Having first dwelt upon the insufficiency of ordinary recruiting to fill the ranks of the Army, he declared his intention of calling on the British Militia to provide 21,000 men, and on the Irish Militia to provide 7000 men, for the Line. The vacancies made through this call and through the discharge of Militiamen who had served their five years were to be filled up by ballotting 36,000 men for England, and procuring by ballot or voluntary enlistment 8000 men for Ireland. It was a heavy demand, as he admitted, but it would render further ballot unnecessary for two or three years. He proposed also to give the men who joined the Line the alternative of enlisting for life if they wished, and to grant them an increased bounty if they did so.

Passing to Windham's Training Act, he declared that he had found it impossible to carry out; but he proposed to use its machinery for classifications and ballots, and if possible to lengthen the training to two if not three years. From thence he hoped to evolve a Local Militia, and so to render the Act really useful. Meanwhile he thought that the Volunteers should be upheld until some decidedly superior substitute to them should

1807. be discovered. He had therefore revived the Inspecting Field-Officers, who had been abolished by Windham, and should encourage the Volunteers to come out on permanent duty. Therewith he introduced bills to enable the Militia to enlist in the Line, and to provide for refilling it upon the consequent depletion.

Castlereagh's expedients were obviously only meant to bridge over a single year until he could devise some permanent scheme. He wished, as he said, to disturb existing arrangements as little as possible. There were of course strong speeches made, condemning resort to the ballot and recommending that if it must be employed it should be for the purpose of re-creating the Army of Reserve. Great objection also was taken, not without reason, to the depletion of the Militia, Addington in particular averring that it had led to the resignation of a vast number of officers in 1804.[1] Windham went back to his old argument that ballot created bounty, bounty rising to excess created new ballot, and so on in a vicious circle until bounties became unendurable; and he urged that he alone had tried to move out of that circle. This might be true ; but it must be said in justice to Castlereagh that he meddled as little as possible with Windham's measures, and that if he introduced drastic treatment of his own, he was compelled to do so by the pressure of the military and political situation abroad.

The bills for permitting enlistment from the Militia into the Army became law on the 13th of August (Ireland, 47 Geo. III. sess. 2, cap. 55; Great Britain, cap. 57). They provided that any number of Militiamen might be enlisted in excess of three-fifths of the establishment of each regiment (sec. 1), a provision which set free 16,327 to enlist in England, 4160 in Scotland, and 8680 in Ireland. If five-sixths of the allotted number came forward at once in any regiment, no more were to be enlisted (sec. 2). If five-sixths did not come forward within thirty days, the Commanding Officer was to explain the terms of enlistment, and, if the number even

[1] *H.D.* 27th July 1807.

then fell below the quota, a book was to be opened to receive men's names for ten days (secs. 5, 6). At the close of those ten days all enlistment without special leave of the Commanding Officer was forbidden for three months, after which three days were to be allowed for volunteering, and so again at the end of the next three months; no man, however, being allowed to offer himself at the end of twelve months after the passing of the Act (sec. 7). No man five feet four inches in height and under thirty-five years of age was to be rejected (sec. 3), and men might enlist for short service or for life (sec. 12). Finally, no man was to be drafted from his chosen regiment against his will. 1807.

The draft from the Militia of Ireland, it must be remembered, was to be in addition to that of 15 per cent annually taken from that force; and was reckoned to deplete it to the extent of 35 per cent. The bounty offered to enlisting Militiamen was £10; and the Duke of York further encouraged the levy by offering an ensigncy in the Line to every officer of the Militia who could bring with him forty volunteers for the Army.[1]

For replenishing the Militia, the Irish Act (47 Geo. III. sess. 2, cap. 56, 13th Aug. 1807) provided for raising a number of men equal to one-half of the established quota, either by ballot or by ordinary enlistment at the discretion of the Lord-Lieutenant; any men in excess of the establishment being retained as supernumeraries (secs. 1-3). A bounty of four guineas was granted to the Colonels for each man, and one additional guinea for expenses, no part of which last was to go to the recruit (secs. 4-6). Any county deficient of its quota after six months was to be fined £30 for every man wanting; but three-fourths, one-half, or one-third of the fine could be remitted if the deficiency were supplied within one month, two months, or three months (sec. 17). Seven-tenths of the expense of finding men to make good casualties was to fall upon the counties (sec. 18).

[1] Castlereagh, *Desp.* viii. pp. 20, 72-75.

1807. The corresponding Act for Great Britain (47 Geo. III. sess. 2. cap. 71) was to the following effect. First, the Act for suspending the ballot was repealed (sec. 1). It was then enacted that within three months of the passing of the Act, a number equal to three-fourths of the quota under the Militia Act of 1802 should be raised (sec. 2). Where new or amended lists were required the time was extended to five months and four months (sec. 8). The fine for exemption was raised to £20; which, or any part of it not falling below half the average price of a substitute, could be paid to the ballotted man who was enrolled in place of the person paying the fine; but the man who accepted the £20, or any part of it, as aforesaid, was not to be entitled to the allowance usually granted to men worth less than £500 (secs. 16-18). The bounty to be given to parochial substitutes was not to exceed £10, and not more than £5 was to be paid to any substitute whatever until he joined his regiment. All fines, unless expended as aforesaid, were to be paid into the Imperial Exchequer (secs. 19, 20). Volunteers were not exempted from the ballot unless they had served the full number of days provided by the Volunteer Consolidation Act of 1804; nor were persons ballotted under the Training Act exempted, nor officers on half-pay, unless they had tendered their services as officers of Militia or Volunteers (secs. 22, 23). Counties, hundreds, or parishes not producing their full quota of men were liable to a fine of £60 for every man deficient, subject to a remission of three-fourths, one-half, and one-quarter if the deficiency were made good within one, two, or three months respectively (secs. 28, 31). Counties that refused to ballot could be subjected to the same fine of £60 (secs. 32, 33). When the full number of men had been supplied, the ballot was to be suspended until the 1st of January 1810 (sec. 34). Finally, the Act was not to apply to London (sec. 27).

Dealing first with the transfer of Militiamen to the Line, it appears that most of the Commanding Officers of Militia behaved very handsomely in encouraging their men to enlist; though as the deficiency of officers in the service increased from 301 on the 1st of July 1807 to 449 on the 1st of April 1808, it must be feared that their subordinates were not equally patient. It must be confessed too that the Militia was not treated fairly in the matter. An order was sent out that, during the thirty days set apart for the enlistment of Militia-men, no officers of the Regular Army must appear near the quarters of any Militia regiment; but the Adjutant-General sent a circular to all the Regular battalions to inform them of the date when the thirty days would expire, and to intimate that their recruiting parties might then go to the Militia regiments, though they "must be careful not to disturb their discipline." Such a caution as was contained in these last words might suffice to save the conscience of the Horse Guards, but could not avert the scenes of riotous drunkenness which inevitably accompanied the treating and other methods of suasion employed by recruiting officers. The whole proceeding was an infringement of the spirit of the law; and it is not surprising that in some quarters it was deeply resented. The Lieutenant of Lancashire, indeed, on receiving directions from the Adjutant-General to admit the recruiting parties, flatly refused to obey them until ordered by the Home Secretary.[1] 1807.

Again, no fewer than thirty-two counties produced five-sixths of their quotas at once, and were consequently excused from producing the remaining sixth. None the less the Secretary of State sent a circular to the Lieutenants asking them to use their influence with the Commanding Officers to squeeze this little residue of men out of them. This was ill received, as well it might be, and in at least one county the request was curtly refused.[2] However, in spite of all drawbacks,

[1] *I.D.* vol. cx. O.C., Dumfries Mila. to S.S. 9th Oct. 1807; vol. cxvi. L.L. Lancs, to S.S. 28th Sept. 1807.

[2] *Ibid.* vol. cxxvii., Circular of S.S. to thirty-two counties, 25th March 1808; O.C. Derby Militia to S.S. 11th April 1808.

1807. the men for the most part came forward willingly. In Hertfordshire the Militia furnished its quota to the Line within a fortnight, and Buckinghamshire, Cornwall, Salop, and Lincolnshire were little, if at all, behind her. The other counties took rather longer to make up their complement, but in only three was there real trouble, namely Cumberland, Caermarthen, and the Isle of Wight. The reluctance of the Cumbrians, which was set down to the "particular disposition of Cumberland men," was overcome without much difficulty; but in the Isle of Wight the Colonel reported that the case was hopeless. Cambridgeshire, strangely enough, held back for a time because the men were not allowed to enlist in the Marines. The Line, so the Commanding Officer reported, was not popular, excepting the Ninety-fifth,[1] but the Marines were greatly sought after. The ultimate result was that the English Militia sent to the Line 15,262 men out of 16,327 qualified to enlist, the Scottish Militia 3890 out of 4160, and the Irish 8353 out of 8680; making a total of 27,505 out of 29,167.[2] Upon the whole, Castlereagh had every reason to be satisfied with the behaviour of the Militia.[3]

[1] This of course was the present Rifle Brigade, already, after seven years of life, a distinguished corps. Evidence abounds that the Light Division could always obtain the pick of the recruits from the Militia.

[2] *Military Transactions*, Supplement, p. 16. But in the Castlereagh *Desp.* (viii. 125) the figures given state the British quota at 19,832, and the Irish at 8556; the British enlistments at 19,118, and the Irish at 8353; and the totals at 27,471 men enlisted out of a possible 28,388; leaving a deficiency of 714 for Great Britain, and 203 for Ireland.

[3] *I.D.* vol. cxiv. L.L. Herts, to S.S. 6th Sept.; vol. cvi. L.L. Bucks, to S.S. 15th Sept.; vol. cxx. O.C. Salop Mila. to S.S. 13th Sept.; vol. cxvi. O.C. North Lancs, Mila. to S.S. 28th Aug.; vol. cviii. O.C. Cornwall Mila. to S.S. 2nd Sept.; vol. cvi. O.C. Cambs Mila. to S.S. 20th Sept.; vol. cvii. L.L. Caermarthen, to S.S. 16th Dec. 1807; vol. cviii. O.C. Cumberland Mila. to S.S. 16th Sept.; vol. cxiii. O.C. I. of Wight Mila. to S.S. 20th Sept. 1807. Return in *C.J.* vol. lxiv. p. 502. The details of men deficient are, *Englana*:—Cardigan, 5; Caermarthen, 41; East Devon, 163; Pembroke, 23; Westmoreland, 9; West Suffolk, 27; 1st West

The replenishing of the Militia, however, was a very different story. In the first place, the levy was delayed by the necessity of making out new lists in almost every county, so as to include boys who had grown up since the last ballot, and to enable Volunteers to work out their exemption. Then there were very thorny questions raised as to the meaning of the sections which governed exemption. The reference in the new Act was to the Volunteer Consolidation Act of 1804, which required that returns of effective Volunteers should be furnished on the 1st of August and 1st of December. Was it sufficient for a Volunteer's exemption that he should have served for sixteen days during the previous eight months or the full number of twenty-four days in the previous twelve months? Such was the kind of question from county after county which flooded the Secretary of State's office for days; and finally it was decided, by very strict construction of the law, that no Volunteer should be exempted unless he had attended drill eight times between the 1st of April and the 1st of August.[1] This decision probably seemed severe, but it was lenient compared with the suggestion of the Lord-Lieutenant of Surrey, who did not love the Volunteers: "Will not all the Volunteers, if they attend all their drills before the 1st of December, be exempt from any ballot after it? If so, why not direct all ballots to be taken before the 30th of November? It can be done." The worthy nobleman did not gain his point; but he was not to be troubled by Volunteers much longer. 1807.

Another hideous complication arose out of the various changes of attitude and legislation in respect of

York, 185. *Scotland*:—Aberdeen, 12; Dumfries, 61; Edinburgh, 13; Forfar, 109; Inverness, 6; Ross, 19; Stirling, 7. *Ireland*:—Fermanagh, 3; Kerry, 68; Kilkenny, 1; Leitrim, 40; Limerick, 1; Longford, 90. Of the number deficient 453 men were due from seven English counties, 227 from as many Scottish counties, and 203 from six Irish counties.

[1] *I.D.* vol. civ. Minutes of G.M. Aberdeen, 29th Oct.; vol. cvi. Minutes of G.M. Ross, 14th Oct.; vol. cxv. L.L. Kent, to S.S. 2nd Nov. 1807.

1807. the Militia since the war began. It will be remembered that Addington at once called out the Supplementary Militia, and that Pitt, by the Permanent Additional Force Act, enacted that the Supplementary Militia should be absorbed, and the Militia generally reduced to its ordinary establishment under the Act of 1802. It will be remembered further that, by the Volunteer Consolidation Act of 1804, Volunteers were not exempted actually from the *ballot*; but any Volunteer on being ballotted could show his certificate of efficiency, and thereby obtain exemption from service in the Militia. His name, however, was retained on the ballot-list, so that, if he ceased to be effective, he could be called up for service, and if his name had actually been drawn for the Militia, he was liable, in this case, to fill the first vacancy that occurred in the Militia. In 1807 there were many Volunteers in this predicament, owing partly to Windham's reforms, partly to a selfish calculation that, if there were to be no more ballot, it was not worth while to work for exemption. Now arose the question whether such men could be forced to fill the vacancies caused by Castlereagh's Militia Transfer Act and Militia Augmentation Act. The vacancies had not been brought about in the ordinary way, but by wholesale sweeping of the Militiamen into the Line; and, moreover, Castlereagh, after thus reducing the Militia by *three-fifths* of its ordinary quota, had ordered the loss to be more than made good by calling up *three-fourths* of the ordinary quota under the ballot. Was it reasonable that Volunteers drawn under a former ballot and then exempted but since become ineffective, should be called upon without fresh ballot to make up deficiencies thus artificially created? The question, after much argument, was submitted to the Law-Officers of the Crown, who decided that such men were not legally liable to fill such artificial vacancies, though they were liable to fill natural vacancies if their county's Militia, at the time when Castlereagh's Act was passed, was short of its ordinary establishment under the Act of 1802. On the other hand, any men ballotted in future, and exempted as effective Volunteers, would, on ceasing to become effective, be liable to supply any vacancies which might then exist, or might hereafter arise.[1] 1807.

Another question, which was more easily decided, was this:—Was a man who had found a substitute in the Army of Reserve, liable to be ballotted under Castlereagh's Act, since under 43 Geo. III. cap. 123, such men were exempted from the Militia?[2] The answer was decisive. The Army of Reserve Act had been repealed; therefore the Act above quoted was no longer in force, and such men were liable to be ballotted.[3]

Yet another trouble, which exercised the Deputy-Lieutenants sorely, and not for the first time, was the standard of height. The Militia Act of 1802 fixed the standard at five feet four inches. The Act 43 Geo. III. cap. 100, sec. 2, enacted that no substitute, personal or parochial, should be rejected if he were five feet two inches in height, provided that he were otherwise fit for service. Some Lieutenants and their Deputies, not unnaturally, construed this to mean that principals were to be five feet four inches high, and substitutes five feet two inches. Others, quite indifferent as to the physical quality of their men so long as they could produce them in some shape or form, took five feet two inches as the standard for all; while others again, being conscientious public servants, rejected men under five feet four inches. By all the folly of having two coexistent standards was impartially denounced, until the question was finally set at rest by the decision of the Secretary at War that the standard of five feet two inches was now universal.[4]

Lastly, an old failing at the Home Office was brought to light by a sarcastic letter from a Deputy-Lieutenant

[1] *W.O. Mila. E.B.* 784, Sub-div. Clerk of Leominster to Sec. at War, 10th Nov. 1807.

[2] *W.O. Mila. E.B.* War Office to J. Allen, 12th Nov. 1807.

[3] See page 35.

[4] *I.D.* vol. cxviii. O.C. Northampton Mila. to S.S. 2nd Nov. 1807; vol. cxx. L.L. Somerset, to S.S. 4th Dec. 1807; *W.O. Mila. E.B.* W.O. to Major Durbin, 23rd Nov. 1807.

1807. of Somerset. "On the 14th of August last," wrote this indignant gentleman in October, "an Act was passed for *speedily* completing the Militia. It has not reached the Deputy-Lieutenants yet, nor have they any reason to expect it, unless you order copies to be sent without delay."

Under such initial difficulties was the ballot of 1807 set on foot. Even at the risk of wearying the reader, I have not shrunk from setting down legal difficulties which have long been dead and can never rise again, in order to show how infinitely the natural obstacles to the levying of recruits may be increased by hasty and ill-considered enactments, and even more by additional Acts passed to amend and explain the same. The root of the matter, of course, lay in the absence of a definite policy, the inevitable result of which was the hurried abandonment of one set of expedients, and the equally precipitate adoption of another set. But though it is too much to expect of human wisdom that it can foresee all the ingenious tricks which a people may discover for the evasion of an unpopular duty, yet there are far too many signs of sheer blindness and carelessness in all the legislation which so far has passed under review. And it must be remembered that every doubt as to the state of the law seriously impeded the progress of the levy. Every legal question was hotly discussed before it reached the Secretary of State, setting all the authorities within each Lieutenancy at variance, embroiling Lieutenancies with their neighbours, raising ill-feeling between commanders of Militia regiments and county magnates, and embittering the perennial strife between the civil power and the military. It is a reproach to our statesmen that such friction should still have abounded after fourteen years of almost unbroken war.

VIII

Let us now turn to the progress of the ballot itself. There was, of course, a rush for substitutes; and crimps and insurance companies drove a roaring trade. Crimping, indeed, reached such a height that it was carried on not only by publicans, parish officers, and such like, but by privates, non-commissioned officers, and even officers of the Army, Militia, and Volunteers; nor was there one who failed to make from £5 to £15 out of every substitute that he provided. In one case a man was engaged for the Warwick Militia by a corporal for a bounty of £10; the corporal sold him to a sergeant for £18; the sergeant made him over to a crimping publican for some unrecorded price; and the publican finally disposed of him to a parish officer for £27:6s. Indeed, parochial officers lay generally at the mercy of the professional crimps, who controlled the market by laying hold of the substitutes, selling them to one another, and keeping them in pay until the unhappy parishes, rendered desperate by fines and repeated ballots, were driven at last to give them their own price. 1807.

Nevertheless parishes were not without resources of their own. Their principle was, very naturally, to avoid above all things the burden of supporting the Militiamen's families; and consequently they always preferred to enlist single men. They would take any boy who could reach the standard of height and pass a medical examination, rather than the finest of married men. In Warwickshire the military officers complained loudly that the Deputy-Lieutenants were remiss in the execution of their duty. The Lieutenant who, with all his subordinates, plumed himself upon the methods by which his Lieutenancy was ruled, indignantly repudiated the charge. The General of the district retorted that two hundred children had been furnished as substitutes, who might grow into men, but were at present only fit for drummers.[1] And beyond all question vast numbers of the so-called men all over England were even as these children of Warwick. As crimps the parish officers appear only to have mastered the elements of their

[1] *I.D.* vol. cxlviii. L.L. Warwick, to S.S. 26th Jan.; Maj.-Gen. Cockburn to L.L. Warwick, and to S.S. 6th February 1808.

1807. profession, for we hear of one who engaged a substitute at Warwick for forty pounds, and offered the man as much as fifty guineas if he would lend him the money for five years free of interest. The crudity of this proposal suggests ambition, indeed, but hardly financial genius.[1]

The insurance companies and subscription societies were very prominent in the ballot of 1807. In all counties near London they indemnified the holders of their policies by producing either a fine or a substitute who had cost them less than £20, and who invariably deserted with the £5 which the law permitted to be paid to him. The Lord-Lieutenant of Buckingham deplored the inefficacy of the law to check this evil, and suggested that it might be possible to attack it by invalidating the policies, on the ground that they were not stamped.[2] In Gloucestershire and the Western counties there was a very extensive insurance office which charged three guineas for an insurance of £20, an extravagant premium for which they might well have returned £50. But the London societies spread their branches wide over the country, bribing recruiting-sergeants and non-commissioned officers right and left, and sowing corruption thickly wherever they went. "We shall be glad," runs one of their circulars to the sergeant-majors of Militia, "to receive in Middlesex growing boys five feet two inches high, and men near fifty years of age, unless their age is too manifest. . . . I propose to allow two guineas to the sergeant and his party engaging the recruit, and one guinea to you for each person we may pass from your county; the men or boys to be obtained for us at as low a rate as possible, and in no case to stand us in more than £15 when delivered in London. I should suppose that men refused by your regiment will be afterwards had for £8 or £10; and the whole of their subsistence till they can arrive in town must be borne out

[1] The authority for the statements in the two last paragraphs will be found in *I.D.* vol. cli. C.G.M. Warwick, to S.S. 23rd Jan. 1808.

[2] *I.D.* vol. cvi. L.L. Bucks, 23rd Oct. 1807.

of their bounty. Captain Whittaker, late of the Surrey Militia, being one of the proprietors of this office, . . . will receive all your county can furnish him with."[1] 1807.

[1] *I.D.* vol. cli. C.G.M. Warwick, to S.S. 23rd Jan. 1808. I print the whole circular below :—

"63 Newman Street, London, *Oct.* 5, 1807.

"Sir—As this office has many subscribers in your county, many of whom must of course be ballotted upon us, and as the peculiar circumstances of Middlesex render the C.O.'s of that Militia glad to accept men which the county regiments will reject, I conceive that this office and the Sergeant-Majors of the following counties through which the recruits from Lancashire must pass, viz. Lancashire, Cheshire, Staffordshire, Warwick, Northamptonshire, Buckinghamshire, Bedfordshire, and Hertfordshire, may be of reciprocal advantage to each other, and that too in no small degree. *Therefore* I propose to you in the first place to influence those sergeants who may be detached from the regiment you belong to into Warwick to receive the men under the approaching ballots for that county, to engage for the Middlesex Militia all such persons as may be deemed unfit for your regiment and yet be fit for service.

"For instance, we shall be glad to receive in Middlesex growing boys five feet two inches high, and men near fifty years of age unless their age is too manifest. Those are circumstances which must be left to the sergeants, and which every one of them are of course acquainted with, for which (*sic*) I propose to allow two guineas to the sergeant and his party engaging the recruit, and one guinea to you for each person we may pass from your county ; the men and boys to be obtained for us at as low a rate as possible, and in no case to stand us in more than £15 when delivered in London. I should suppose that being refused by your regiment they will afterwards be had for £8 or £10 ; and the whole of their subsistence till they can arrive in town must be borne out of their bounty.

"Captain Whittaker, late of the Surrey Militia, being one of the proprietors of this office, will be at Manchester for the purpose of recruiting, and will march from thence all the way with the recruits, and receive at Coleshill, Meriden, Coventry, and Dunchurch all your county can furnish him with. The exact day of his being at each of these places, you shall be made acquainted with in due time, for the information of the sergeants, to enable you to collect and deliver their men under your directions. But as the men so engaged by you and received by us may desert before they are enrolled, or by chance not be accepted, the allowance to you and the sergeants can only be made on the return of the party, when, if any should desert or be rejected, they shall either be restored at the place we received them or satisfactorily accounted for. The guinea to you for

1807. The circular proceeded to say that if any of the office's clients in the county needed a substitute, one must be procured as "unlikely to desert as possible, because much of the success of our insurance depends upon our receiving the parochial allowances, which we are only entitled to in case of the substitute actually serving a month."

Compared with this lordly way of doing business, there is a pathetic helplessness in the appeal made by the "Praeses of Delegates of twelve Militia Societies in and about Glasgow" to the Secretary of State. This dignitary complained that the officers appointed to receive substitutes for the Militia regiments gave them no subsistence, and that consequently the Societies were put to the great expense of keeping them alive until they were sent to their battalions. Moreover, a number of ballottable men had been drawn away from the county as substitutes to other counties a hundred miles away, which was contrary to law. "The bounties," so ended the letter, "have been very oppressive, and if the societies are to furnish subsistence too, the burden will be very heavy." The writers apparently had not the slightest idea that they were themselves contravening the law, or at any rate what had been the law, when they called upon the Secretary of State to protect them, though they were ready enough to invoke the Act which prohibited the procuring of substitutes from distant counties.[1]

each man may possibly be better remitted from town; you can receive it, however, in any way you direct.

"Should any person be ballotted upon our insurance funds in your county, all we have to request is, that the sergeants to whom the person ballotted will be directed to apply, will procure, as reasonable as he can, a substitute as likely not to desert as possible, because much of the success of our insurance depends upon our receiving the parochial allowances, which we are only entitled to in case of the substitute actually serving a month, for which we shall make the same allowance to them and to you as for the recruits they may engage for, as for the Militia of Middlesex."

Addressed: To the Sergeant-Major of the Warwickshire (or other) Militia.

[1] *I.D.* vol. cxiv. Praeses of Delegates to S.S. 5th Dec. 1807.

But it need hardly be said that the law upon the one point as upon the other was a dead letter. In Nuneaton notices were publicly issued offering bounties of £30 and £17 respectively for recruits for the Northampton and Leicester Militia.[1] From Berwick the Lieutenant reported without concealment to the Secretary of State in January 1808 that he could not fill the ranks of his Militia from the county. The people were all agricultural; labour being scarce, they were not to be tempted by bounties; and hence he was obliged to recruit "at a distance" with great delay and expense.[2] In Birmingham there was a Major of Volunteers who was also Lieutenant-Colonel in the Leicester Militia, and kept a regular recruiting agency for his Militia in the town. The county of Leicester, it seems, made a practice of encouraging the payment of exemption-fines instead of the production of substitutes. As the fines under the Militia Act of 1802 were payable to the stock-purse of the county's Militia regiment, the Leicester Militia was always in funds, and was not only able but willing to outbid any other county by £5 in the purchase of recruits.[3] But all legislative efforts to secure that the Militia should be a strictly local force were obviously futile, so long as substitution was permitted, and it is needless to multiply examples of the fact. 1807.

For the rest the wild traffic in substitutes literally raged during the weeks of the ballot; and it is probable that in England the national taste for gambling made it a positive enjoyment. In some cases the substitutes firmly declined to engage themselves to serve, unless the whole of their bounty was paid into their hand instead of the £5 which alone was allowed to them by law before they reached their regiments. The Deputy-Lieutenants in Lancashire in vain offered printed papers to their men acknowledging the further sum due to them, and promising to pay it at the appointed time. The Lanca-

[1] *I.D.* vol. cxxii. C.G.M. Warwick, to S.S. 14th Dec. 1807.
[2] *Ibid.* vol. cxxvii. L.L. Berwick, to S.S. 15th Jan. 1808.
[3] *Ibid.* vol. cli. C.G.M. Warwick, to S.S. 23rd Jan. 1808.

1807. shire men would be content with nothing but the whole of the bounty paid down in hard cash; and the Deputies were obliged for a time to adjourn the ballot.[1] Nor was the caution of the recruits wholly unreasonable, for in Nottinghamshire a subdivision clerk absconded with £170, the property of some unfortunate substitutes, which had been kept back from them temporarily in fulfilment of the law.[2] Elsewhere this provision as to payment of the bounty (which was of course designed to discourage desertion) was simply evaded by a private arrangement between the ballotted man and his substitute.[3] Finally, in March 1808 the levy was supposed to be more or less completed, when the following results were published[4]:—

	Quota.	Joined their Regiments.	Enrolled but not joined.	Deficiency to be supplied.
Great Britain	37,557	28,261	4308	4988
Ireland . .	9905	6119	664	3122

From another return it appears that of 26,085 men enrolled in England, 3129 were principals and 22,956 substitutes. Among the counties Middlesex with a quota of 692, Rutland with a quota of 61, and Carnarvon with a quota of 96, produced not a single principal; the Tower Hamlets with a quota of 320, furnished two principals; Leicester with a quota of 480, twelve; Derby with a quota of 667, fifteen; Cumberland with a quota of 436, twenty; the three Ridings of York with a joint quota of 2329, only 106; Staffordshire with a quota of 824, forty-two; Lincolnshire with a quota of 992, fifty-four; and Northumberland

[1] *I.D.* vol. cxvi. Thomas Wilson (D.L. Lancs) to S.S. 26th Nov. 1807.

[2] *Ibid.* vol. cxliv. L.L. Notts, to S.S. 31st May 1808.

[3] *Ibid.* vol. cxxviii. L.L. Bucks, to S.S. 21st March 1808.

[4] This return and the following are printed in *C.J.* 1808 (Appendix), vol. lxiii. pp. 613-614.

with a quota of 480, twenty-seven. Among counties that gave a more creditable account of themselves, Pembroke showed 76 principals out of a quota of 148; Caermarthen 106 out of 299; Herefordshire 127 out of 337; Cardigan 52 out of 174; Sussex 127 out of 466; Suffolk 159 out of 777; Norfolk 182 out of 901; Somerset 183 out of 865; Essex 166 out of 908; Devon 168 out of 899; and Berkshire 94 out of 380. The total sum paid into the Treasury for exemption-fines was £14,958, of which sum over £2000 came from Berkshire, over £2500 from Durham, over £2300 from Sussex, and over £1200 from Hampshire. Monmouth was the lowest contributor with £10, and Cornwall ran her hard with £12; but it is doubtful whether any legitimate deduction can be drawn from these figures. 1807.

The bounties, that is to say, the average prices of substitutes, of which a return was also made, varied from £10 in the Isle of Wight to £16 in Montgomery and Rutland, £30 in Devon and East Yorkshire, £40 in Cardigan and the North Riding of Yorkshire, £41 : 10s. in Northumberland, £44 in Anglesey, and £45 in Monmouth. Throughout Wales, with the exception of Montgomery, bounties ran very high, which possibly accounts for the number of principals produced by one or two counties. But it would be rash to repose too much confidence in these figures, for the transactions between lotmen and substitutes or crimps were by no means always public. It may be mentioned as an example of what went forward that two drummers of the Aberdeen Volunteers paid their Colonel £20 towards the regimental funds, having received £40 apiece to engage themselves as substitutes in another corps.[1]

I pass next to the Volunteers of the United Kingdom, first giving a comparative table in round numbers of their effective strength in rank and file from the 16th of December 1803 to the 1st of July 1807:—

[1] *I.D.* vol. cxxv. Lt.-Col. Finlayson to S.S. 8th Feb. 1808.

1807.	16th Dec.	1803	414,000	of which in Ireland		72,000
	1st July	1804	330,116	"	"	71,895
	"	1805	318,173	"	"	67,074
	"	1806	307,163	"	"	64,085
	"	1807	294,148	"	"	65,942

Thus it will be remarked that they had shown a steady decline in numbers from the first, and that Windham's reforms had really worked no very notable change in their strength. Castlereagh, as we have seen, inclined to give them temporary encouragement; the most solid part of which was permission for corps which had not completed their twenty-six days of drill to go upon permanent duty for not less than ten or more than fourteen days, with full pay for those periods both for officers and men.[1] It was indeed necessary to keep some of the Volunteers in existence, for, owing to the depletion of the Militia, those of Devon, Gloucester, Kent, Hampshire, and Somerset were required to find guards for the French prisoners at Plymouth, Portsmouth, Bristol, and Norman Cross, receiving of course full pay for the duty.[2] There, however, the encouragement ended, for the reports concerning them were not generally very favourable. When the renewal of the ballot was announced, a number of men thronged to join Volunteer corps, but they were not well received, and rightly so. For some time past the Lieutenants had had orders to forward no further offers of Volunteer corps; and this placed them in a difficulty, for such tenders of service were often very numerous. "The people," wrote the Lieutenant of Northumberland, "seem to think that they have the right to become Volunteers by such offers, and to exempt themselves from the present and future ballots." [3] The fact seems to have been that evasion of national duty was now become the sole object of Volunteering. "The Volunteer plan," reported the Lieutenant of

[1] Circular to L.L. 6th Aug. 1807.

[2] Circular to L.L. of the five counties, 22nd Aug. 1807.

[3] *I.D.* vol. cxviii. L.L. Northumberland, to S.S. 13th Aug. 1807.

Surrey, "was at first entered into in a right and proper spirit, but now it has dwindled down to little else than exemption from other services."[1] "When the Volunteers were first raised," wrote a gentleman from Norwich, "I subscribed like other people, as it was conceived that the subscribers were to bear all the expense; and numbers of people enrolled themselves. But when pay was allowed, a new set of men joined, who found that when work was short the Volunteer's pay, added to casual employment, would enable them to live. Half of them are rank revolutionists. Half of them meet in a court at the back of my house, where I hear them damning the King and Parliament. They command their officers and declare openly that they will do what they please."[2] Norwich, it must be remarked, like all manufacturing towns at that time when England's transition from an agricultural to a manufacturing country was accomplishing itself, contained a somewhat turbulent population; and the damning of Parliament, though a serious symptom in those days, has become a mere commonplace in these. But that men should command their officers is an evil thing in every generation; and there had always been too much of it among the Volunteers. 1807.

In the Isle of Wight in this same year the privates of a troop of Yeomanry (which were then reckoned Volunteer cavalry) had declined to serve any longer if a certain officer were admitted, maintaining in defiance of Act of Parliament that every officer must be regularly proposed and approved by the corps at large. The Commanding Officer therefore resigned, whereupon the troop elected an officer of their own choosing and tried to put him into command.[3] The old idea, that Volunteers could do as they pleased, never wholly perished, and indeed actually received countenance from the Courts of Law. In the spring of 1807 the Richmond Volunteers were on parade, when a sergeant took occasion

1 *I.D.* vol. cxxi. V.L. Surrey, to S.S. 2nd Sept. 1807.

2 *Ibid.* vol. cxxiv. Norfolk, Thomas Howes (undated) to S.S.

3 *Ibid.* cxiii. V.L. Hants, to S.S. 8th Oct., 19th Nov. 1807.

1807. to strike Colonel Drew, the Commanding Officer. Drew returned the blow with the flat of his sword, and caused the sergeant to be disarmed and turned out. The sergeant thereupon brought an action against the Colonel, when Mr. Justice Heath laid it down that Drew had no right to take the sergeant's sword, and that the sergeant had a right to defend it. He therefore summed up against Drew, and the jury brought in a verdict of £200 damages with £300 costs.[1] This was probably the heaviest blow struck at the subordination of the Volunteers throughout their existence; and it fell just at a time when discipline particularly needed to be strengthened. It was now discovered also that there had been gross abuses in connection with the allowances granted to the Volunteer corps for the maintenance of their arms; and a circular was issued to intimate that in future these would be granted only for such arms as were certified by the Inspecting Field-Officers to be in good repair.[2] In Wiltshire it seems that good reason existed for extraordinary wear and tear of muskets; for the Volunteers, weary of waiting for the invasion of the French, had turned them to the destruction of game and rabbits, an operation which was probably little less perilous to the King's subjects than invasion itself; and had certainly not been contemplated when the weapons were issued.[3] In fact whatever the Volunteers may have been in 1804, they stood revealed in 1807 in their primitive condition as an armed rabble.

With this stern fact before him, Castlereagh spent the winter of 1807 in devising means for replacing this rabble by something which should return better value for the money expended upon it. Meanwhile the year closed with a stroke of misfortune, which was hardly redeemed by real and effective success in another quarter. The expedition returned from Buenos Ayres wrathful and humiliated after a desperate fight in the

[1] *I.D.* vol. cxxi. L.L. Surrey, to S.S. 18th April 1807.

[2] Circular to L.Ls. 8th Aug. 1807.

[3] *I.D.* vol. cxxii. C.G.M. Wilts, to S.S. 12th Dec. 1807.

streets of the city, wherein the men had covered themselves with glory and the General with disgrace. Rather more than a thousand officers and men had fallen in the course of these ill-conceived operations, so wantonly initiated by Popham; but the remainder to the number of nearly 8000 were at least restored to England for future campaigns. From Copenhagen also the force had returned, fortunately little abridged of its original strength. It had done its work, which was not very arduous, by the capture of Copenhagen and of the Danish fleet, and was quite fit for further campaigns elsewhere. The whole affair had been well managed, especially on the part of the Cabinet; and the thrust, as was testified by the wrath of Napoleon, had sped home and undone his ambitious schemes in the Baltic. Still the outlook was gloomy, and Ministers could hardly guess that this was the darkest hour before the dawn, and that another year would see Napoleon irretrievably committed to the fatal blunder which brought about his fall. 1807.

CHAPTER IV

I

1808. At the opening of the year 1808 the progress of the Regular and Reserved Forces was shown to be as follows, the numbers including the rank and file only :—

	Establishment, 1st Feb. 1808.	Effective Strength, 1st Feb. 1808.	Effective Strength, 1st July 1807.
Cavalry . .	28,792	26,520	26,315
Infantry . .	198,327	178,295	156,561
Artillery . .	25,662	24,781	24,071
Militia . .	95,823	77,164	77,790
Volunteers .	...	296,669	294,378

Besides this, it was reckoned that 10,000 recruits had been enrolled for the Militia, but had not yet joined headquarters. Upon the whole, therefore, there was a solid increase to the Army of about 22,000 men, and to the Militia of about 9000 men.

On the other hand, the Commander-in-Chief reported and proved up to the hilt that the short service, increased pensions, and other reforms introduced by Windham had failed completely to fulfil his promise that they would suffice to keep the ranks of the Army filled solely by voluntary enlistment. The number of men raised by voluntary recruiting in 1806 and 1807 was much larger absolutely than in previous years, but not so relatively to the number of parties employed. Yet provision for additional pensions had already swelled the expenses for Chelsea and Kilmainham by £200,000 annually; and this sum would be still further augmented within a few years as the periods of service of the various batches of men began to expire. Lastly, constant changes of station made it impossible to apply accurately the rules for the increase of a man's pay after each term of seven years' service, particularly in conjunction with the privilege that two years' service in the East and West Indies should count as three. In those days men had a passion for shifting from regiment to regiment as often as they had opportunity, and it was impossible to register their movements so closely as to do justice either to them or to the public. 1808.

Castlereagh, on receiving this report, very magnanimously urged every consideration that could be brought forward in favour of Windham's system; but the Horse Guards met the statements and arguments with facts and figures which were neither to be controverted nor ignored.[1] Accordingly, when the Mutiny Bill came before Parliament, in March 1808, Castlereagh was obliged to represent that short service, though it might answer for work in Europe, was impossible for a country which had to supply so many foreign garrisons as England. Of 204,000 Regular troops in the Army, 70,000 were engaged for short service; 36,000 of them, enlisted during the past twelve months, would all be lost in seven years, and in fact limited service could not cover its own waste. He mentioned incidentally that the great increase of recruits gathered by voluntary enlistment had been due really to an extraordinary cause. Windham had threatened to disband the whole of the fifty-four second battalions formed by the Army of Reserve, unless they were increased to four hundred men apiece within six months, and this menace had led the officers of these battalions to make unusual exertions lest they should be relegated to the half-pay list. He therefore moved a clause, not to sweep away short service altogether, but to allow recruits the option

[1] Corresp. in Supplement to *Military Transactions*, Appendix 18.

1808. of enlisting for a term or for life as they might prefer.[1] He carried the House with him. The Mutiny Act of 1808 bound every recruit to serve until legally discharged; but short service none the less remained as an alternative open to such men as preferred it.

Windham, as was natural, stood up for the system which he had introduced, setting forth his side of the question in a series of thirteen propositions, with a vast array of figures all tending to show that recruits were better, cheaper, and more numerous under his scheme than under any other. Castlereagh, unfortunately, had yet more facts and figures to his hand to overthrow these in a series of counter propositions; and it must be confessed that in the duel of statistics he came off the better.[2] In fact there was no gainsaying the unpleasant truth that, without some such heroic measure as the quadrupling of the private soldier's daily pay, it was impossible to keep the ranks of the Army filled without some form of compulsion; and Castlereagh was profoundly convinced that it was imperative not only to maintain but to increase the Army. Enforced service abroad was out of the question; but enforced service at home was consecrated by constitutional usage and confirmed by the Militia Acts. The Army of Reserve had been an experiment in another department of compulsion, but it had not been successful. Practically the only resource, therefore, was to turn the Militia once more into a recruiting depôt for the Army.

To this end Castlereagh had been maturing his plans for increasing the Militia at the expense of the Volunteers. His idea was to select first all that was good of his predecessor's schemes, and to graft upon that stock a new shoot of his own; and he therefore put forth the following suggestions, the figures being, with one exception, reckoned for England only :—

1. To keep 100,000 Volunteers only of the best description, *in Great Britain*, and those chiefly in large towns and populous manufacturing districts, where men would

[1] *H.D.* 8th March 1808. [2] *Ibid.* 13th Aug. 1807.

be glad to turn to them in order to evade other service; the State imposing on them such conditions as would make them a cheap, useful, and efficient force. 1808.

2. To create 200,000 Sedentary Militia, to be trained for twenty-eight days annually, but not to leave their counties except in case of invasion or rebellion.

3. To train, under Windham's Training Act, 200,000 men, and make them liable to serve in the Line in case of invasion.

Though he set down these three descriptions of force in the order thus given, he intended originally that the two first should be based upon the last, that is to say, upon the Training Act. He found fault with Windham's measure upon three principal grounds—viz. that Windham had offered to pay the men called out for exercise an equivalent for the loss of their time and labour, which the country could not afford; that it was impossible to provide adequate training for men within the space of twelve months; and that, though it was obviously useless and dangerous to bring large bodies of men together unless previously organised and provided with officers, it was impossible conveniently to find officers for so large a number as 200,000.

He proposed, therefore, to establish the following principles as the basis for a new system of training:—

1. That instruction in the use of arms should be imposed upon all able-bodied men between eighteen and thirty as a positive duty, to be enforced by fine; and that every parish should keep a list of men between those ages.

2. That the State should provide the means and discharge the expenses of instruction, but allow no pay for attendance at drill. Every effort, however, should be made to train in their own parishes men who lived at a long distance from the places of assembly.

To facilitate the teaching, the Government was to distribute and employ drill-sergeants in all the counties, taking them from the permanent staff of the Sedentary

1808. Militia (whose organisation will presently be explained), give them charge of a certain number of firearms, and pay them five shillings apiece for every man certified by proper inspectors to be perfected in the use of the firelock. Men so passed were to be exempt from further drill for three years, after which they would be required to renew their certificate to prove that they were still completely trained. Men not certified as efficient were to be mustered once every six months in their parishes, and, if found not to be trained, were to be fined ten shillings, with an increase of ten shillings at every half-year until their certificate had been gained. If (so he argued) men found that they *must* train themselves under penalties, they would soon organise themselves into squads and companies for their own convenience.

From the men thus trained, he proposed to form the Sedentary Militia by annual ballot; for after their previous instruction they would find twenty-eight days' drill in the year sufficient to make them fairly expert in the higher branches of exercise. They were to serve for three years, and then be exempt from further service until their turn came round in rotation; but they were to complete their three years' service even if they passed the military age during the course of it. Exemptions were to stand as under the Additional Force Act. Ballotted men were to be allowed to find a substitute upon paying a fine, but such substitute was to be also a trained man of military age; and if he were ballotted during his term of service as a substitute, he was to serve first his three years as a substitute, and then proceed with his three years as a principal. The Sedentary Militia was to be organised in battalions of 1000 rank and file, with a permanent staff of an adjutant, a sergeant-major, a quartermaster-sergeant, twenty sergeants, twenty corporals, and twelve drummers. At every ballot there was to be drawn not only the full number required from the ranks, but a supplementary number of one-third or fourth of the establishment, who were to be liable to fill vacancies in the order in which they were drawn. The Sedentary Militia were to be at liberty to enter the Army, Navy, Marines, or Regular Militia, the places of men who enlisted being at once filled out of the supplementary quota. Its number would be 200,000 men for England, and a proportionate number for Scotland; the full strength to be arrived at gradually, and the Volunteers to be reduced as the Sedentary Militia increased. 1808.

The Regular Militia was to be ballotted for as under the existing Acts, neither the trained men nor the Sedentary Militia being exempt, but the men being still chosen between the ages of eighteen and forty-five, so as not to throw too heavy a burden upon a limited class. "Necessity," he wrote, "may lead hereafter and consequently justify us in applying the principle of conscription more directly, but in the first instance our object should be to make the service of the Sedentary Militia as little onerous as possible, and to try what resources can be drawn by proper encouragement and voluntary enlistment from a body so constituted."[1] But the Regular Militia, through the additional facility of procuring men by enlistment, would be much strengthened; and, as Castlereagh observed, "a corps of this description seems an indispensable ingredient in the Army of a state which must reduce its military force suddenly in time of peace, and call it forth as suddenly upon the recurrence of war."

Finally, the Regular Army, when the system was perfected, would be kept up partly by ordinary recruiting, partly by Volunteers from the Sedentary Militia, and in the third place by a school to be established on a large scale for the reception of boys, who should pass two or three years there in education before being attached to regiments. He conceived that both parents and parishes would be glad to send children to such an institution if

[1] This sentence is faithfully transcribed, so the faults in it must not be ascribed to the author. Castlereagh's English was always detestable.

1808. they were assured that they would be educated first, and not compelled to bear arms too soon. The term of service for such boys would be seven years, reckoning from their attainment of the age of eighteen.

All the recruits were to have the option of enlisting for short service or for life, without limitation as to place. Men engaged for life would be thrown principally into first battalions; men engaged for a limited term into second battalions. Thus the difficulty of relief for foreign garrisons would be overcome, and any advantages derivable from short service would be retained. All alike would be liable to foreign service; and if it were necessary to levy a large number of men by ballot, they would be received into the second battalions, from whence they could be tempted to re-engage for longer service.

In round numbers Castlereagh reckoned that the complete armed force of England would ultimately attain to the following strength:—

Navy, Marines, and Sea Fencibles . .	150,000 men
Army and Regular Militia . . .	350,000 men
Volunteers (Great Britain) . . .	100,000 men
Volunteers (Ireland)	80,000 men
Sedentary Militia (England) . . .	200,000 men
Sedentary Militia (Scotland) . . .	100,000 men
Trained Men	400,000 men
	1,380,000 men[1]

or more than half of the 2,000,000 men liable to service under the Levy en Masse Act.

Here at last was a plan for effecting that which was

[1] Castlereagh, *Desp.* viii. pp. 113-124. I suspect some of these figures to have been mistranscribed. In the earlier part of the memorandum Castlereagh gives the Army and Regular Militia at 300,000 jointly, which would reduce the above total to 1,330,000. Moreover, the calculation of 100,000 Sedentary Militia for Scotland against 200,000 for England is excessive, the Scottish Militia being to the English Militia as 1 to $5\frac{5}{8}$. The true estimate for Scotland would therefore be about 35,000 men. The total would then stand at 1,295,000 men.

really needed—national training in arms; the ideal which had been foreshadowed in the elder Pitt's original Militia Act of 1757. It is very evident too, from one of the sentences which have been quoted, that Castlereagh designed it to be permanent, and to be valid in peace as in war. Endless embarrassments, difficulties, and disasters would have been averted if it could have been erected and maintained in the form which he suggested; but this was not to be; and when he laid his Local Militia Bill before Parliament it was shorn of very much of its usefulness. None the less his speech in introducing it was so statesmanlike that it is worth while very briefly to abstract it here. 1808.

He began by saying, most rightly, that the Regular Army must be his first care, and took credit to himself for having by his measures added 40,000 men to it. Omitting the Artillery, the Regular Army and the Militia in the British Isles numbered 200,000 men. If every company in the Regular Infantry were raised to 100 men, 50,000 more soldiers could be admitted; and it would be of great advantage to have these men ready trained without occasion for a ballot. This could be done by establishing a Local Militia (it will be observed that the phrase Sedentary Militia had been discarded), with forty-eight days' drill near their homes, and twenty-one days of embodiment in their own counties. The Volunteers would suffice if they were always as efficient as at present, but it was necessary to organise a *permanent* force of the same strength. Then in the First Line there would be the Army and Established Militia; in the Second the Volunteers; and in the Third a Local Militia which need not exceed six times the Established Militia, that is to say, 320,000[1] men in Great Britain. Add to this 70,000 effective Volunteers in Ireland; and there would be 400,000 trained men, ready to fall into the Line and Militia if required. The effective Volunteers in Great Britain numbered 290,000, of which 240,000 were under arms at the last inspections. To

[1] The number should be 309,000.

1808. bring these 290,000 to 320,000, only 30,000 men were wanted; but the deficiency was so unequal in different districts that not fewer than 60,000 would answer the purpose. He proposed therefore to create a Local Militia of 60,000 men, to be gradually increased as the Volunteers diminished, and to supersede them in time of peace. The force would be raised by ballot, but only in districts where sufficient Volunteers, or men between the ages of eighteen and thirty-five, did not spontaneously come forward. To encourage such voluntary offers, he would give a small bounty to those who entered the new force of their own will; and he hoped also to tempt gentlemen of rank to join as officers. The qualifications of the Regular Militia would be required of captains but not of subalterns. Service would be for four years, and always within the county except in case of invasion. When a ballot was held, no substitutes would be allowed, the case of the Provisional Cavalry having given warning against such a course. The fine for exemption would be so great as to discourage men from paying it; and finally all insurance against personal service would be made penal. The force would be cheaper, man for man, than Windham's levies, and would finally reach the number of 400,000 men. With such a force, and 200,000 regular troops, the Empire would be secure.[1]

It will be observed that though Castlereagh hinted that he looked forward to the disappearance of the Volunteers, he adroitly dissembled his true feelings concerning them; so much so that he brought down the usual denunciation of them from Windham. But Windham's chief quarrel with the measure was that Castlereagh had practically adopted his Training Act, only altering the number of days' training, and incorporating the men into battalions, whereas he himself wished to keep them as a great reserve to be passed straight into the Line. He also declared that Castlereagh had other designs than merely making good the

[1] *H.D.* 12th April 1808.

deficient number of Volunteers, because a circular had been issued to stop all further increase of that force. To all this Castlereagh responded with much tact that he had borrowed a great deal from Windham's Training Act, and was not the least ashamed of it. Upon the whole, the opposition to the Bill seems to have been half-hearted, though more than one member urged consideration of an alternative plan suggested by Lord Selkirk. This was to call up all young men from eighteen to twenty-five years of age, train them for three months in their first year and for smaller periods in subsequent years, until at twenty-five they became exempt. Castlereagh disposed of this by saying that it would destroy the whole system of quotas, and bear very unequally upon the counties unless the Volunteers were at once abolished. And it must be remembered always in connection with Castlereagh's scheme, that he had inherited the "fleeting and inapplicable mass" from his predecessors, and that its existence was a perpetual bar to any but a very gradual reorganisation of the people for military purposes. 1808.

The Local Militia Bills became law on the 30th of June (48 Geo. III. cap. 111, Scotland, cap. 150). They enacted that a Permanent Local Militia should be enrolled in Great Britain, not to exceed, together with the Volunteers, six times the quota of the Militia under the Militia Act of 1802, that is to say, not to exceed 308,934 men; and that deficiencies among effective Volunteers should be supplied by Local Militiamen (secs. 1-3). Only men between the ages of eighteen and thirty were to be ballotted; and no substitution nor bounty to ballotted men was to be allowed (sec. 8). Sick or infirm persons could be exempted by two Deputy-Lieutenants under medical certificate (sec. 11). Ministers of religion, schoolmasters, and practising doctors were likewise exempted; also men who were serving, or had served, in the Army of Reserve or had found a substitute or paid the fine for exemption from service therein. Men who were in the like case in

1808. respect of the Regular Militia were exempt for four years after the expiration of their term of service, or for six years from the date of the enrolment of their substitute (sec. 13). Articled clerks and apprentices, poor men with fewer than three children born in lawful wedlock, and persons under five feet four inches in height but not under five feet two inches, though exempted from the Regular Militia, were liable to serve in the Local Militia (sec. 14); but ballotted apprentices might not enlist in the Army without their master's consent (sec. 15). Ballotted men were to be sworn to serve for five years unless sooner discharged (sec. 16). Any ballotted man not presenting himself to be enrolled was to be fined £30; or £20 if his annual income were less than £200; or £10 if his income were under £100; which fines were to be paid to the Paymaster-General of the Forces, and were to give exemption for two years only (sec. 17). Persons imprisoned for not paying these fines were liable to serve for their full term of four years after expiration of their period of imprisonment (sec. 18). Ballotted men engaging to serve in Volunteer corps at their own expense were entitled to remission of half the fine, but if they failed to continue to serve for four years, they were liable to forfeit treble the sum remitted, and to serve in the Local Militia (sec. 20). Persons paying the fine were required to declare that they had not insured themselves against such payment; and on refusing so to declare, or on making a false declaration, were to forfeit thrice the amount of the fine, with alternative of three months' imprisonment. The penalty for insuring persons against fines was a fine of £50 (secs. 22, 23). When men between the ages of eighteen and forty voluntarily enrolled themselves in any parish, the ballot was to be held only for the number deficient of the quota; and such voluntary recruits were to receive a bounty of £2 : 2s., which, however, they were to forfeit if they enlisted in the Regular Army within two years (secs. 24, 26, 27). Members of Friendly Societies were not to be prejudiced by entering the Local Militia, whatever the rules of the Societies (sec. 25). Corps of Volunteer Infantry, irrespective of age, might transfer themselves bodily to the Local Militia, with the King's approval; also Artillery Volunteers and Yeomen; but any vacancies remaining after such transference were to be supplied by ballot if not filled voluntarily within three months. All transferred Volunteers were required to declare that they had received no bounty exceeding two guineas (secs. 29, 30). On assembling for exercise Local Militiamen were entitled in the first year to one guinea, and in subsequent years to half-a-guinea for necessaries; also to a further guinea on being called out or embodied under any Order in Council or proclamation under the Act (sec. 31). Persons serving in the Local Militia were entitled to the same exemptions from the Regular Militia as the Volunteers had received under the Training Act, also to two years exemption after the end of their four years' service, unless their turn to be ballotted came round earlier (sec. 32). The Local Militia could be formed into battalions and regiments, and a proportion of the regimental staff kept on permanent pay. Officers were to rank after those of their grade in the Regular Militia; but no higher title than Lieutenant-Colonel Commandant was to be held, except by Lords-Lieutenant and officers who had held the rank of Colonel in the Regular Army or Militia (secs. 34, 35). Officers of Volunteers transferred with their corps to the Local Militia retained their rank, but were forbidden in any case to take rank above a Lieutenant-colonel in the Regular Army (sec. 36). The Local Militia could be put under the command of General Officers, and called out for annual training for not more than twenty-eight days, and to no greater distance than an adjoining county (sec. 38). Men could remove from the Militia of one county to that of another on giving notice to their Commanding Officers (sec. 39). In case of invasion or rebellion the Local Militia could be embodied and marched to any part of Great Britain (sec. 40). It could also be called out by the Lord-

1808.

1808. Lieutenant to suppress riots, when its assembly was limited to fourteen days only and was to be counted as part of its training (sec. 42). In both of the above cases it was to be entitled to the same pay as the Regular Militia, and the wives and families of the men were likewise entitled to parish relief (secs. 43, 44). Local Militiamen might enlist in the Army, Navy, Marines, and Regular Militia except during the period of annual training; and the vacancies thus created were to be filled up like all other vacancies for the Militia, any suspension of the ballot for the Regular Militia notwithstanding (secs. 45, 46). Counties were liable to a fine of £15 for every man deficient of their quota on every 14th of February, subject to remissions of two-thirds and one-third of such fines if the deficiency were made good before the 14th of March and 14th of April respectively (secs. 47, 48). Finally, there was inserted at the instance of Whitbread[1] a section for the relief of men who had paid fines or found substitutes for the Army of Reserve, and had since been compelled to serve as principals under Castlereagh's Act of 1807 for completing the Militia (sec. 47).

It will be observed that the Act in its final form varied somewhat from the original plan sketched by Castlereagh, most notably in the omission to provide a body of supplementary men for the immediate filling of vacancies. The invitation to entire Volunteer corps to enrol themselves as Local Militia was also a concession, though possibly a wise concession, which marred the original idea of composing the new force wholly of young men, who should have received their elementary instruction under the Training Act. There was, moreover, as shall be seen, another weak point in the loose wording of the sections concerning the "marching-guinea." But, on the other hand, it converted at a stroke a large number of uncontrollable men into corps which could be disciplined and compelled to obey orders; and this was a great step in advance. More-

[1] *H.D.* 2nd May 1808.

over, it will be noticed that the experience of the past was wisely turned to account in the drafting of the Act. There were to be no more doubts as to the worth of exemptions purchased for the Militia, the Army of Reserve, or any other Additional Force; no more questions whether men could be ballotted to fill vacancies or recruits could be enlisted into the Army; no more trouble with the tricks of Friendly Societies. Moreover, the total abolition of substitution was an incalculable gain, though in reality the reform only carried out the original intention of the elder Pitt's Militia Act of 1757. This deserves to be lifted into prominence as perhaps the most notable point in the whole of our administrative military history. 1808.

It will be convenient, before touching upon other topics, to follow up the construction of the Local Militia during the summer of 1808, intimately connected as it is with the history of the Volunteers. At the opening of the year the Government seemed inclined to continue its favours to the latter force, for it issued a circular on the 2nd of April to say that the Volunteers might come out again on permanent duty during 1808 for not more than fourteen, or fewer than ten, days, with the same allowances as in 1807. But within five days there came out another circular to say that in many Volunteer corps the difference between the effective numbers and the establishment was so great that a new establishment must be made, and that meanwhile all corps were provisionally limited to the number of men actually enrolled on the 1st of April. This, no doubt, was the circular to which Windham alluded in his speech; and it intimated pretty clearly that Volunteer corps below a certain strength would be swept out of existence without a chance of completing themselves so as to avert the evil day. Two days before the Local Militia Act received the Royal assent, another circular of the 28th of June warned all commandants of Volunteers that unless they sent in their muster-rolls within fourteen days of the 1st of August, their corps

1808. would lose the privileges of effective Volunteers and become subject to the ballot for the Local Militia. There was to be no delay, no evasion, no parleying. The "fleeting inapplicable mass" must become stable and applicable, or it would find itself turned into Local Militia.

Then came the question whether the Volunteer corps would or would not as a rule transfer themselves bodily to the Local Militia. Speaking generally, they seem to have been somewhat backward in doing so. In some cases the officers were willing enough, but their men would not follow them. In Suffolk the Helmington battalion was ready to furnish ten officers but only three men. In the same county the transfer of the Risbridge battalion was wrecked by the conduct of two captains, who were incensed because their Commanding Officer refused to recommend one of them for promotion to major. It is satisfactory to know that in accordance with the recommendation of the Colonel this corps was at once disbanded. In Sussex the Volunteers as a body declined to have anything to do with the Local Militia; and in Nottinghamshire some revolted from the very name and could not be won over. In Ross likewise they stood haughtily aloof until they discovered that their parishes would be liable to heavy fines, when, like true Scots, they begged hastily to be transferred, and offered even to sacrifice their bounty if permitted to do so. In Kent the Volunteers dissolved themselves in dudgeon in all directions; and for a quota of 7776 no fewer than 5074 needed to be ballotted. In Lancashire over 5000 Volunteers accepted service in the Local Militia, but even so compulsion was necessary to force nearly 7000 more into the ranks; and a certain number, until brought to their senses, positively refused to be ballotted. In Lincolnshire again it was necessary to invoke the ballot for nearly half of the quota. On the other hand, there were many counties in which the spirit was very much better. Caermarthenshire, Denbigh, and Wiltshire produced the whole of their men without a ballot; Hampshire did very nearly as well; and in Devon, whose full quota was 9000, over 8000 Volunteers converted themselves into Local Militia. In all it seems that in seventy-six counties of Great Britain it was necessary to raise only 32,810 men by ballot.[1] Upon the whole, therefore, the Volunteers, though poor of spirit in some counties, came forward as well as could be expected; and they were encouraged by the latitude which the Act gave them to enrol voluntary recruits in the Local Militia, and so to draw in stragglers from corps which, as complete bodies, had no relish for the new service.[2] In Wales it seems probable that the readiness of the Volunteers to accept transfer to the Local Militia was due to the poverty of the officers; for in Pembroke the Lieutenant pleaded hard for a corps to be continued in the status of Fusiliers, since the officers were chiefly 1808.

[1] Return in *C.J.* vol. lxv. p. 620. Unfortunately eleven counties furnished no return.

[2] *I.D.* vol. cxxxviii. S.S. to L.L. Herts, 30th Dec. 1808; vol. cxlvii. L.L. Suffolk, to S.S. 1st, 23rd Aug.; O.C. Risbridge Vols. to S.S. 3rd Aug. 1808; vol. cxlviii. L.L. Sussex, to S.S. 17th Nov. 1808; vol. cxliv. O.C. Notts Loyal Vols. to S.S. 16th July 1808; vol. clxvi. L.L. Kent, to S.S. 20th Nov. 1808; vol. clxviii. Minutes of G.M. Lancs, 18th Jan.; Two D.Ls. of Ormskirk to S.S. 20th Feb. 1809; vol. clxix. Lincs, Return of 10th Jan. 1809; vol. clvi. L.L. Caermarthen, to S.S. 22nd Feb. 1809; vol. clix. L.L. Denbigh, to S.S. 3rd Jan. 1809; vol. clxxvi. L.L. Wilts, to S.S. 21st Jan. 1809; vol. clxiv. L.L. Hants, to S.S. 28th Feb. 1809; vol. clx. L.L. Devon, to S.S. 5th Feb. 1809; *Entry Book*, vol. xliii. S.S. to Lord Rolle, 25th Jan. 1809.

I append a return of the county of Devon of 19th July 1809, which is interesting as showing the part played by a single county.

Men liable to Militia service (exclusive of men serving)		14,692
Yeomanry and Volunteers exempt . . .	11,454	
Enlisted in Army, Marines, and Sea Fencibles	2258	14,682
Clergy, etc., exempt	970	
Infirm men		9190

There is thus a deficiency of ten men unaccounted for.

It must of course be remembered that Devon, with the sea on both sides, and with a large naval arsenal, furnished a large number of seamen and marines. Unfortunately I cannot furnish the like returns for other counties, which would probably be equally creditable.

1808. farmers' sons, and subalterns were not to be obtained unless all (as was the rule in Fusilier regiments) enjoyed the same rank and pay. The wealth of Lancashire, on the other hand, may account for the fact that the county considered the change to the status of Militia as a degradation. In this case no defect more damning to the whole principle of the Volunteers as founded by Pitt and Addington could possibly be instanced.

Meanwhile the process of weeding out inefficient Volunteer corps proceeded steadily, with the result that some curious specimens were discovered. One of the Inspecting Field-Officers held a review of the South Elmbridge Company, which possessed arms for seventy-two men. Five men only appeared on parade; and the inspector approached the Commanding Officers of the Kew and Ham Volunteers in order to obtain returns of their numbers. One of them returned no answer whatever; and the other replied that he had resigned, and that his corps had not attended the last inspection.[1] It was for such useless and absurd bodies as these that the Office of Ordnance had been plagued to find arms. Another rather pathetic but very ridiculous case was that of the Somerset House Volunteers, formed for the defence of that building only, and commanded, for its sins, by Colonel Richard Brinsley Sheridan. Somehow Sheridan could never remember to issue orders for his corps to be inspected, with the result that it forfeited its exemptions from the Militia ballot. The officers in despair appealed to Lord Titchfield, the Lord-Lieutenant, who, with a dry humour that was characteristic of him, reported as follows on the 10th of September. "I have written two letters to Colonel Sheridan (in July), one a private letter to Carlton House, where I believe he resides; the other a public one directed to him in London. I cannot tell whether either has reached him, for I have received no answer. I shall be much surprised if I ever do receive any answer." No such surprise was in store for Titchfield; but in February 1809

[1] *I.D.* vol. cxlviii. I.F.O. Surrey and Kent, to S.S. 7th June 1808.

Sheridan wrote to him, pleading hard for indulgence to the Somerset House Volunteers, quite as if no one but himself had ever given thought to the subject, and without a word in acknowledgment of the Lieutenant's letters.[1] 1808.

Turning now to more serious matters, it must be noted that Castlereagh's boast that he had added 40,000 men to the Army was no idle one. Altogether in 1807 and the first three months of 1808 there were raised some 19,000 men by ordinary recruiting, and 26,000 from the Militia, making in all 45,000 men against a casualty list for 1807 of 14,570 men. This meant a solid gain of about 30,000 men; and though many of them had engaged themselves for seven years only, they were under no restraint as to foreign service. There was therefore a respectable force to hand for offensive operations over sea; and as fate willed it, there was an excellent opportunity for such a force to act in 1808.

The first expedition despatched by the Government in that year was a body of about 10,000 men under the command of Sir John Moore, which was sent to Sweden with some vague idea of defending that unlucky kingdom. Its real mission seems to have been to make a show of adherence to a faithful but half-witted ally; for it was too weak to be of any service, and, in view of the fact that it had been consigned to a lunatic, was hampered, not unreasonably, by restrictions which made it utterly useless. Accordingly it sailed to Sweden in May, and sailed back in July; and meanwhile new work had appeared for it in another quarter. Napoleon in the winter of 1807-8 had invaded Portugal and Spain, and in May 1808 the Spanish nation had risen in insurrection and sent emissaries to beg for help from England. General Spencer was already at or about Gibraltar, afloat with some 4000 troops; and though Moore had not yet returned from Sweden, there were men enough to spare for a little campaign in Portugal.

[1] *I.D.* vol. cxlii. Officers of Somerset House Volunteers to S.S. 13th July; L.L. Middlesex, to S.S. 10th Sept. 1808; vol. clxix. Sheridan to L.L. Middlesex, 12th Feb. 1809.

1808. The effective strength of the Army on the 1st of June was, exclusive of artillery, as follows :—

In the British and Channel Islands .	107,022	rank and file
In Heligoland	302	,, ,,
In Madeira	1612	,, ,,
Gibraltar, Malta, and Sicily . .	24,282	,, ,,
West Indies	20,308	,, ,,
North America	7818	,, ,,
East Indies and Ceylon . . .	19,776	,, ,,
Goree, 224 ; New South Wales, 536 .	760	,, ,,
On passage	4454	,, ,,
With Moore, 10,871 ; with Spencer, 3704	14,575	,, ,,

Of the troops at home the greater number were second battalions, there being in fact but two first battalions in England, four in Scotland, and nine in Ireland. It is not surprising, therefore, that when in July Sir Arthur Wellesley was despatched to Portugal with some 9000 troops, the whole of his infantry (nine and a half battalions) was, with the exception of half a battalion of Rifles, drawn from Ireland. He was reinforced in August by seven more battalions, three of them second, and four of them first, amounting to about 4000 men in all, and with these added to Spencer's force was fought the campaign of Roliça and Vimeiro.

The Convention of Cintra brought the operations to an unfortunate end ; and the recall of all the generals who were concerned in it threw the command into the hands of Sir John Moore. In the course of the autumn and winter Castlereagh increased his force to some 42,000 men, British and German ; and with 33,000 of these Moore moved north-eastward from Portugal to join the Spanish armies, but, finding that they had been hopelessly beaten, finally decided to make the dash upon Napoleon's communications which has made his name famous. On the 16th of January 1809 he fought the action of Coruña, and on the following day the wreck of his army embarked for England, where it disembarked a little over 26,000 strong.[1]

[1] I am indebted for these figures concerning Moore's army to Oman's *History of the Peninsular War*, i. 646.

II

On the 25th of January 1809 Castlereagh, after a very handsome tribute to Moore, introduced a new Bill to enable the Militia to enlist into the Army. He was not without good justification. The casualties for the year 1808 had been 17,183, and against these figures ordinary recruiting had produced only 10,477 men and 2486 boys. On the other hand, the Spanish insurrection against Napoleon, kindled by the spontaneous impulse of a proud and gallant people, had roused the greatest enthusiasm in England. Nine battalions of Militia, the Bucks, the Durham, the Hants, the Hereford, the Leicester, the Pembroke, Flintshire, Merioneth, and Carnarvon, had volunteered for active service in Spain within a few weeks after the insurrection became known in England.[1] Moreover, the diversion of Napoleon's troops to Spain had drawn great numbers of his men from Germany; while the capture of one of his corps at Baylen had heartened all the armies that he had ever defeated. Austria was arming with feverish haste to take her revenge; and even in Prussia, crushed and humbled to the dust, free corps were organising themselves to strike at the first favourable moment. The time, therefore, seemed propitious for a great effort to overthrow the conqueror who for so long had dominated Europe. 1809.

Castlereagh said nothing of all this in introducing his Bill, but remarked simply that it was now ascertained that the easiest and swiftest way of increasing the Army was to draw men from the Militia. The Act of 1807 had encouraged the transfer of 29,000 men from the Militia to the Line, and in twelve months over 27,000 had been transferred. He had asked the country for 45,000 to fill the gaps in the Militia, and in six months

[1] *C.C.L.B.* 8th Aug. 1808; *I.D.* vol. cxxxvii. L.L. Hants, to S.S. 26th Sept.; L.L. Hereford, to S.S. 14th Oct.; vol. cxxxix. L.L. Leicester, to S.S. 14th Aug. 1808; *W.O. Mila. E.B.* 21st July, 1st, 3rd, 10th Aug. 1808.

1809. 41,500 had joined their regiments. He proposed, therefore, once again to encourage Militiamen to enlist in the Army to such an extent as to leave, as in 1807, three-fifths of the establishment untouched. But whereas in 1807 it was necessary not only to complete the establishment but to raise men in excess, in this year it would be necessary only to cover deficiencies, so that for England only 24,000 would be called for instead of 36,000. He purposed if possible to dispense with the ballot, and to throw the expense of raising these men not upon the counties but upon the public. He would therefore in the first place try to gather the necessary Militia recruits by voluntary enlistment, offering a bounty of ten guineas from the Imperial Treasury. If a ballot were found necessary, he would give this sum to the ballotted man, either as a bounty if he served himself, or as a subsidy towards the price of a substitute. He hoped that the county gentlemen and Colonels of Militia would forward the levy, since the expense was to fall upon the Imperial Treasury and not on the counties; and upon the whole he was sanguine that the ballot would be unnecessary and that general recruiting for the Army would not be injured.

These proposals, of course, met with some opposition. Tierney saw no occasion to increase the Army until the House knew on what service it was to be employed, and Lord Milton declared that to make the Militia fill the ranks of the Regulars was nothing less than conscription for the Army.[1] On the other hand, Colonel Wood of the Middlesex Militia declared that he and his fellow-commanders had overcome their prejudices against the system, inasmuch as by furthering it they could best serve their country. Bounties, observed the Colonel, were not high; for he had lately got thirty men for eight guineas apiece—a statement of delightful effrontery, since as a matter of fact he was employing an agent in Norwich to gather recruits from the Local Militiamen, to the exasperation of that county and to the infraction

[1] *H.D.* 25th Jan. 1809.

of a whole volume of Militia Acts.[1] Against this Mr. Giles declared that the Militiamen drafted into the Line had cost the country in bounties £28 a head, or £726,000 in all, one-third from general taxation, one-third from private individuals, and one-third from the landed interest; and that some cheaper way ought to be found.[2] 1809.

The Bills for transferring Militiamen to the Line became law on the 13th of March (49 Geo. III. cap. 4; Ireland, cap. 5). The men to be enlisted were not to exceed such number as should leave three-fifths of the establishment intact; but when the number of men in any regiment in excess of three-fifths of the present establishment should be less than two-fifths of the establishment in 1807, such two-fifths might enlist (secs. 1, 2). If five-sixths of this number were willing to enlist at once, no more were to be engaged without the Commanding Officer's consent (sec. 3). If the five-sixths did not enlist within thirty days, the Commanding Officer was to explain the terms of enrolment and allow enlistment for a further seven days, after which there was to be no more enlistment, excepting with his consent, for one month. Then three more days were to be given; then after another month's interval three more days; and after that three more periods of three days at intervals of three months (secs. 6-9). The remainder of the provisions were the same as in the Act of 1807; but an amendment was added in an Act for Completing the Militia (49 Geo. III. cap. 53, sec. 32) empowering the King to appoint two more periods of three days each at any time after the 1st of August for the enlistment of Militiamen into the Line from any regiments that had not supplied their full numbers. The quotas of men thus permitted to enlist amounted to 18,130 for England, 3654 for Scotland, and 6708 for Ireland, or 28,492 men in all.

[1] *H.D.* 2nd Feb. 1809; *I.D.* vol. cxliii. L.L. Norfolk, to S.S. 24th Dec. 1808.

[2] *H.D.* 24th March 1809.

1809. Meanwhile, at the Horse Guards there had been thought out a further plan for the improvement of the military force of the country, to which the enlistment of men from the Militia was but auxiliary.

The proposal was to increase every regiment of the Line to two battalions; the first battalions to be for unlimited service as to time and place, and of the strength of 800, 1000, or 1200; the second battalions to be uniformly 1000 strong, composed of men obtained by ballot, but officered by officers of the Regular Army only, who would pass to the first battalion according to their rank. This would give a "disposable" force of about 100,000 men, and a force for home defence of the same strength, but having the advantage over the Militia, that the officers would be thoroughly trained.

The rest of the armed strength of the country was to be distributed into Local Militia, Yeomanry, and Volunteers only, the Regular Militia passing out of existence.

The Volunteers should be in corps not less than 600 strong, and entirely self-supporting, so as to be of no expense to the public except for their arms and for their pay when called out on permanent duty, at which time they ought to be subject to martial law.

The Local Militia should be formed on the same principle as the rest of the Army, the establishments being equalised so far as the populations of the counties permitted. The arrangements for calling them out for training should be such as to make the service as little burdensome as possible, so that the country gentlemen might be encouraged to hold commissions. The Local Militia should in every case assume the uniform, colours and equipment of the regiment of the Line belonging to its county, and in fact become a part of it. The men of the second battalions should be encouraged by bounties to extend their services to their first battalions, and those of the Local Militia in like manner to the second battalions. Probably enough men would come forward voluntarily to fill the gaps in the second battalions, but if not the ballot must be resorted to; for the essence of the plan was that the second battalions should be kept complete. Thus a real and useful connection would be established between the different branches of the military force; the regiments of the Line would be closely connected with the counties whose names they bore; and the Militia would become what it ought to be constitutionally—the basis of the national force. Only thus could the recruiting for the Army be placed on an assured and permanent footing. The amount of the force thus produced would be— 1809.

Infantry of the Line for general service, exclusive of Guards, Veteran battalions, and Sixtieth . .	100,000
Second battalions, limited to service in the British Isles	100,000
Local Militia, at least	200,000
Yeomanry	32,000
Volunteers	100,000
Total (all foreign corps excluded) . .	532,000[1]

This memorandum, which bears the signature of Sir Henry Calvert, the Adjutant-General, expanded the scheme proposed by the Commander-in-Chief in 1807. It anticipated, as will be at once remarked, the territorial system which at present obtains in the Army; and there can be no doubt of its soundness in many respects. It was an absurdity to have two descriptions of Militia, one of which in practice only duplicated the second battalions of the Line, and competed with them for recruits; and the division of the forces into the Regular and Movable Army recruited by voluntary enlistment, and the Sedentary Army recruited by ballot without power of substitution, would have been more intelligible, more business-like, and more efficient. Castlereagh, however, seems to have shrunk from the change, and though, as shall in due time be seen, the Local Militia practically displaced the Volunteers, yet no steps were taken wholly to abolish the Regular Militia.

[1] Castlereagh's *Desp.* viii. 194-197.

1809. The levy of Militiamen for the Line opened well, though, as in 1808, some few counties hung back, Inverness in particular declining at first to produce a man, while others came forward readily with their quota. By the 1st of June 16,429 of the 28,492 had enlisted; namely, 13,002 from England, 1050 from Scotland, and 2377 from Ireland, England contributing a far larger proportion of her quota than the sister Kingdoms. On the 25th of May 1809 the effective strength of the Regular Army was returned as 219,874 rank and file, including 31,077 foreign troops, of which 107,857 were at home, and 112,017 abroad; the largest detachment abroad being a force of 22,000 men in Portugal, of which more shall presently be said. Besides these there were in the three Kingdoms 65,524 Militia, making a total force of 285,398 rank and file, or, including sergeants, trumpeters, and drummers, but *not* including officers, 301,598 non-commissioned officers and men.

It remained, therefore, to fill up the gaps in the Militia, for which purpose were passed two Acts (49 Geo. III. cap. 53 for England; cap. 56 for Ireland). The former provided for raising Militiamen equal to one-half of the quota of 1802 (25,245 men) before the 1st of October 1810 (sec. 1). Until the 1st of June 1810 voluntary recruits might be enlisted for the Militia by beat of drum for a bounty not exceeding twelve guineas, such recruits to have not more than one child born in wedlock, and to be placed in respect of the support of their families on the same footing as substitutes (secs. 2, 3, 5). After the 1st of June all deficiencies were to be filled by ballot; and preparations for this ballot were to be made if any deficiencies existed on the 1st of April 1810 (secs. 7, 8). The fine for exemption was fixed at £20. The bounty to ballotted persons or to substitutes from the 1st of June to the 1st of September 1810 was to be ten guineas, but parish officers were empowered to raise volunteers for the same bounty until the 1st of September 1810 (secs. 14, 15). Counties

not providing their quota by the 1st of October 1810 were 1809.
to be fined £40 for each man deficient (sec. 24), which fines, together with the £20 exemption-fines, were to be paid over to the Imperial Exchequer (sec. 34). Power was reserved to the King to order a ballot at any time before the 1st of June and after the 1st of October 1810 to complete the Militia (sec. 36); but, after the men had been raised, the ballot was to be suspended until the 1st of January 1812 (sec. 29).

The process of raising Militiamen by beat of drum seems to have gone on fairly quietly, though occasionally there was trouble. London, as usual, was forward in attempting to steal men from other counties. Thus the Tower Hamlets Militia sent a recruiting party, without any beating order, to Stroud in Gloucestershire, where they offered a reward of a guinea to any man who would bring them recruits for their regiment. Recruits having been brought in, received five guineas on the spot, were sent up to the regiment, and from thence were at once sent back on furlough to their homes, with the intimation that they too would receive a guinea for every recruit that they in their turn should produce. By this ingenious method the Tower Hamlets enlisted numbers of men at a cheap rate, leaving the people of Gloucestershire enraged but impotent.[1] Another difficulty was that under voluntary enlistment a parish often provided more than its quota, and thus as a reward for its patriotism incurred an undue burden for the support of the Militiamen's families.[2] But on the whole the complaints were few, and matters seem to have proceeded with great smoothness.

In Ireland (49 Geo. III. cap. 56, 3rd June 1809) the men for completion of the Militia were to be voluntarily enlisted, at a bounty not exceeding eight guineas (sec. 1). Counties not producing their quota within twelve months were to be fined £30 for every man deficient. But over and above this an Irish Militia Consolidation

[1] *I.D.* vol. clxiv. L.L. Glos. to S.S. 4th Aug. 1809.
[2] *Ibid.* vol. clxiv. L.L. Glos. to S.S. 8th Dec. 1809.

1809. Act was introduced on the 6th of February by the Chief Secretary, Sir Arthur Wellesley, though in great measure prepared by Castlereagh in 1805.[1] Hereby the Irish Militia was appointed to consist of thirteen battalions of six companies each, two of seven companies, ten battalions of eight companies, one of nine companies, and six of ten companies, or 24,100 men. No regiment was to have more than 100 rank and file in a company (secs. 2, 9). Militiamen enlisting into the Regulars, except under a special Act, were liable to six months' imprisonment (sec. 63). Full machinery for the ballot was authorised, but the Lord-Lieutenant was empowered to allow the Militia, or any vacancies therein, to be supplied by voluntary enlistment (sec. 130); or to authorise parochial assessments for money to raise men in lieu of the ballot (sec. 124). This last was the most important provision in the Bill for Ireland, for, whereas it had been a temporary expedient before, it was now made a perpetual possible substitute for the ballot, which had always been a source of trouble in that country.

Next, some amendment was needed for the Local Militia Act, for which purpose Castlereagh introduced a Local Militia Act Amendment Bill on the 27th of March. His speech showed how rapidly this new force had been developed. In all there were now 250 regiments of Local Militia in Great Britain; 184 with 149,440 men in England, 66 with 45,721 men in Scotland, making together 195,161 men, or an average of nearly 800 men to each battalion. Of these 125,000 had passed into the Local Militia from the Volunteers, and 50,000 or 60,000 had been voluntarily enlisted. But the bounty of two guineas to every such voluntary recruit had been found too heavy; and Castlereagh proposed to leave it to the parishes to assess themselves spontaneously and give what bounty they might choose, not exceeding one guinea a man, which sum was ultimately increased in the Act to two guineas. There was another trouble, though it is not mentioned in the report

[1] Castlereagh's *Desp.* viii. 40-43.

of Castlereagh's speech, namely, that the recruiting sergeants of the Army had been unable to resist the temptation to enlist Local Militiamen during the period of training ;[1] an evil which also required to be checked. Accordingly the Act, when passed on the 12th of May, contained the following provisions (49 Geo. III. cap. 40). Voluntary enlistment for supplying deficiencies was permitted at any time (sec. 2), and vacancies in the Local Militia were to be filled at once without orders from headquarters, irrespective of the suspension of the ballot for the Regular Militia, or of the fact that the Local Militia and Volunteers in any county might, taken together, exceed six times the quota of the Regular Militia (sec. 3). Local Militiamen were allowed to enlist in the Regular Militia (but of their own counties only, 49 Geo. III. cap. 129, 21st June 1808). The enlistment of Local Militiamen, during the period of training, into the Army or Regular Militia was forbidden under penalty of a fine of £20 (sec. 6). Powers were given to the Deputy-Lieutenants to make new apportionments of quotas among parishes and districts, and to regulate the inequalities of numbers in the divisions of the counties (secs. 8-10). The section (26) of the original Act as to the bounty of two guineas to voluntary recruits was repealed ; and powers were given to the parochial authorities to offer any bounty up to that sum ; but the bounty to Volunteers transferring themselves to the Local Militia was done away, unless such Volunteers were actually serving before the present Act was passed (secs. 11-14). Volunteers transferred to the Local Militia were exempted from service in the Regular Militia (sec. 15). Non-commissioned officers, drummers, and bandsmen of the Local Militia were forbidden to enlist in the Regulars without consent of their Commanding Officer (sec. 28).[2]

1809.

[1] *I.D.* vol. cliii. Col. Whitbread (Beds.) to S.S. 26th April 1809.

[2] A second amending Act (49 Geo. III. c. 82) was also passed later in the session, but contains nothing essential to our purpose.

1809. It will have been gathered from Castlereagh's speech quoted above that the Volunteers had declined as the Local Militia increased; and in June those that were not genuinely self-supporting received their death-blow in an intimation that no further allowance for clothing would be granted to Volunteer Infantry.[1] Little more therefore will remain to be said of this force, though, curiously enough, the services of the Volunteers were really needed in Cornwall in February 1809. A transport containing 240 soldiers of Junot's army, which was bound to France in pursuance of the Convention of Cintra, came into Penzance in a sinking state. The men on board her were out of all discipline and control, and threatened to break out of the ship and land. The Volunteers in the district were therefore hastily called out to overawe the Frenchmen and to patrol the countryside; so that on this occasion it may be said that they were of real value.[2] But from this time forward they were wholly eclipsed by the Local Militia, which now demands a slight review.

Windham's criticism of the new force was that it contained, no doubt, a fine body of men; but were they soldiers? To this it can only be answered that, if they were not in some measure soldiers, the Volunteers, from which two-thirds of them were sprung, must have been incurably inefficient. Out of the 195 battalions, 116 came out for a month's or a fortnight's training during 1809, which was a creditable number considering that the Local Militia was only called into being on the 30th of June 1808. In any case they furnished a useful number of recruits to the Army and Regular Militia. In June 1809 a circular was issued empowering Lords-Lieutenant to offer a bounty of eight guineas to all men who would join the Regular Militia; and from the Bucks regiments alone nineteen men were collected in a few days. The Lord-Lieutenant of that county also suggested and obtained approval of a useful and

[1] Circular to the L.Ls. 30th June 1809.

[2] *I.D.* vol. clviii. L.L. Cornwall, to S.S. 23rd Feb. 1809.

economical reform, namely, that the recruits should be called out for a period of training half as long again as that of the rest of the battalion.[1] But indeed it may be said that Buckinghamshire, under the guidance of the Grenvilles, was always one of the foremost counties for any patriotic work. From Denbigh the Lieutenant reported that his Local Militiamen were ready to enter the Army without any bounty or solicitation.[2] In fact, though no sufficient evidence exists absolutely to prove the fact, it should seem that a number of young fellows no sooner found themselves obliged to serve, without option of finding a substitute, than they became ready to make the Army their profession in earnest. 1809.

Nevertheless there was, as it happened, a great deal of trouble with the Local Militia during 1809. In Aberdeen the people of Garioch rose tumultuously to prevent the enrolment of their quota; and the Deputy-Lieutenants only accomplished their duty at great personal risk and under the protection of a military force.[3] But this isolated outbreak was of small importance compared with a turbulent spirit which appeared in all parts of the Kingdom. It seems that certain women, by whom inspired it is impossible to say, made it their business to tramp from regiment to regiment of the Local Militia, trying to excite riots. The pretext for disturbance was a pretended right of the men to the guinea allowed under sec. 31 of the Act to provide them with necessaries—"that fatal clause," as the Lord-Lieutenant of Carnarvon termed it—and certainly as a pretext it proved very successful. There were petty mutinies in various quarters, of which many were hushed up; though some record of the more serious remains. At Ely a Cambridgeshire regiment, after perfectly orderly behaviour for twenty-seven days, turned against their Commanding

1 *I.D.* vol. clv. L.L. Bucks, to S.S. 27th June; 21st Dec. 1809. I have been unable to discover the circular alluded to, but its existence and purport are proved by the former of these letters.

2 *Ibid.* vol. clix. L.L. Merioneth, to S.S. 10th June 1809.

3 *Ibid.* vol. ccxxxvi. L.L. Aberdeen, to S.S. 2nd Jan. 1813.

1809. Officer upon the twenty-eighth, threatening him with their bayonets and with cries of "no knapsacks"; the grievance being that some of the captains, following the custom of the Volunteers, had given the men their guinea, while others had spent it upon knapsacks and so forth. It was necessary for the Lord-Lieutenant to go down in person to explain matters to the men, after which five ringleaders were tried by regimental court-martial and flogged. In Merioneth again the men were discontented because the money was spent on knapsacks instead of being placed in their hands. In Hertfordshire the Archenfield Local Militia, at the instance of a sergeant, rose against their officers for no apparent reason, but doubtless owing to trouble over the wretched guinea; and all the townspeople joined the mutineers in a disorderly riot. Once again it was imperative to flog four men, though the Commander-in-Chief left it to the Colonel to remit any excess over one hundred lashes. In Taunton a far more serious affray arose from the attempt of a corporal and several men to rescue a prisoner from the guard-room. The townspeople joined in the riot; one of the officers was wounded by the bayonet of one of the ringleaders, and order was not restored until the Thirteenth Light Dragoons, the Taunton Rifle Corps, and the recruiting parties in the town had turned out in arms. The cause of the trouble could not be traced. There was no complaint about the marching-guinea; and on the morning of the day the battalion had done no more work than a march of five miles to the Commandant's country house, where he treated them to bread and cheese and beer. In fact the riot seems to have been due to a kind of infection of disorder which ran all through the Local Militia—most of them, it must be remembered, converted Volunteers—during the last fortnight of June. However, the Commandant at Taunton was equal to the occasion. He assembled the regiment, disarmed it, summoned a drum-head court-martial which sentenced the leader to 500 lashes and four more men to 100 apiece; tied up the leader on the spot to receive 175 lashes, remitted all the remainder of the punishments, and within twelve hours was able to report that discipline had been restored.[1] 1809.

So much for the strength of the forces in 1809; it is now time to look to the employment of them abroad. First, it must be noted that in the spring of 1809 Austria declared war upon France, and the Archduke Charles advanced against the French Army while it was not yet concentrated. This diversion compelled Napoleon to recall troops from Spain; and Sir Arthur Wellesley, who had been sent back to Portugal in command of a force of some 21,000 rank and file, which was presently raised to some 33,000, was able for a time to take the offensive and fight the compaigns of the Douro and Talavera. The latter of these, chiefly owing to the sickly state of his army in the valley of the Guadiana, was somewhat costly in the matter of casualties.[2] Moreover, Minsters, unable from dearth of specie to send more troops to the Peninsula, despatched in July an expedition of 40,000 men to the Scheldt, where the incompetence of the Commander assured failure to an enterprise whose success was, at best, extremely doubtful. The climate played havoc among the rank and file and made the campaign extremely costly. Add to this the facts that General Beckwith, having been reinforced by four battalions in November 1808, attacked and captured Martinique with 10,000 men in February 1809; and that General Stuart was able to embark 11,000 men for

[1] *I.D.* vol. clxxiii. O.C. East Staffs, L.M. to L.L. 30th June 1809; vol. clvi. L.L. Cambs, to S.S. 25th June 1809; vol. clix. L.L. Merioneth, to S.S. 1st July 1809; vol. clxv. Sir H. Hoskyns to L.L. Hertford, 20th June 1809; vol. clxxiii. O.C. West Somerset L.M. to S.S. 27th June 1809.

[2] The return of casualties in the Peninsula, 31st March to 25th December 1809, was:—

Dead	4931
Deserted	349
Discharged	41
Total	5321

C.J. vol. lxv.

1809. raids upon the French in Naples and Calabria; and it will be seen that in all some 84,000 rank and file, or say 95,000 of all ranks, were employed in offensive operations during this year, though with lamentably small results.

Meanwhile, apart from Walcheren, the country had encountered a series of misfortunes. First, the Duke of York had been forced by the scandals concerning Mrs. Clarke to resign the post of Commander-in-Chief; and the weight of this blow to the military administration can only be appreciated by students who know what the Army was before the Duke took it in hand. Again, the Ministry had been broken up, and Castlereagh, the ablest man that ever controlled the War Office, had been driven from it. Spencer Perceval had become Prime Minister; Castlereagh's place had been taken by Lord Liverpool, a sound, sensible man, whose reputation is far below his desert; and Palmerston had been appointed Secretary at War. Moreover, the Austrian attempt to break down the power of Napoleon had proved a failure. Wagram had forced her to a humiliating peace; and the Emperor of the French was free once more to turn all his force against Spain. The only comforting feature in the situation, known only to a few in England, and hardly apprehended by them, was that Russia had not thrown in her lot against Austria with a whole heart, as her alliance with France required of her. In England, therefore, all was grumbling and discontent; and the denunciations in Parliament of the fiasco of Walcheren were hardly more bitter than the criticisms concerning Wellington and his campaign of Talavera.

III

In such a temper of the nation the tone of all opponents whether to the new or to the old Government in Parliament was, not wholly without excuse, to the last degree captious. When, therefore, the Army Estimates were brought forward there were loud cries for petty economies. However, Palmerston carried his estimates, and, since the Government was bent on prosecuting the war in the Peninsula and had taken 30,000 of the Portuguese Army into pay, it remained to be seen how the ranks of the forces were to be filled. 1810.

The casualties in the Regular Army for 1809 numbered 21,630, one of the highest figures attained in the course of the war. The chief source of recruits lay in the Militiamen who had been called upon to enlist in the Line by the Act of 13th March 1809. The number allowed to enlist from the Militia of Great Britain had been 21,784; and of these by the same day of 1810 there had been raised 15,331, leaving a deficiency of over 6000. There was, however, still the quota of the Irish Militia to be added, over and above Ireland's usual contribution of 3000 to 4000 men annually; besides which there had been raised by ordinary recruiting 9675 men and 2045 boys. Thus there were men enough to carry the Army through another year of war.

With the Militia matters were not quite so prosperous. The number required to fill the vacancies caused by enlistments into the Regular Army was, it will be remembered, 25,245 men in Great Britain; and these according to the Act were to be raised by voluntary recruiting until the 1st of June 1810, and after that date by the ballot. This lenient, though perhaps politic, method of dealing with the Militia was not wholly successful, for on the 24th of January 1810 the deficiency was still 18,512, showing that only 6733 men had been obtained in eight months. This, of course, could be made good by the ballot; but one troublesome drawback to the system was that patriotic parishes which showed zeal in providing recruits gained thereby no advantage against the time when the ballot should come. An Act was therefore passed (50 Geo. iii. c. 24) to enable the Justices and Deputy-Lieutenants to make a just apportionment of the recruits among the parishes, so that no hardship should ensue either from this cause, or in respect of the support of the enlisted

1810. men's families. It was further enacted, for the prevention of abuses, that the provisions of the Mutiny Act as regards the enlistment of apprentices should apply to the Militia.

The Government, from leniency towards the counties and to give them time to prepare their lists, prolonged the time for voluntary enlistment to the 30th of June; but the ballot was duly applied to complete the Militia after the 1st of July; and the usual crop of troubles at once sprang up. In many counties it seems that there was something like a revolt of the Deputy-Lieutenants and Justices, "whose conduct and language checked the operation of the law." From others there were pathetic appeals that the bounty of £10 to parochial substitutes, which was ordered to cease on the 1st of September, might be prolonged to the 1st of October, owing to the time consumed in making out new ballot-lists.[1] But the Act reserved no power to the Crown to do this; and the aggrieved counties were fain to submit to the inevitable. Where new ballot-lists had not been made out, there were still more formidable obstacles. In Inverness twenty-eight indignant tradesmen complained that they had all of them been drawn for the Militia, to the omission of many others who had not been included in the ballot because the lists were two years old. They alleged further that the number of constables had been doubled from forty to eighty within the past eighteen months to secure exemption for a certain number of young men; and they appealed frantically for new lists, because trade, since they had been ballotted, was at a standstill.[2] In another subdivision of the same county the ballot failed completely. Several of the lotmen disappeared or deserted; others raised legal objections which procured them bill after bill of suspension from

[1] *I.D.* vol. clxxx. L.L. Linlithgow, to S.S. 2nd August 1810. Eight more counties made the same request.

[2] *Ibid.* vol. clxxix. Enclosure in David Macpherson to S.S. 24th Aug. 1810. Memorial of a subdivision of Inverness to S.S. Dec. 1810.

the Supreme Court until the last day of the ballot had expired. Their suits were all of them dismissed with costs; but meanwhile they had gained their point and were safe until the next ballot. 1810.

This, however, was but one manifestation of the general hatred of the Militia in Scotland. The Vice-Lieutenant of Bute reported at the end of October that the Arran division could not possibly produce its quota owing to the invincible aversion of the people from personal service; and he requested that the Militia might be completed by ballot and that the exemption-fines might be applied, as in former cases, to the purchase of substitutes. He added that the people had begun to claim exemption as seafaring men, and that if this claim were allowed it would be preferred by the entire population, whereas, if his recommendation were accepted, the fines would certainly be forthcoming, for there was an insurance company ready to oblige its clients with the money for a premium of four guineas a year.[1] Nairn, again, one of the counties that had pleaded for extension of the time wherein the ten-guinea bounty might be granted, declared that without this privilege she could not raise her quota of men. "The business," added the unfortunate Lieutenant, "is so intricate, owing to the number of Acts of Parliament, that scarcely two counties have acted upon them under the same construction." Perth begged likewise for postponement of the ballot.[2] In Lanark matters were so far behind-hand that even a fortnight after the time for the ballot had expired, the new lists had not been distributed to the Deputy-Lieutenants. This was due in part to certain legislation of 1804 which deprived the Lieutenancies of Scotland of the power to remunerate their own servants, and made it in consequence exceedingly difficult to get the work done. But, unlike the other counties, Lanark lamented the prolongation of the

[1] *I.D.* vol. clxxix. V.L. Bute, to S.S. 30th Oct., 27th Nov. 1810.

[2] *Ibid.* vol. clxxix. L.L. Nairn, to S.S. 2nd Sept. 1810; vol. cxcii. L.L. Perth, to S.S. 20th June 1810.

1810. enlistment by beat of drum for one month, and the consequent loss of power during that month to raise parochial substitutes for ten guineas.[1] Edinburgh made a like complaint of the suspension of the ballot during June. In Midlothian only seven men had been raised by beat of drum, and most of the ballotted men had paid fines instead of finding substitutes, which did not deliver the parishes from the fine of £40 for every man deficient. Private bounties for substitutes, added the Vice-Lieutenant, had in some counties reached the height of £50; and this was confirmed by the Lieutenant of Fife, who reported that he had raised the quota for his county, but that bounties had indeed exceeded the above figure, the £50 paid being in addition to the ten guineas allowed by the Act, so that the total amounted to £60 : 10s. In consideration of the circumstances the Vice-Lieutenant of Edinburgh begged that the fines of £20 paid for exemption might be accepted as part of the penalty of £40 levied on the county for every man deficient. He pleaded in vain. To one and all of these requests that the law might be wrested to one side or another in their favour, there could be but one reply—that the Secretary of State could grant no dispensations from Act of Parliament.[2]

In England there were difficulties of much the same kind as in Scotland. In Buckinghamshire the Lieutenant urged that a short Bill should be passed to extend the time for the ballot until March 1811, so that recalcitrant counties might be brought to their senses by heavy fines. His own quota was nearly complete, but in his virtuous indignation he omitted to mention that some of his men had been raised at Leicester, where the crier had been sent round to offer forty guineas apiece for three or four men for the Buckinghamshire Militia. In Berkshire the Lieutenancy took upon itself to ballot men after the 1st of October, and would not set them

[1] *I.D.* vol. clxxxvii. L.L. Lanark, to S.S. 19th Oct. 1810.

[2] *Ibid.* vol. clxxxiv. L.L. Edinburgh, to S.S. 3rd Oct.; vol. clxxxv. V.L. Fife, to S.S. 25th Aug. 1810.

free without the Secretary of State's order.[1] In Cardigan a new and unexpected complication came to light. The county had duly supplied its quota of men under the Act of 1809, but the Militia was still short of its strength by eighty-four men; the Government having calculated its last contributions to the Line upon the assumption that its regiment was up to its establishment, whereas 102 men were wanting to complete it.[2] In Lancashire there was as much trouble with the Deputy-Lieutenants as with the people. The mercantile community at large had come to an amicable agreement that apprentices should enlist when trade was slack, and be claimed by their masters when trade was brisk. The rest of the population, stricken with envy of so happy a solution of a difficult problem, bound their sons, brothers, and cousins apprentices *pro forma*, so as to be able to claim them likewise whenever they were wanted. Thus in Lancashire military service was converted into a kind of out door relief, which could be repudiated as soon as suited the convenience of the recipient. The case of the Deputy-Lieutenants was different. Always highly critical in the North as to the interpretation of Acts of Parliament, possibly because they were unwilling to execute them, the Deputies were divided in opinion as to the construction of the last Act for completing the Militia. The enactment, so argued one party, was designed to procure men by the 1st of October: after that date there could be no fresh ballot; and therefore the payment of the fine of £40 would exonerate any parish from further operation thereof. On the contrary, contended the opposite party, the intention was that the ballot should be continued until the men were supplied, and then suspended until the 1st of January 1812. The question was carried to the Secretary of

1810.

[1] *I.D.* vol. clxxx. L.L. Bucks, to S.S. 14th Oct.; vol. clxxxix. Subdiv. Clerk, Leicester, to S.S. 24th Aug.; vol. clxxx. L.L. Berks, to S.S. 22nd Oct. 1810.

[2] *Ibid.* vol. clxxxi. O.C. Cardigan Mila. to S.S. 11th March 1810.

1810. State, who laid it down that both sides were wrong. No ballot, he wrote, can be held after the 1st of October until the 1st of January 1812 without the King's special directions; but if such directions be given, payment of the fine will not exonerate the parishes in default.[1]

Once again I must apologise for quoting at length the difficulties raised by the construction of the enactments that so rapidly succeeded each other in these times. The judgment of the Secretary of State, quoted immediately above, shows how drastic this particular Act really was. Practically it said to the counties: "You shall produce so many men for the Militia by a certain day, or you shall pay a fine of £40 for every man deficient, and still be liable to produce them later on." But the Act did not say so in so many words, and possibly Ministers refrained from inserting any phrase which should exactly convey such a meaning, in the hope that they might not be compelled to enforce this particular interpretation of it. If this were the case, they were greatly disappointed. So many Acts dealing with the Militia, some in full force, some obsolete, were before the Lieutenants and their Deputies, to say nothing of the complications produced by the establishment of the Local Militia, that they became very pardonably confused. They therefore either construed the Acts according to the precedents known to themselves, or wrangled over their true meaning, or in the last resort unanimously lost their tempers, and shrank from putting the measures into force. The exaction of a fine for men not raised was, according to the Militia Act of 1802, in the nature of a composition which balanced the two sides of the account; and it would have been better in the first instance to have made it perfectly clear that what held good in 1802 was not intended to apply to 1809. The natural

[1] *I.D.* vol. clxxxvii. L.L. Lancs, to S.S. 20th Feb.; Lord Stanley to S.S. 25th Sept. 1810; *H.O. Mila. E.B.* S.S. to L.L. Lancs, 28th Sept. 1810.

consequence of these doubts, and of the bad blood engendered thereby, was that in 1810 there were levied, instead of the 18,512 men still required to complete the number laid down by the Act, no more than 14,934. Of these 6055 had been raised by beat of drum and 8879 by ballot, and of the latter 797 only were principals against 8082 substitutes.[1] 1810.

The Local Militia appears to have stopped short somewhat in the progress made at the beginning of 1809. Whitbread stated in the House of Commons that half of that in his own county, Bedford, had never been out on permanent duty nor received their clothing, while in other counties none whatever had been called out for training. The Government seems to have been uneasy about its expense, which was set down at £16 a man annually; and it was further alleged that military duty was unsettling the men for their ordinary pursuits.[2] Accordingly an Act to amend the Local Militia Act was passed on the 18th of April (50 Geo. III. cap. 25), which contained the following provisions.

In case of reduction of the permanent staff, commandants were empowered to engage other non-commissioned officers at a reduced rate of pay (sec. 1). The days of exercise to qualify Volunteers for exemption from service in the Regular and Local Militia were reduced from twenty-four to eighteen annually (sec. 2). The fine of £15 upon counties for every man deficient of the quota on the 14th of February was suspended, though it was to be enforced for every man not present at the annual training (sec. 5). Constables were required to make returns of deficiencies on the 14th of November, and the counties were obliged to make them good before the 14th of February on pain of a fine of £15 (sec. 6). Local Militiamen who enlisted in the Line and made no declaration of the bounty that they had received, in order that the same might be refunded, were subject to a fine of twice the amount of the bounty, to be

[1] *C.J.* vol. lxvi. p. 561.
[2] *H.D.* Whitbread's Speech, 1st March 1810.

1810. stopped from their pay (sec. 7). Local Militiamen who were members of Friendly Societies were not to be subject to fines imposed by such societies for non-attendance during their period of service (sec. 13). Apprentices were forbidden to transfer themselves from the Volunteers to the Local Militia without their masters' consent (sec. 14). It was further ordained that military offences of Local Militiamen should be triable by court-martial, whether their regiment was embodied or not (sec. 3).

It will have been noticed that the Government resolved to save money in the first instance by reducing the number of days' training for the Volunteers rather than for the Local Militia; but early in 1810 an order was issued for the reduction of the permanent staff of the Local Militia, as an initial economy, and the first section of the Act above quoted was intended to comfort commandants under the bereavement of their favourite non-commissioned officers.[1] But unfortunately there were other matters besides economy to be attended to, for which no provision was made in the Act. The original measure, binding men, as it practically did, to personal service by ballot, bred in those liable to serve not only considerable stubbornness, but an amazing talent for evasive trickery, while at the same time developing deplorable weakness in some of the Lieutenancies. In Kent over seventy ballotted men refused either to pay the fine or to serve; and the Lord-Lieutenant wrote to ask the Secretary of State what was to be done, though the Act distinctly said that such men could be imprisoned and were liable to serve after their imprisonment. Again, several wealthy tradesmen of Maidstone, on being drawn for the Local Militia, consented to be enrolled, but, on the day before the training began, took the bounty to enter the Regular Militia, and so excused themselves for not attending. They

[1] I have been unable to find this order or circular, but its issue is proved by *I.D.* vol. cxcii. O.C. 4th Oxford L.M. to S.S. 5th Jan. 1810.

were astute enough, however, to agree with the recruiting officer of the Regular Militia that they should be allowed to find a substitute; and when the transaction was completed they declared that it was cheaper to take the bounty and find a substitute for the Regular, than to pay a fine for two years' exemption from the Local, Militia. It must be acknowledged that the ingenuity of these men did them considerable credit, and lent great force to Sir Harry Calvert's contention that there should be only one description of Militia. But Kent was remarkable for providing knotty questions for the Secretary of State. In this same year it possessed a parish in which every man liable to ballot was serving or had paid the fine for exemption, but which none the less had not produced its quota of men for the Local Militia; and there arose the point whether or not it was liable to a fine for every man deficient.[1] In Lancashire again the Lieutenancy, writhing under the ballot, submitted to the Secretary of State so many suggestions for dispensing with it, that in despair he expressed himself as unable to interfere with the local details of enforcing the Militia Acts.[2] 1810.

Another great difficulty arose from desertion. The Commandant of the 1st Devon Local Militia forwarded to the Home Office a handbill advertising for no fewer than seventy-seven deserters from his regiment. There were some doubts, he said, as to whether they could legally be convicted of desertion, not having appeared at the last training; and, if they could not, he expected not to muster half of his men at the next. The Secretary of State was able to assure him that under the Militia Act of 1802 these men were liable to a fine of £20, or six months' imprisonment;[3] but it was one of the curses of the Local Militia Acts that instead of

[1] *I.D.* vol. clxxxvii. L.L. Kent, to S.S. 8th Feb., 6th June 1810.

[2] *Ibid.* vol. clxxxvii. L.L. Lancs, to S.S. 22nd March; *H.O. Mila. E.B.* S.S. to L.L. Lancs, 7th May 1810.

[3] *Ibid.* vol. clxxxiii. O.C. 1st Devon L.M. to S.S. 14th Oct.; *H.O. Mila. E.B.* S.S. to O.C. 16th Oct. 1810.

1810. giving commandants, who at best were only amateurs, a plain code for the government of their regiments, it was constantly referring them to Militia Acts and Volunteer Acts of which they had no knowledge.

Yet another besetting sin of the Local Militiamen, a sin begotten of cupidity, was to enlist as Volunteers or as substitutes in the Regular Militia of other counties than their own, contrary to the law. Such men of course received good bounty; but the only penalty was imprisonment for "neglecting to appear at the place of exercise" as Local Militiamen. In at least one case such an offender gave information against himself in order to keep his bounty at the cost of imprisonment, thus exemplifying once more the error of keeping two different descriptions of Militia simultaneously.[1]

In Scotland there was occasionally unpleasantness because some corps of Local Militia had carried with them the habits acquired when they were Volunteers, particularly in cases where independent companies, each under its own petty magnate, had been united into battalions. In one battalion of this kind some of the captains were Deputy-Lieutenants, and as such assumed the right to control the Commandant. On one occasion when their Commanding Officer's views did not coincide with their own, they formed a meeting of the Lieutenancy and delivered to the men their arms, accoutrements, and camp equipage, contrary to his orders and indeed contrary both to Act of Parliament and the King's regulations; and the unhappy Commandant, submitting at the moment "to avoid the appearance of dissension," carried his sad story to the General of the District, who forwarded it to the Secretary of State.[2]

But the greatest obstacle of all with which commandants of Local Militia had to contend was the undisguised hostility of the population in many quarters towards the force, and the efforts of violent men to

1 *I.D.* vol. clxxx. L.L. Bucks, to S.S. 3rd June 1810.

2 *Ibid.* vol. clxxxvii. O.C. Kirkcudbright L.M. to G.O.C. Scotland, 7th May 1810.

prevent the Act from being executed. In the Cinque Ports the magistrates faithfully and courageously did their duty in collecting their Local Militiamen amid daily insults and menaces. In the Romney division not a man would serve nor pay the fine; but the magistrates at once issued warrants against the recalcitrants, and in Hastings, Pevensey, and Tenterden they succeeded in enforcing the Act. They ordered the recruits to Dover; and the men were peaceably and contentedly approaching the town when the people of Dover waylaid them, and either persuaded or intimidated them into returning home. Some of them were retrieved and taken to Deal barracks, as the only chance of training them, and the rest were warned that they were deserters and that unless they presented themselves within a fortnight they would be treated as such.[1] In other quarters the old supposed grievance about the "marching-guinea" or allowance for necessaries, reduced after the first training to half a guinea, was again made the pretext for mutinous outbreaks. More than one commandant was nervous lest the men should claim the whole of it in cash, though the Secretary of State had directed it to be spent, as the law intended, upon necessaries. The question was complicated by the fact that in many of the regiments of Regular Militia, which from long standing and good management possessed a heavy stock-purse, it had been the custom to pay the men the half-guinea without any deductions.[2] It seems, moreover, to have been the fact that, at any rate in some quarters, the men could purchase necessaries for themselves more cheaply than their officers could purchase for them.[3] However that may be, it is certain that the rank and file, in spite of Acts of Parliament, regulations, and the punishment 1810.

[1] *I.D.* vol. clxxxii. Clerk to Magistrates of Cinque Ports to Lord Warden, 18th Sept. 1810.

[2] *Ibid.* vol. clxxxv. O.C. Glamorgan L.M. to S.S. 22nd March 1810.

[3] *Ibid.* vol. clxxxvii. L.L. Kirkcudbright, to S.S. 18th June 1810.

1810. of rioters in 1809, still harboured a vague notion that they had the right to this allowance in cash without deductions, and that, if it were withheld, they were being defrauded. No man likes to be cheated, and no men enjoy it less than those who spend their lives in endeavouring to get the better of their neighbours. No class is so suspicious as the waged class, and thus its feelings are easily worked upon by unscrupulous men.

The first mischief occurred at Bath, where the regiment of West Mendip Local Militia, usually a loyal and orderly corps, was assembled for training. On the morning of the 16th of May the men on receiving the order to march refused to move, but presently obeyed, and went without further ado through a field-day, at the close of which the Commandant addressed them on the subject of the marching money, read out the words of the Act of Parliament concerning it, and apparently satisfied them thoroughly. On returning to the town the Commandant ordered the leading sections to be marched as prisoners to his lodgings, where he intended to read them a lecture. The regiment thereupon broke its ranks as if to rescue them, but was checked by its officers; and the prisoners were then marched to gaol. In the evening the men paraded, perfectly sober and orderly, expressed regret at their behaviour of the morning, and begged for release of the prisoners, to which the Colonel replied he would make no conditions, but that their treatment would depend on the behaviour of the regiment. There would have been no more trouble but that the rabble of Bath came up,[1] led away a few of the worst characters, and, going with them to the gaol, forced the doors and released the prisoners. Then all order was lost. The Colonel, attempting to re-arrest one of the prisoners, was threatened by the bayonets of his own men. His officers were attacked by the

[1] The letter says that they had "Burdett" upon their hats; that very absurd person being the popular champion of liberty at the moment.

mob; and the whole town was in uproar, until the Lancashire Regular Militia arrived from Bristol to restore order. Then the Local Militia came to their senses and, though the populace was still raging, escorted the prisoners back to gaol. Two of them were then tried by court-martial, sentenced to fifty lashes, tied up before the whole regiment, without the slightest sign of indiscipline, and pardoned at the last moment. The riot lasted for three days; and the sympathies of the lower class were so entirely with the mob, both at Bath and at Bristol, that the Lancashire men were hardly allowed by their landlords to leave the houses in which they were billeted, and indeed in some cases were obliged to force the doors.[1] 1810.

Within a few days this was followed by another mutiny of the Upper Tivy Local Militia of the county of Cardigan, which had been assembled for twenty days' training at Aberystwith on the 10th of May. The men were quite orderly and contented until a newspaper arrived with an account of the riot at Bath. The Commanding Officer at once published in regimental and company orders the King's Regulations as to the expenditure of the half-guinea for necessaries; but on parade that day there were signs of insubordination, though after the reading of the Regulations to the men once more in the Colonel's presence, these disappeared. The parade was then dismissed, and the leaders in disobedience, on expressing contrition, were pardoned, with the exception of one man who was tried by court-martial and sentenced to three hundred lashes. Upon this the Colonel received warning from several individuals that he and his officers would be murdered if the sentence were carried out; and this was no vain threat, for Aberystwith was a kind of Alsatia, a home of the lawless, full of men who could serve their country but would not, nor might be constrained to do so but by an armed force.

[1] *I.D.* vol. cxciii. O.C. West Mendip (Somerset) L.M. to S.S. 17th, 18th May; G.O.C. Western District, to S.S. 20th May 1810.

1810. On the 30th of May, the last day of the training, the Colonel formed a guard of twenty-seven trustworthy men to take charge of the prisoner, and dismissed the rest to their homes. They cheered the Colonel, and many of them left the town that evening. In the course of the night the Colonel was warned that an attempt would be made to rescue the prisoner, whereupon he repaired to the guard-room himself with his pistols, and ordered in ball-cartridge. Nothing, however, happened until next morning, when the prisoner was tied up for punishment in a courtyard at the back of the guard-room, the Colonel intending only to inflict a few lashes to bring the man to his senses. One of the mob thereupon jumped on to the wall of the courtyard, and at this signal the rabble without discharged a shower of stones upon the small party within. Several men of the guard were badly hurt, and the remainder, losing their tempers, fired at every man who appeared on the wall until their ammunition was exhausted. The prisoner was hastily unbound lest he should be killed by stones, and the Colonel withdrew his party into the House of Correction hard by, which the rioters, among whom were a few Local Militiamen, at once assailed with every missile that they could find, swearing that they would murder the Colonel and officers. At last the Colonel went out alone, when the populace incontinently took to its heels, and the little party marched out triumphant with its prisoner to the Colonel's quarters. None of the mob were injured, but many of the officers were badly hurt, one of them indeed dangerously; and the Commanding Officer could only write that "after thirty years' service he had always found that these marching-guineas led to mutiny." "But," he added, "it was not the guineas but the punishment of a mutineer which led to the riot, in which there were engaged all the scum of Aberystwith, but only about thirty Militiamen."[1]

[1] *I.D.* vol. clxxxi. O.C. Upper Tivy L.M. to L.L. Cardigan, 1st June, 23rd July 1810.

There were other mutinies in the Local Militia in Wiltshire, Warwickshire, and Worcestershire in the course of the summer and winter, all nominally due to the miserable marching-guinea, but all obviously excited and stimulated by the townspeople. In Worcestershire, indeed, the Commanding Officer had spent only one shilling of the half-guinea in necessaries, and was prepared to give the balance to the men; but even so there ensued a riot, to suppress which it was necessary to call in a battalion of Regular troops.[1] It will be seen that an effort was presently made to end the trouble about the marching-guinea once for all; but this did not go to the root of the matter. The heart of the mischief lay in the general aversion of a large section of the population from all obedience and subordination whatever. Such aversion still exists, and is encouraged by the ignorant and foolish, who would gladly place arms in the hands of all Volunteers that ask for them, forgetting that undisciplined men in numbers are neither more nor less than a mob, and that an armed mob is the most dangerous of all. Yet these same men, if they chance to suffer from the insubordination of Regular troops, are always the first to cry out against the indiscipline that they themselves have encouraged. 1810.

It remains now to summarise briefly the offensive operations of England in the course of 1810. These consisted in the West Indies of the attack and capture of Guadeloupe early in the year; in the Mediterranean, of some petty work in the Ionian Islands; in the East, of the capture of Banda, Amboyna, and Bourbon; and in the Peninsula, to which Napoleon was now again able to devote the greater part of his force, of the defensive campaign which is identified with the names of Bussaco and Torres Vedras. By reason of the number of troops, over 20,000, engaged in operations within the

[1] *I.D.* vol. cxcvi. L.L. Warwick, to S.S. 22nd Nov.; O.C. Wilts L.M. to S.S. 10th June; vol. cxcvii. O.C. Worcestershire L.M. to S.S. 28th May 1810.

1810. tropics, the losses from sickness were considerable, and the casualties for the year amounted to 19,498. The effective strength of the Army for 1810 had been returned at 199,062 British, and 38,390 foreign and colonial, cavalry and infantry.[1] The artillery, British and foreign, numbered 25,245; making a total of 262,697 rank and file of the three arms. Apart from men enlisted from the Militia, there had been recruited by ordinary means 7367 men and 1728 boys. In all 4092 men and 3773 boys joined the Regular Army (exclusive of foreign troops) during 1809 and 1810, making, together with the Militiamen, 44,700 recruits in all; while the casualties in those two years amounted to 41,128. Thus the net balance showed 3572 men to credit, so to speak; but if the 3773 boys were not counted as men, then the net loss on the two years was 201.

IV

1811. Upon the introduction of the Army Estimates Palmerston stated the Regular force of the Empire at roughly 235,000 men,[2] of which 211,000 were fully effective. The casualties he reckoned, including those of the foreign corps, at 22,000 to 23,000 annually. He dared not reckon the proceeds of ordinary recruiting at more than 11,000 a year for British troops, and 4000 a year for foreign troops; leaving a deficiency of 7000 to 8000 men. How was that deficiency to be supplied? The establishment of the Militia for Great Britain and Ireland was 92,000 men, and the effective strength 84,000, besides which 5000 to 6000 more were due from the ballot. He proposed, therefore, to reduce the Militia of the United Kingdom to its old establishment of 1802, namely 70,000; and for this purpose to allow a number not exceeding 10,000 men

[1] Not including 30,000 Portuguese in British pay.

[2] The return for 25th Jan. 1811 gave the figure at 234,594, foreign and Colonial corps (excepting the Portuguese Army) included.

to enlist voluntarily into the Line. Hereby no new ballot would be needed until the end of 1812. In the matter of expense he pointed to over £300,000 saved in the past year by curtailing the annual term of exercise for the Volunteers, and added that he now proposed also to reduce the training of the Local Militia to fourteen days annually. 1811.

Palmerston's plan for raising men was entirely approved by Castlereagh, who, however, wished in the first place to encourage volunteers from the Militia by continuing the support of the families of the enlisting Militiamen, which hitherto had ceased from the moment that they entered the Line; and in the second to recruit the Militia as far as possible for a fixed bounty, lower than that given to the Regulars. For the English at large he adhered to the existing system of a Regular Army for offensive operations over sea; a Regular Militia to occupy the principal garrisons and advanced positions against invasion; and a Local Militia to assemble under their protection for the repulse of the enemy. Finally, he urged the advantages of making it possible to transfer British Militia to Ireland and Irish Militia to England in rotation, so that all the regiments might in succession take a turn of service in the sister islands.

Accordingly a Bill for permitting a certain number of Militiamen to enlist was introduced, and passed with no great difficulty. Windham was dead, but a few of his followers still advocated his plans for voluntary enlistment only, coupled with short service; to which Mr. Ryder replied that short service was still optional with recruits, but that not one-fourth of them cared to avail themselves of it, though the difference in bounty for limited and unlimited service amounted only to the difference between five guineas and six. The Bill therefore became law on the 11th of April (51 Geo. III. Great Britain, cap. 20; Ireland, cap. 30). It provided that 5714 men from the English, and 1142 from the Scottish Militia should be allowed to enlist in

1811. the Line; and in Ireland fifteen men from every company (cap. 20, sec. 1; cap. 30, sec. 4). In Great Britain the Secretary of State was to ascertain annually the number of men (not exceeding the above total in all) to be enlisted from each regiment of Militia, which number was not in any case to rise above one-seventh of the quota of 1802; and he was to signify it before the 1st of February to the Commanding Officer of every regiment (sec. 3). A greater number might be enlisted by the King's order in cases where counties had not contributed to the Line the full quota allowed to them under former Acts, and had therefore an excess of men over the establishment laid down by the present Act (sec. 4). In Ireland, if the full quota were not enlisted in any one year, the deficiencies might be added to the quota of the next year, and enlisted together with it (cap. 30, sec. 5). Commandants of Militia were to explain the terms of enlistment into the Line to the men within two days of receiving the order, and men were to be allowed to enlist for the seven days immediately following; after which, at intervals of not less than a fortnight, periods of three more days apiece were to be appointed for enlistment (secs. 6, 8).

The remainder of the provisions dealt with the reduction of the Militia; so it will be well first to state that, by an Order in Council of the 11th of March, the ballot had been continued in such counties as had not completed their quota of Militia to the establishment laid down by the Act of 1809; and that on the 4th of April there had been passed an Act (51 Geo. III. cap. 17) validating all enrolments under ballots held, without such order, after the 1st of October 1810. The deficiency under the Act of 1809 was therefore in process of being made good; and it was now enacted under 51 Geo. III. cap. 20, that fines incurred by parishes for men deficient on the 1st of October 1810 should be remitted to the extent of three-fourths, one half, and one-third, if the men were produced by the 1st of June, 1st of July, and 1st of September 1811 respectively (sec. 21). When the men required under the Act of 1809 had been raised, the ballot was to be suspended until 1st July 1813 (sec. 23); and Militiamen might thenceforth be raised by beat of drum for a bounty of twelve guineas, of which part was to go towards the expense of obtaining the recruit, and part to be paid into his hand (secs. 23, 25). Boys of fourteen and upward could, by the King's order, be enlisted to a proportion not exceeding one-fourth of the whole number of men required for the year; their standard of height to be fixed by regulation (sec. 26). The Militia of Great Britain after the passing of this Act was to be gradually reduced to the quota of 1802; but the King was empowered to order supernumeraries to be raised by beat of drum in numbers equal to that of the men enlisted into the Line in each year under the present Act; which supernumeraries were to be taken to fill no vacancies except those of the men so enlisted into the Line (secs. 29-31). Officers and non-commissioned officers, who would become supernumerary upon this reduction, could be ordered to remain with their regiments; and special arrangements were made for supernumerary field-officers (secs. 33-35). The King, after the reduction of the Militia as aforesaid, was empowered to order a number of men, equal to that which had been allowed to enlist into the Line, to be raised by ballot in each county, whether such number should have enlisted or not; and if a ballot were so ordered, all vacancies from death, discharge, etc., were to be filled according to the provisions of the Militia Act of 1802 (sec. 36). A bounty of ten guineas was to be paid to every ballotted man, whether principal or substitute, and no further allowance whatever (secs. 37, 38). Deputy-Lieutenants were to apportion the voluntary and ballotted recruits among the various parishes (secs. 39, 40); and Local Militiamen were permitted to enlist into the Militia of their own counties (sec. 41). Lastly, support to the families of Militiamen raised after the passing of this Act was to

1811.

1811. be discontinued, except in the case of ballotted men who were enrolled as principals (sec. 20).

These enactments for England and Ireland, as will have been remarked, were a new departure, inasmuch as they provided for a fixed annual draft of, roughly speaking, 10,000 men from the Militia into the Line, which draft, if not complete in one year, could be made good in the next; and it was obviously intended that, if possible, the equivalent for this draft should be voluntarily enlisted every year into the Militia so as to silence all invidious statements that men were being ballotted or conscribed for the troops of the Line. Thus at length effect was in part given to Sir Harry Calvert's recommendations of 1809; and though the two descriptions of Militia, the Regular and the Local, were still preserved, the first was reduced to its peace establishment, and the ballot was reserved, except in cases of emergency, for the latter only.

A further important step in respect of the Militia was an Act to permit the interchange of the British and Irish Militias, pursuant to Castlereagh's advice (51 Geo. III. cap 118). Hereby it was enacted that in future all Militiamen should be engaged to serve in any part of the British Isles—that in fact there should no longer be a Militia of Great Britain and a Militia of Ireland, but one Militia of the United Kingdom (secs. 1-6). No British corps was to continue in Ireland, nor Irish corps in England, for more than two years successively; and at no time was more than half of the British Militia to be in Ireland, or more than one-third of the Irish Militia in England, except in case of rebellion or invasion. Moreover, British or Irish Militia who had once served in the sister Kingdom were not to be liable to serve there again except in rotation after an interval of four years or six years respectively (secs. 8, 9). No corps was to be called upon to serve in a sister Kingdom without the King's orders. The King was empowered to accept voluntary offers of the present Militia so to serve; and existent Militiamen voluntarily engaging for service in any part of the United Kingdom were to receive a bounty of two guineas. It was specially provided that Commanding Officers should explain to their men that there was no compulsion (secs. 10-14). 1811.

Meanwhile the ballot, prolonged by royal order for the completion of the Militia under the Act of 1809, continued during the opening months of 1811, and was not furthered by the fact that no bounty to ballotted men was now granted by Government. In Scotland the proceedings were still delayed by petty actions brought against the Lieutenancies by lotmen, by endless ingenious pleas for exemption, by the absconding of ballottable men until the ballot was over, and by the old dispute with the Barons of the Exchequer over the payment of the Lieutenancies' clerks and other servants. The price of substitutes, also, had risen to an appalling height. In Forfar it was reported to range from £50 to £80; and the county declared itself unable, even by rigid enforcement of the law, to produce its quota. Nevertheless there were signs that, either from better feeling or from hard necessity, there was rather less reluctance in Scotland to serve in the Militia, for Sutherland among her quota furnished sixty-six principals as against four substitutes. On the other hand, in Skye and other parts of the west coast men prepared to emigrate to Carolina rather than serve their country; and one gentleman in Haddington had formed so low an opinion of the zeal of his compatriots that he recommended the Secretary of State to discharge the whole of the Scottish Militia. "You have 11,000 men in Scotland," he wrote, "doing nothing, and unwilling to volunteer for the Line as they will lose support for their families, which is the great inducement to them to serve. If you were to discharge the 11,000 you would get 9000 recruits, for most of them are weavers who cannot get work." [1]

In England matters were little different. In Man-

[1] *I.D.* vol. cc. L.L. Inverness, to S.S. May, 12th June; Angus Mackintosh to S.S. 5th July 1811; vol. cci. O.C. Berwick Mila. to S.S. 12th March. Return of men raised in Sutherland under

1811. chester the fines paid for deficiencies in the number of men amounted to £7200. In Brecon the price of substitutes rose above £60; and in Staffordshire it became so prohibitive that the Lieutenancy suspended enrolment for a time in the hope, which was fulfilled, of lowering it. In Yorkshire a Deputy-Lieutenant suggested a general commutation of service for money, to be paid by hundreds and even larger districts within the county, as a certain means of raising men at less cost and with less oppression, and of diminishing the abuse of insurance. The method had, he said, been practised, though prohibited by law, and when exercised by honourable Colonels had been found beneficent both to the regiment and the county. Thus, even in the ninth year of the war, the one idea of filling the Regular Militia was still to find substitutes, or in other words to compete with the Regiments of the Line for recruits at enormous expense to individuals and local bodies. Yet the Government continued to prefer this system to that advocated by Calvert; and though at this distance of time it seems utterly to be condemned, we should perhaps be rash to infer that it was wrong in practice. I can only account for Ministers' adherence to it upon the hypothesis which I have already suggested, that the strong element of gambling which it contained was palatable to the people.[1] It must be added, however, that when the ballot was ended and enlistment by beat of drum restored, the Government did its best to ease matters by allowing every Militia regiment to recruit its full proportion of boys, and left the standard of their height to the untrammelled judgment of Commanding Officers.[2]

Act of 1809, 9th Jan. 1811; vol. ccvii. L.L. Forfar, to S.S. 23rd Feb. 1811; vol. ccxx. Mr. J. Brown, Haddington, to S.S. 15th April 1811.

[1] *I.D.* vol. ccxi. T. Stanley to Attorney-General, 12th March (enclosing memorial from Manchester); vol. ccxvi. L.L. Staffs, to S.S. 4th Jan.; vol. cci. L.L. Brecon, to S.S. 27th April; vol. ccxx. Sir J. Duckett (Yorks) to S.S. 20th March 1811.

[2] Circular to O.C. Militia Regts. 15th July; to O.C. 1st Somerset Militia, 4th Sept. 1811.

In the matter of volunteering for the Line the Militia seems to have shown laudable alacrity, supplying 11,453 recruits, or 1143 in excess of the number required of them, in the course of the year 1811. In the West Middlesex Regiment so many above the full quota offered themselves on the first day that it was possible to select the best from among them;[1] and this is the more remarkable, for the operations in the Peninsula had not yet assumed the brilliancy to which they were later to attain. Other corps were equally forward;[2] though some of course held back; but the policy of asking for a small number of men only was in this year successful. Nor were the regiments, as a body, less ready to volunteer for duty in Ireland. Some hesitation was shown at first, for there was nervousness among principals lest they should commit themselves to service beyond their covenanted term; but they were speedily reassured when they learned that strict faith would be kept with them. The Home Office, however, when inviting offers from the various corps made one very foolish mistake by omitting to mention that the men serving in Ireland would be paid in Irish currency, which was below the British currency in value. No doubt the purchasing value of the Irish currency in Ireland was equal to that of the British in England; but Commanding Officers, after representing to their men in good faith that they would receive the same pay and allowances, felt greatly the awkwardness and humiliation of having to explain to them, after they had volunteered their services, that their pay would be reduced. The War Office, which also sent a circular upon the subject to the Militia regiments, was careful to make the matter clear; and the Home Office was quite inexcusable for neglecting to do so. It was just such folly as this that shook the faith of the forces in 1811.

[1] *I.D.* vol. ccxii. O.C. West Middlesex Mila. to S.S. 3rd May 1811.

[2] *Ibid.* vol. ccviii. O.C. N. Hants Mila. to S.S. 2nd May; vol. ccxiii. O.C. Montgomery Mila. to S.S. 1st May 1811.

1811. the Government, led them to regard every offer with suspicion, and brought about mutinies and riots.[1]

Turning next to the Local Militia, it must first be observed that it was greatly increased by further dissolution or transference of Volunteer corps during 1811. Indeed the surviving Volunteer and Yeomanry corps were none of them called out upon permanent duty during this year, and therefore disappeared in great measure from the public view. What increase the Local Militia may have gained hereby, there are unfortunately no returns to show; but it is evident that it was now settling down, and was accepted as the backbone of the national forces. There was one faint echo of the trouble over the marching-guinea in the course of the summer;[2] and there was one very bad case of an officer who sold his uniform at the end of the training in 1810, but retained his commission, in order to escape the ballot for the Regular Militia, until the outset of the training in 1811.[3] There was also some trouble still with Local Militiamen who enlisted illegally, for the sake of the bounty, into Regular Militia regiments of other counties, and then appealed to their Commanding Officers to reclaim them for the Local Militia; but the Government seems to have abstained deliberately from taking measures to check this evil.[4] Still, generally speaking,

[1] *I.D.* vol. cci. L.L. Bucks, to S.S. 9th July; vol. ccix. O.C. Hereford Mila. to S.S. 1811.

[2] *Ibid.* vol. cciii. O.C. Stirling L.M. to S.S. 4th June 1811.

[3] *Ibid.* vol. ccxvii. L.L. Somerset, to S.S. 14th June 1811.

[4] The following letter from the O.C. Notts Mila. to S.S. 10th April 1811 (*I.D.* vol. ccxiv.) will show the extent of this practice. "Several men of my regiment enlisted into the Regular Militia of other counties, I believe with fraudulent intentions. Last year a sergeant of the Derbyshire Militia enlisted four of my men, knowing that they belonged to my regiment; and my Adjutant tells me that fifty have enlisted into other Militia regiments, and that ten of them have written to him to be claimed. What am I to do? These men have clearly acted illegally; but if I seize them I shall injure the recruiting service, probably protect men who have been guilty of perjury and fraud, and encourage others to do the like." To this the Secretary of State answered that the Regular Militia must, under 49 Geo. III. cap. 129, be discharged if claimed. "If you

the conduct of the force seems to have improved greatly, while the Lieutenancies shrank less than before from executing the Act for keeping it up to strength. In Buckinghamshire the Deputy-Lieutenants did not hesitate to draw a young gentleman, past eighteen years of age, upon the foundation of Eton College, for the Local Militia, a proceeding which called forth a noble and dignified protest from the Provost. To this the Secretary of State replied that, though there was no legal provision to exempt the lad, who must therefore pay his fine or be enrolled for four years, yet he would take care that no hardship should come of it, and, in case a new Militia Act were required, would consider the propriety of giving exemption to students upon eleemosynary foundations.[1] But this was by no means all. The Local Militia began to display a fine and enterprising spirit. When the Cornish Regular Militia volunteered for service in Ireland, the 4th Cornwall Local Militia offered to do duty for it in England during its absence; and in the course of the summer the Banff Local Militia, 1074 strong, tendered itself for service in any part of the world, and the Berkshire for service in the Peninsula.[2] 1811.

The operations of the year were confined to the capture of Mauritius and Java in the Far East, and to the campaigns in the Peninsula which are remembered by the names of Barrosa, Fuentes d'Onoro, and Albuera. The casualties for the year numbered 19,019. The recruits raised by voluntary enlistment amounted to 9532 men and 1940 boys, or 11,472 altogether, which, added to 11,453 men transferred from the Militia, made

deem it necessary to claim them [note this evasion of responsibility on the part of the Secretary of State] you will transmit to the Home Office such particulars as are necessary to bring the men to condign punishment."

[1] *I.D.* vol. cci. Provost of Eton to S.S. 8th May 1811; *H.O.M.E.B.* vol. xlvii. S.S. to Provost, 11th May 1811.

[2] *I.D.* vol. cciii. L.L. Cornwall, to S.S. 13th June 1811; vol. cc. V.L. Banff, to S.S. 23rd July; O.C. Berks L.M. to S.S. 30th June 1811.

1811. a total of 22,925, or, deducting boys, 20,985 soldiers added to the Army in the course of the year. The net gain, therefore, was 1966 for the year 1811. The casualties among the foreign troops raised the total by 2000, but against this was to be set an aggregate of 4795 foreign recruits enlisted.[1] The Army, therefore, at the outset of 1812 was in a strong position, and all the stronger since it had regained in 1811 an excellent Commander-in-Chief in the Duke of York.

V

1812. The estimates for 1812 provided for an establishment of 245,446 Regular British infantry and cavalry of all ranks, and nearly 27,000 artillery; of which number about 68,000 only, including 15,000 of Veteran and Garrison battalions, were to be employed at home. Roughly speaking, therefore, there were about 145,000 effective British and Colonial troops employed beyond sea, over and above some 30,000 foreigners—half of them of the King's German Legion—and the Portuguese army of 30,000 men. Besides these again the establishment of embodied Regular Militia was set down at 103,000, and of Local Militia at 240,000; but these figures are certainly far in excess of the actual numbers. Reducing them, however, to 250,000 jointly, there still remained a force of at least 300,000 well and fairly well trained troops, besides Volunteers, for home defence. In all, therefore, the armed forces of Britain must have amounted to nearly 500,000 really effective men.[2]

The strain upon the resources of recruiting was, however, beginning to be felt so strongly that on the 20th of April a short Act was passed to enable a proportion not exceeding one-fourth of the Militia of Ireland,

[1] *H.D.* vol. xxi. p. 898.

[2] The effective strength of the Army (including foreign and Colonial Corps) and Regular Militia for 25th January 1812 is returned at 320,940. Allowing 180,000 for Local Militia, Yeomanry, and Volunteers (a very moderate estimate), we get the full 500,000.

as of England, to be raised from boys of fourteen years of age and upwards (52 Geo. III. cap. 29). In addition to this the ordinary recruiting service was reconstituted, according to a plan long desired by the Duke of York, and more zealous officers were appointed to carry on the work. 1812.

A more important measure was an Act passed on the same day to consolidate and amend the Local Militia Acts (52 Geo. III. cap. 38, England ; cap. 68, Scotland). Hereby it was enacted that the quota for England should be 163,188, and for Scotland 30,724, or 193,912 men in all (secs. 14, 162, 166, and 169), which, added to the really efficient Volunteers of London and other great towns, would make, roughly speaking, 250,000 men. In counties where the present quota was smaller than the number of men serving, the men in excess were to continue to serve, but no vacancies were to be filled up until the number had been reduced to the level of the quota (sec. 15). When, however, the quota was greater than the number of men at present serving, no further enrolment was to take place so long as the Local Militia and effective Volunteers together were equal to six times the quota of the Militia as fixed in 1802 (sec. 16). When the number serving was less than the quota, Volunteers between the ages of eighteen and thirty, and having not more than two children under fourteen years of age, were allowed to transfer themselves to the Local Militia, receiving two guineas bounty if they had been effective on the 12th of May 1809, and had continued so ever since; and such transferred Volunteers were exempted from service in the Regular Militia (secs. 17, 18). Artillery Volunteers and Yeomanry might also transfer themselves to the Local Militia ; but vacancies in the Yeomanry were not to be filled by ballot unless they remained for six months unfilled by voluntary engagement (sec. 20). The men were, as before, to be ballotted from those between eighteen and thirty years of age on the Militia lists (sec. 23) ; and no man under thirty was to be made a special constable (sec. 25).

1812. Parishes might be grouped together for convenience of ballotting (sec. 28). The clauses forbidding insurance and substitution were re-enacted ; but voluntary recruits might be accepted, and parishes could levy a rate to pay them a bounty of not more than two guineas (secs. 34-36). Persons voluntarily enlisting themselves, if between the ages of eighteen and thirty-five, with not more than two children, and five feet two inches in height, could avert the ballot to the extent of their numbers (sec. 37). Exemption was granted, over and above the persons in the former Acts, to poor men with more than two children and to students on an eleemosynary foundation. Men who had served by substitute in the Regular Militia or in any additional force were exempted for four years after the expiration of their period of service, and men who had served in person for six years (sec. 38). Men already enrolled in the Local Militia were exempted from the ballot for the Regular Militia for two years after the expiration of the period of service, unless they neglected to attend training; but men enrolled after the passing of this Act were to be exempt for one year only (secs. 39, 40). The fine for exemption was, as before, £30, reduced to £20 for men with annual incomes of less than £200, and to £10 for those whose income fell below £100. Payment of the fine or personal service ensured certain exemption for two years (sec. 44, and cap. 116, sec. 1). Men imprisoned for not paying their fine could be compelled to serve their four years after the term of imprisonment had expired (sec. 45). Deputy-Lieutenants might re-apportion quotas in cases where they seemed inequitable (sec. 48). Vacancies were to be filled up by fresh ballot, the parish to supply the vacancy of a man promoted to be non-commissioned officer being chosen by lot, unless the promotion were due to the reduction of another non-commissioned officer to the ranks (sec. 60). Special directions were given as to the timely ballotting of men to fill the place of those whose term of service was expired (sec. 61). The enrolment of servants was

not to vacate contracts with masters, unless the servant 1812.
did not return to the same master as soon as possible after the end of the training. Any dispute concerning wages under the value of £20 might be settled by a Justice of the Peace, who had power to levy distress if the money were not paid as he decided (sec. 62). Local Militiamen were allowed to enlist into the Line, with the exception of non-commissioned officers and musicians, who could only do so with their Commanding Officer's consent, and of apprentices, who needed to obtain their master's consent (sec. 65). All vacancies were to be filled up as appointed in sec. 60, even though the ballot for the Regular Militia might be suspended; but voluntary recruits, as in sec. 37, were allowed to enter until the quotas fixed by the present Act were complete (sec. 66). The Local Militia was to be formed into companies of not less than sixty, or more than one hundred and twenty privates, with three officers; and these, where the numbers in the county sufficed, were to be organised into one or more regiments of not more than twelve or less than ten companies; or, failing this, into battalions of not more than seven or less than four companies. Regiments of eight hundred men and upwards were to have four field-officers; corps of 480 to 800 men, three field-officers; battalions of less than 480 men, two field-officers; and corps of three companies, one field-officer. Corps of five companies and upwards were allowed to have a Light, or a Grenadier company; to regiments of eight companies and upwards, both Light and Grenadier companies were permitted, each with two lieutenants instead of lieutenant and ensign. Every company over ninety strong might have three subalterns (sec. 68). Officers in excess of the establishment at the time of the passing of the Act could be retained (sec. 69). Counties could be divided into districts for the supply of different corps within them (sec. 62). Local Militia upon embodiment were entitled to the same pay and allowances as the Regular Militia; with a grant of 10s. 6d. a man in the first year, and 5s. 3d. a man in subsequent years, for necessaries

1812. (sec. 86). The annual training was to be for not more than twenty-eight days, and the men could not be ordered to march outside their own counties (sec. 88) unless the Lieutenant recommended for convenience of training that the regiment should be assembled in an adjoining county (sec. 90), and except in case of invasion or insurrection (sec. 123). Offences committed during the training could be tried afterwards (sec. 95). Local Militiamen, when embodied, could be subjected to stoppages for linen and necessaries, not exceeding fourpence a day (sec. 102). Men absenting themselves from training were to be treated as deserters and liable to a fine of £20 or six months' imprisonment (sec. 105); but their vacancy was to be filled up by ballot if they were absent for three months, though they were none the less liable to serve if they returned (sec. 106). A proportion of non-commissioned officers could be kept on permanent pay by the King's order (sec. 116); and these could be called upon to raise voluntary recruits for the Regular Army or Militia (sec. 119). Commanding Officers were required to make out a list of men, of the age and standing prescribed by sec. 17, who were willing to prolong their service for a bounty not exceeding £2 : 2s.; and such men were to be enrolled as volunteers for the place or parish for which they originally served (sec. 135). The King was empowered to increase the Local Militia to six times the quota of the Regular Militia, on summoning Parliament within fourteen days (sec. 156). Counties were to be fined £15 for every man deficient of their quota on the 14th of February every year (secs. 176, 177); and the payment of this fine was to be accepted in discharge of its duty in raising and training men (sec. 185). Local Militiamen actually serving were exempted from payment of rates towards these fines.

The most important novelties in this Act were, first, the reduction of the strength of the Local Militia, and, secondly, the power given to Local Militiamen to prolong their service, which was justly criticised in Parliament as an abandonment of the original principle of putting the whole population through the ranks. It was defended on the ground that it would produce a more effective force, avert the need for calling men from their ordinary avocations, and save £100,000 a year. No doubt at so critical a time these were important considerations; and yet it was a great misfortune that Ministers should have yielded to them. For the first time Castlereagh had compelled the country to recognise that it was the duty of every able-bodied citizen in the prime of life to be trained to arms, and had introduced legislation, none too drastic, to enforce that duty. Yet the Act vitiated this good service, first by admitting Volunteer corps without regard to the age of the Volunteers, and, secondly, by allowing men who were ready to do their duty to take the place of men who were not. In both cases they admitted the very principle which they professed to repudiate—that of substitution—and this was a most objectionable compromise. It was unstatesmanlike since it took no thought for the future, whereas Castlereagh had designed the Local Militia to be a permanent force; and it was unnecessary, because the country was still conscious that its fate was uncertain and could only be assured by a great effort. 1812.

The truth seems to have been that Government had not foreseen an embarrassment which was bound inevitably to show itself when, as was the case in 1812, the four years' service of the first batch of Local Militiamen should expire. As the entire force was created practically at the same moment, it followed necessarily that the entire force became entitled to its discharge at the same moment, and that consequently, unless a certain number of men were allowed to re-engage, no old soldiers would be left to leaven the raw recruits. An officer in the Edinburgh Local Militia pointed out a remedy for this by suggesting that every man on reaching the age of eighteen should, as a matter of course, be enrolled in the Local Militia, and that some machinery should be devised for the automatic enlist-

1812. ment and discharge every year of a certain fraction of the men liable to service.[1] In the absence of such machinery the Lieutenancies were at a loss to know what to do. Many of them recognised the importance of making the Local Militia a means of national training; but on the other hand the officers naturally clamoured for a few old soldiers to be left to them. Here, however, a further difficulty arose. A bounty was to be allowed under the Act to every Local Militiaman who extended his service, but the bounty was to be paid not by the counties but by the parishes. Now when the Volunteers transferred their services to the Local Militia, it had frequently happened that through the zeal and good example of the gentry one parish had contributed every able-bodied man to the service, while its neighbour, from want of natural leaders, had contributed none. The Local Militiamen of the zealous parish were ready and eager to re-engage for a further period of service; but the parochial ratepayers felt it to be a poor return for their patriotism that they should be subjected to an extra tax for bounties because they had provided more men than their neighbours for defence of the country; and complaints upon this account were very common.[2]

However, in spite of these drawbacks and of some perilous reforms wrought by the new Act, the Local Militia appears to have passed through the year 1812 very quietly. Some Commanding Officers dreaded the abolition of the marching-guinea and the change which gave Local Militiamen exemption for only one instead of two years from the Regular Militia ballot; but on the other hand the grant of relief to their wives and families in all circumstances, the exemption from the duty of acting as peace-officers, and the promise, if

[1] *I.D.* vol. ccxxvi. Sir A. Muir Mackenzie to the Lord Chief Baron, 24th Dec. 1812.

[2] *Ibid.* vol. ccxxvii. C.G.M. Glamorgan, to S.S. 16th Sept. 1812, one specimen which must serve for many. The Sec. of State expressly disclaimed the provision of the bounty from the Imperial Exchequer in a letter to L.L. Caithness, 14th Aug. 1812, *H.O.L.M. E.B.* vol. liv.

they were called out on active service, of freedom to carry on their trades in every town in the Kingdom, seem to have reconciled the men to these unpopular conditions.[1] The Local Militia was frequently employed in suppressing riots in Cheshire, Lancashire, Yorkshire, and Derbyshire during the course of the year, but there was no trouble in the force itself. It is true, however, that the Lieutenancy of Cheshire recommended that the Stockport and Macclesfield Local Militia should not be assembled, owing to the disturbed state of the district and the probability that every private in the corps was more or less concerned with the causes of the unrest.[2] The force had, in fact, definitely settled down to its work; and there seemed to be good prospect that, if permitted to remain in existence, it might yet serve its purpose of giving military training to the whole nation. 1812.

The continued separation of the Local Militia from the Regular Militia, nevertheless, remained a source of weakness and of friction. The restriction of the Local Militia to men between eighteen and thirty years of age, and the exemption of these men, even for one year after their term had expired, from the ballot for the Regular Militia, naturally tended to throw service in the Regular Militia chiefly upon men over thirty years old, who were for the most part married, husbands and fathers. The only possible remedy would have been to blend the two Militias into a single Militia of two classes, to make all the younger men pass through the Local Militia as a matter of course, and to give them no exemption from the ballot for the Regular Militia. Moreover, personal service only, and not service by substitute, in the Regular Militia, should have availed to earn exemption from service in the Local Militia. Had the war been prolonged it is possible that the

[1] *I.D.* vol. ccxxviii. O.C. 4th Lanark L.M. to S.S. 8th Sept. 1812.

[2] *Ibid.* vol. ccxxiii. Minutes of G.M. Cheshire, 25th April; vol. ccxxix. Printed Minutes of Lieutenancy of Lancs, 1st May; vol. ccxxxv., O.C. Sheffield L.M. to S.S. 18th April 1812.

1812. organisation might have been perfected ; but, as things were, the initial blunders of Addington and Pitt had consumed in foolish experiments the years which might have been devoted to the building up of a sound and permanent system.

For the rest, this year 1812 was the great year of the war, which saw most of the armies of Europe march into Russia under the banners of Napoleon, to return not again except as a scanty remnant. In Spain the operations had been marked by a series of brilliant British successes at Ciudad Rodrigo, Badajoz, and Salamanca. The Army in the Peninsula had been reinforced in the course of the year by over 20,000 men, exclusive of nearly 11,000 drafts sent out to make good the waste of war ;[1] and though the greater part of these had not joined the Army until after the battle of Salamanca, they were nevertheless upon the spot ready for the next campaign. Moreover, for the first time a detachment from the enormous garrison which was kept idle in Sicily had been withdrawn for service upon the east coast of Spain. The time was come for a great effort ; and the country was fully alive to the importance of making that effort. One cloud only obscured the general brightness of the outlook. Long disputes with America over the British maritime code had at length culminated in war.

The casualties among the British troops for the year 1812 amounted to 20,313 ; and among all the troops in British pay, to 29,562.[2] In the course of the year there had been obtained by ordinary recruiting in the United Kingdom 12,563 men and 1869 boys, making a total of 14,432 ; and as many of the boys enlisted in former years must by this time have grown to men's

[1] *H.D.* Lords, Lord Wellesley's speech, 12th March 1813.

[2] Another return in *C.J.* gives the figure as 26,687. Palmerston in his speech (*H.D.* 8th March 1813) explains the discrepancy as due to the fact that disabled men sent home from the seat of war were struck off the effective list, and not immediately accounted for upon their arrival in England.

estate, it may be assumed that the actual gain was not far short of 14,000 men. Besides these the Militia had contributed its full quota of 9927 men, making in all little short of 24,000 men gained in the course of the year. Additional battalions had been furnished to the amount of 5300 men; two new Fencible battalions had been raised for defence of Canada; additional Veteran Battalions, British and foreign, had been formed for the employment of men who, though unfitted by wounds or injury for service in the field, were equal to work in garrison. Moreover, the establishment of foreign corps had been raised by 2000 men. Altogether Palmerston was able to state in the Commons that against the 29,562 casualties suffered during 1812, he could set 39,762 men, British and foreign, added to the Army; making a net gain of 10,200 effective men, four-fifths of them indeed foreign, but 2000 British. 1812.

VI

The full establishment of Regular troops of all arms, British and foreign, voted for the year 1813 was 314,531; of which the foreigners numbered 33,203.[1] Their effective strength was, on the 25th of January 1813, 255,876; of which 203,000 were British, and the remainder foreign and Colonial. The establishment of the Regular Militia was 93,210 men, and its actual strength 71,000; that of the Local Militia, as fixed by the Act, was 193,912. The Volunteers had continued to dwindle during 1812, until Huskisson in debate described them as a merely nominal force, except in Ireland. The infantry,[2] with the exception of a few corps in Middlesex, Surrey, Kent, Devon, Gloucester, Hants, and Northumberland, was finally dissolved by a circular of 17th March 1813, their weapons being 1813.

[1] In 1812 the figures had been 304,896 and 32,525.

[2] Its strength is given in a return of 6th March 1812 as 49,436 effective rank and file; or 30,000 below its establishment.

1813. required to arm the insurgent Prussians against Napoleon.[1] The Yeomanry, on the other hand, was left untouched; indeed later in the year Ministers announced that they desired to increase its efficiency, and to that end encouraged the incorporation of all isolated troops into regiments, offering also the pay of Regular cavalry to all which would come out for twelve days' permanent duty annually.[2] The Government was evidently awaking to the fact that the Yeomanry was a far more valuable force than the Volunteers, of which it had formerly been reckoned a part.

The military measures brought before Parliament in the spring were comparatively unimportant. The Militia of the Stannaries had complained that they were not allowed to enlist into the Line,[3] having volunteered in vain for service as a complete regiment in the Peninsula; and an Act was accordingly passed to enable them to enlist, to the proportion of one-seventh of the quota of 1802 (53 Geo. III. cap. 20; 23rd March 1813). A short amending Act was also passed to alter slightly the dates for holding the ballots for the Local Militia, to allow battalions of the force to consist of no more than six companies, and to regulate the appointment of the quotas in counties where there were effective Yeomanry and Volunteers (53 Geo. III. cap. 28, England; cap. 29, Scotland). A short Act to amend the Militia laws was also passed (53 Geo. III. cap. 81; 2nd July 1813), which enacted that a Volunteer, whose corps had been discontinued by Royal order, should not be liable to serve in the Militia if drawn for the ballot while he was an effective Volunteer (sec. 4). The King was further empowered to order supernumerary Militiamen to be raised by beat of drum to the proportion of one-half of the quota fixed by 51 Geo. III. cap. 20; and Commanding Officers of Militia were authorised to raise men

[1] Circular to L.Ls. of England, 17th March 1813.

[2] Circular to L.Ls. 29th Oct. 1813.

[3] *I.D.* vol. ccxxxiii. Warden of the Stannaries to Col. Lemon, 18th Nov. 1812.

by beat of drum at the headquarters of their regiments, or within ten miles thereof, even though such headquarters should be remote from their own county (secs. 6, 7). The number of men enlisting into the Line in counties having more than one regiment of Militia was restricted to one-seventh of the establishment of the Militia, irrespective of the number actually serving; but if, on the 24th of January in any year, the actual number of men serving, after deduction of the quota allowed to enlist into the Line, exceeded the establishment, such excess of men was to be allowed to enlist also (secs. 8, 9). For the first time since the war began no special provision was necessary for raising recruits; and the existing machinery worked smoothly and well. Nevertheless, one or two regiments of Militia began to show signs of exhaustion, or at any rate of unwillingness to furnish their quotas of men to the Line; for between the 1st of April and the 25th of November 1813 the Militia furnished no more than 9095 recruits, out of its appointed 10,000, for the Regular Army.[1] Ordinary recruiting, however, flourished astonishingly under the new regulations, producing in the course of the year 12,824 men and 1874 boys, or an average of a full thousand men a month. 1813.

It must, however, be noted that some of these recruits were obtained by exceptional methods. In order to increase the force in America the Militia of thirteen Scottish counties, and of Wicklow, South Lincolnshire, West Suffolk, South Hants, and West Norfolk, received permission to enlist men for the Forty-Ninth Foot for service in North America only, with an assurance of discharge within six months of a general peace; of a grant of fifty acres of land to privates, sixty acres to corporals, and seventy-five to sergeants; and of a free passage for their wives and families to Quebec within twelve months of the husbands' departure.[2]

[1] Return in *C.J.* vol. lxix. p. 638.

[2] The English and Irish regiments above named, together with the Fife, Perth, Berwick, Kirkcudbright, and Ross regiments, were

1813. There was some little trouble with the Scottish Militia in some quarters, owing to the claim of a great many substitutes to be discharged on the completion of ten years' service. It seems that this was the result of a regular agitation set on foot by some pettifogging lawyers in various parts of Scotland; but the wording of the Act was so plainly adverse to any such claim, that the men were easily persuaded of their folly, and the mischief was stamped out with little trouble.[1]

Another and more serious difficulty was that the system of maintaining the Regular Militia by voluntary enlistment began to show signs of breaking down, even though the bounty offered to both boys and men was ten guineas.[2] The provision in the Act of 1813 which allowed Commanding Officers to recruit men at their regimental headquarters, wherever they might be stationed, was intended to remedy this failing, but it is extremely doubtful whether it did so. Commanding Officers were loth to destroy the local character of their regiments by taking in aliens from other counties; and in cases where their numbers were fallen very low, they asked rather to be sent back for a time to their county town than for power to enlist recruits in a strange land.[3] On the other hand it appears that Highlanders would follow a Highland Militia regiment to any quarter, and refuse to enlist in any other.[4] But the concession granted by the Act of 1813 was vitiated for

informed at the same time that on the 1st of June they might offer the following bounties to men who would enlist in the Regular infantry:—viz. to men who were serving before the 1st of April, 14 guineas for life service and 10 guineas for limited service; to men who had served only since 31st March, 10 guineas for life service and 6 guineas for short service. *I.D.* vol. ccl. Circ. of S.S. 14th May 1813.

[1] *I.D.* vol. ccxxxvi. O.C. Banff and Inverness Mila. to S.S. 29th Jan., 11th, 26th Feb., 23rd March; vol. ccxxxvii. Lieut.-General Wynyard to A.G. 2nd Jan. 1813.

[2] *Ibid.* vol. ccxli. Commdt. Edinburgh Mila. Depôt to S.S. 7th Oct.; S.S. to Commdt. 11th Oct. 1813.

[3] *Ibid.* vol. ccliii. O.C. Beds. Mila. to S.S. 7th Jan. 1814.

[4] *Ibid.* vol. ccxxxviii. O.C. Ross Mila. to S.S. 17th Feb. 1813.

purposes of recruiting by the standing order which forbade Local Militiamen to be enlisted in any Regular Militia but that of their own county.[1] It was useless to give commanders power to invite recruits outside their counties when all the finest young men, being absorbed by the Local Militia, were withheld from them. In truth, the competition between the Local and the Regular Militia had become acute, and the Commanding Officers of the latter began to complain bitterly. "The Local Militia has become a source of patronage to its commanders," wrote the Colonel of the Cardigan Militia. "Lately sixty young men offered themselves to one of our County Local Militia regiments. The Commanding Officer took forty of them, and discharged that number of undesirable men. Hence the ballot for the Regular Militia falls on old and married men, in fact, on the rejected of the Local Militia. If they serve in person, they are fit for nothing; and their substitutes from the manufacturing districts desert." From Lancashire came a similar remonstrance owing to the difficulty of raising Regular Militiamen by beat of drum. "Exemption from the Militia ballot draws the finest young men to the Local Militia, because if they wish to enlist from thence into the Line, they can do so when they please. These men if ballotted [for the Regular Militia] would serve; or they would enlist in the Line or Regular Militia rather than risk losing the bounty. As it is, service in the Regular Militia is forced upon men to whom it is almost ruin, or they must give enormous bounties to substitutes."[2] 1813.

These were serious symptoms; and not less formidable was the depleted condition of some of the Militia regiments in consequence of the heavy drafts required from them by the Line, and the discharge of

[1] *I.D.* vol. ccxl. O.C. Devon Mila. to S.S. 11th July; S.S. to O.C. Devon Mila. 12th July 1813.

[2] *Ibid.* vol. ccxli. O.C. Glamorgan Mila. to S.S. 20th Jan.; vol. ccxxxviii. O.C. Cardigan Mila. to S.S. 26th Feb.; vol. ccxliii. O.C. 1st Lancs Mila. to S.S. Feb. 1813.

1813. principals upon the expiration of their term of service. The Adjutant of the Notts Militia reported that he had five hundred men who had never handled a firelock, and fourteen sergeants out of thirty-one who were new to their work. He therefore begged that he might be allowed to give his non-commissioned officers seven days of preliminary instruction before the training;[1] but his letter was not even answered. Many other regiments must have been in much the same condition, but no heed appears to have been taken of them. Events were moving fast in Europe, and Ministers appear to have left all minor details to chance. Members of disbanded Volunteer Corps complained loudly, and not unreasonably, that after all their years of service they had lost their exemption from the Local Militia ballot through no fault of their own. Ministers expressed regret. They had hoped that the ballots would have been over before the time appointed for the dissolution of the Volunteer Corps; but as it was not so, the Volunteers must take the consequences.[2] Moreover, as the Regular Militia ballot recommenced on the 1st of July 1813, the Volunteers became subject to that also, with the alternative of paying from £30 to £40 for a substitute.[3] Emphatically the last state of the Volunteers was worse than the first.

But there was much excuse for ignoring such small matters as these, for as the year waned disaster upon disaster befell the hated Bonaparte. Prussia had turned upon him early in the year; Sweden had followed her later; and in August Austria at last threw in her lot against him. Two long and chequered campaigns were ended in October by the decisive overthrow of Napoleon at Leipsic; and in November the wreck of his army

[1] *I.D.* vol. ccxlvi. Adjt. Notts Mila. to S.S. 20th March 1813.

[2] *Ibid.* vol. ccxlviii. Geo. Jackson (Surrey) to S.S. 23rd April; S.S. to Geo. Jackson, 26th April 1813.

[3] *Ibid.* vol. ccl. L.L. York West Riding, to S.S. 25th April 1813.

retired across the Rhine. A few weeks earlier Wellington, having utterly defeated Joseph at Vittoria in June, had crossed the Spanish frontier into France; and on the 10th of November he drove Soult from the lines of the Nivelle with heavy loss. A week before, on the 4th of November, Parliament met and Castlereagh announced that the time was come for a supreme effort. First he intimated that, in spite of all the country's exertions, the Army and Militia were as strong numerically as ever; for improved attention to the health and discipline of the troops had so greatly reduced casualties, including desertion, that they amounted to little more than 12 or 14 per cent in time of war, whereas they had formerly amounted to 10 per cent even in the profoundest peace. As a matter of fact, the returns show that in spite of heavy casualties in the Peninsula, the effective strength of the Regular troops, British and foreign, was 260,797 on the 25th of September 1813, against 255,876 on the 25th of January 1813; while the strength of the Militia during the same period had been reduced only from 71,055 to 69,886. The casualties for the year, according to Castlereagh's estimate, would not exceed 30,000; but while he thought that ordinary recruiting would continue to be successful under the new system, he doubted the adequacy of the supply that would be derived from the Militia. Since 1805 that force had furnished close upon 100,000 men to the Army, and the 70,000 men, of which it was at the highest computation composed, were for the most part ready to enter the Line. But some of them were unfit for foreign service, and he did not therefore wish to send the regiments bodily out of the country, but to allow them to give men enough to the Line to enable England to maintain her present attitude. He would therefore leave at least one-fourth of each regiment at home; but would offer a small additional bounty to tempt the rest to enlist, and if a certain number accepted service, would permit their officers to go with them. In addition to this, he proposed to allow a certain number

1813. to serve abroad as Militiamen in Provisional Battalions, so that their wives and families could enjoy parochial support during their absence, their service abroad being limited to Europe, and their Commanding Officers to be Colonels of Militia. As to numbers, he proposed to take from the Regular Militia the 10,000 men allowed every year by law, a further quota of 10,000 in advance, and 6000 to 8000 men due from certain counties which had not produced their full quota in former years. These, added to the numbers obtained by ordinary recruiting, would, he hoped, bring the year's supply to 40,000 men. For the rest he intended to allow Militiamen to count previous service in the Militia towards their pensions, and to give pensions also to Militia sergeants, in order to encourage men to enlist.

The Bill was unopposed upon any ground even by the most hardened sticklers for constitutional nicety, and it duly became law on the 24th of November (54 Geo. III. cap. 1; for the City of London,[1] cap. 17; for the Stannaries, cap. 20). Hereby the King was empowered to accept voluntary offers from three-quarters of the actual number of men in any Regular Militia regiment of the United Kingdom, to serve in any part of Europe (sec. 1). A bounty of eight guineas was to be given to all non-commissioned officers and men who made such offer, and they were to be sworn to serve in any part of Europe during the remainder of the war and until six months after the ratification of a definitive treaty of peace (sec. 2). The proportion of officers to be accepted was as follows :—

From any regiment providing 900 men .	3 field-officers
From any regiment providing 600 men .	2 " "
From any regiment providing 300 men or three-quarters of its actual strength .	1 " "

A proportion of other officers might also be accepted (sec. 4). The men volunteering on these terms might

[1] Another Act (54 Geo. III. cap. 38) was passed to allow a proportion of the London Militia to enlist in the Line.

be formed into provisional battalions (sec. 5). No officer of Militia was to rank with the Regulars higher than as a Lieutenant-Colonel of Militia; and if sufficient Militia officers did not offer themselves, the King might appoint others (secs. 6, 7). The Militia officers accepting service under the Act were entitled to half-pay, and their widows to pensions (sec. 8). All ranks of Militiamen were to be subject to the Mutiny Act (sec. 9); but in other respects they were to retain their immunities and privileges, provision for wives and families, etc. (sec. 10). In the case of men enlisting into the Line, the King could grant commissions in the Regular Army to Militia officers in the proportions of a captain, lieutenant, and ensign for every hundred men; and five sergeants and six corporals could likewise be enlisted for every hundred privates. Officers could be allowed also to smaller numbers of men enlisted. Such companies could be attached to existing battalions of the Line, or massed together into additional battalions (sec. 12). Their officers were to be entitled to half-pay (sec. 18). Commanding Officers of Militia were empowered to refuse, on sufficient cause shown, to discharge Militiamen anxious to enlist in the Line; and no clerk or bandsman could be enlisted without the consent of the Commanding Officer (secs. 14, 15). No man was to be drafted from the regiment in which he had enlisted without his own consent (sec. 16). The number of men to be enlisted for service in any part of Europe was not to exceed 30,000 men, nor three-fourths of the actual strength of any regiment (sec. 19). 1813.

Another Act (54 Geo. III. cap. 10, 6th Dec. 1813) enabled the Regular Militia to be employed in any part of the United Kingdom without reference to the restrictions in 51 Geo. III. cap. 118. Yet another (54 Geo. III. cap. 12) empowered the King to augment his foreign force by the addition of eighth, ninth, and tenth battalions to the Sixtieth Rifles; and a third (54 Geo. III. cap. 19) authorised the King to accept offers of Local Militia to serve out of their counties until the

1813. 25th of March 1815, for not more than forty-two days in the year, such service to be treated as part of the annual training, and, if it exceeded twenty-eight days, to be accepted in lieu of it.

These measures were, of course, one and all of them revolutionary and adapted for an exceptional and extraordinary crisis only; but they do not seem to have been very successful. The Local Militia, on the whole, though there were a few exceptions, offered to extend its services all over the United Kingdom in accordance with the Act; but the Regular Militia by no means displayed any great alacrity to extend its service to Europe. In the first place, the Government seems to have made a mistake in offering two different kinds of service to the Militia, for the officers did not know to which to encourage their men. They assumed that the Government would prefer recruits for the Line pure and simple, and used their influence accordingly, with the more readiness since a smaller number of men, according to former regulations, entitled Militia officers to a commission in the Regular Army. It was therefore a shock and a surprise to them when they were informed that Ministers preferred men to engage for the Provisional Militia Battalions, and would accept no offer from officers unless they brought eighty privates with them.[1] But apart from this, the men were generally unwilling to serve in the Provisional Militia battalions except on various conditions, such as being left with their own company-officers or field-officers, and the like. Thus in the Cornish Militia at one moment 107 men were ready to serve abroad as Militiamen on one day, but only 80 a fortnight later, though 154 willingly enlisted in the Line. In Westmoreland, on the other hand, nearly 200 men came forward to serve abroad as Militia; whereas in Cumberland there were only 17 men ready to accompany 14 officers. In Denbigh the

[1] S.S. to O.Cs. of 27 Militia regiments, 6th, 9th, 11th, 13th, 14th, 15th, 18th, 20th, 23rd, 30th Dec. *I.D.* vol. ccxli. Staff officers of Glamorgan Mila. to S.S. 9th Dec. 1813.

officers and men tendered their service in large numbers; but they withdrew their offer unanimously as soon as they learned that their Colonel, Sir Watkin Wynn, would not be allowed to accompany them; and instead sent 67 recruits to the Line.[1] In the South Devon Militia every officer and most of the non-commissioned officers volunteered to go abroad if they could do so with three-fourths of their men; but the privates, who were mostly substitutes of ten years' service, were disinclined to move unless they received some reward for all the work that they had done. The East Devon Militia, which had long shown prejudice against enlistment into the Army, sent one man to the Line only; and in the North Devon, though 11 officers came forward to form a Provisional Battalion on condition that 300 men would join them, only 21 men were forthcoming. In Dumfries 14 officers and 6 men volunteered for Militia service abroad and one man for the Line.[2] In Forfar the officers presented themselves in a body, but only two men would consent to serve abroad either as Militiamen or in the Line.[3] In Lancashire the men would have nothing to do with extended service in the Militia, and declined to enter the Line unless they could choose their own regiments.[4] But it is useless to multiply instances. Suffice it that, with a few notable exceptions, the Militiamen were disinclined for service, as such, abroad; and that ultimately after much difficulty and confusion, owing to the withdrawal of many men upon second thoughts from their engagements, there were formed by the end of February only 1813.

[1] *I.D.* vol. ccxxxix. Return of Cornish Mila. 2nd Dec., O.C. Cornish Mila. to S.S. 12th Dec.; O.C. Cumberland Mila. to S.S. 3rd Dec.; O.C. Westmoreland Mila. to S.S. 28th Nov.; L.L. Denbigh, to S.S. 11th Dec. 1813.

[2] *Ibid.* vol. ccxl. O.C. S. Devon Mila. to S.S. 27th Nov.; Returns of East and North Devon Mila. 27th Nov., 1st Dec.; Returns of Dumfries Mila. Nov. 1813.

[3] *Ibid.* vol. ccxli. O.C. Forfar Mila. to S.S. 9th Dec. 1813.

[4] *Ibid.* vol. ccxliii. O.C. 1st and 2nd Lancs Mila. to S.S. 2nd, 3rd Dec.; Return of Lancs Mila. 7th Dec. 1813.

1813. three Provisional Battalions, the First under Lord Buckingham, 979 of all ranks; the Second under Colonel Bayley, 925 of all ranks; and the Third under Colonel Sir Watkin Wynn, 881 of all ranks. This last, it must be noted, could not have been completed unless Sir Watkin had been placed in command, for, as has been seen, not a man of the Denbigh Militia would go abroad without him.[1]

Altogether the Provisional Battalions were a failure, partly because the Militia officers obtained better terms by taking their men to the Line; partly because neither officers nor men were disposed to serve abroad except as complete battalions; and partly because, between drafts for the Army and the competition of the Local Militia, the patience of the old constitutional and most long-suffering force was fairly exhausted. The men formed into Provisional Battalions numbered, without deducting officers, little more than 2700. The Militiamen enlisted into the Line from the 25th of December 1813 to the end of the war in June did not exceed 3243. Thus the total contribution of the Militia to the Regular Army during the first six months of 1814 may be set down at 6000.

[1] The three battalions were formed as follows :—

First.	Buckingham's.		Second.	Bayley's.		Third.	Wynn's.	
Bucks Mila.	415	all ranks.	Leicester	284	all ranks.	Denbigh	135	all ranks.
Wilts	93	,,	W. Middlesex	417	,,	Derby	125	,,
Northampton	180	,,	E. Suffolk	35	,,	Hereford	110	,,
1st Surrey	32	,,	Sussex	94	,,	Westmoreland	162	,,
2nd Surrey	118	,,	Wilts	95	,,	2nd W. York	349	,,
Worcester	141	,,						
	979			925			881	

W.O. Mila. E.B. S.S. to Buckingham and Bayley, 14th, 29th Jan.; to Sir W. Wynn, 31st Jan.; to Buckingham, 24th Feb. 1814. It must be remarked upon these figures that Cambridgeshire had offered 94 men and failed to produce any, and that Derby had at first offered 328 N.C.Os. and men. *I.D.* vol. ccxxxviii. Return of Cambs Mila. 1st Dec. 1813; Return of Derby Mila. 28th Nov., 13th Dec. 1813. On the other hand, Lord Buckingham wrote to the Sec. of State on 18th Jan. 1814 that he made up his contingent of the Bucks from 415 to 470 (*I.D.* vol. ccliii.), which would raise the strength of his battalion to 1034.

Ordinary recruiting in the first six months of the year produced 5375 men and 754 boys. The casualties for the same period cannot be ascertained, being made out for the whole year, and including vast numbers of discharges made after the signature of peace; but as the deaths alone for the year amounted to over 12,000, it is reasonable to suppose that the casualties for six months from death, discharge, and desertion reached at least that total. The effective strength of the Army, in rank and file, had been, exclusive of foreign and colonial troops, 1814.

On 25th June 1813 . . .	211,397
On 25th Dec. 1813 . . .	219,351
It was on 25th June 1814 . . .	209,158

With the prospects of peace near at hand from the moment of Napoleon's abdication in April, it is not fair to draw too strict deductions from any of these figures, though it must be remembered that we were still at war with America. It must also be recollected that Castlereagh's measures at the end of 1813 were by admission desperate, and not designed to meet more than a temporary emergency. Nevertheless it must, I think, be admitted that the war was brought to a close before the problem of recruiting the British Army had been finally solved.

CHAPTER V

1814. UPON a review of the whole matter it may seem at first sight that a variety of opposing conclusions may be drawn from the facts set forth in the foregoing pages. Opponents of compulsory service, for instance, can point to the constant break-down of the ballot, to the unfairness and oppression which it caused, and to the success of voluntary enlistment even for the Militia. Advocates of Volunteers, again, may adduce the readiness of that force to go upon permanent duty, and its alacrity in turning out upon the few occasions when a real or false alarm demanded its service. But the whole question of the recruiting of our military forces must be judged not by isolated occurrences, but by the whole mass of events and the general trend of legislation from the beginning to the end of the war.

The initial mistake of Addington and his colleagues was that they did not make the increase and maintenance of the Regular Army their first object—did not perceive, in fact, that all military measures which are not framed with the ultimate purpose of benefiting the Regular Army are not only useless but positively prejudicial. Thus they allowed substitution in the Militia Act of 1801, though the exclusion of the principle, in the case of men enlisted for home defence only, would have been perfectly legitimate, and the number of Militiamen called for—70,000 or, including the Supplementary Militia, 94,000 for a population of fifteen millions in the United Kingdom—certainly cannot be considered oppressive. By the express words of the

Act these 94,000 were forbidden to enlist in the Regular Army, and as they consisted chiefly of substitutes, they simply deprived the Army of that number of recruits. Having thus drained the recruiting market heavily to produce a defensive force, Addington in the second place bethought him of the Regular Army, and tried to call the Army of Reserve into existence to supply it; the said Army of Reserve being simply additional to the Militia, formed once again by ballot, with the principle of substitution again admitted, and differing from the ordinary Militia only in that the men were allowed to enlist in the Regulars. This done, he allowed the Volunteers to take the bit between their teeth and to mass themselves in extravagant numbers; and then proceeded to reduce the ballot-lists to skeletons by exempting all Volunteers both from Militia and Army of Reserve. As he was unprepared with rules to govern this mob of men, which had sprung into existence against his wish, his Home Secretary was obliged to introduce, by sidewinds and sly devices, regulations which gave rise to endless friction and discontent, and yet were powerless to enforce discipline. It is not too much to say that to the end of the war our military system never recovered from the mischief wrought by Addington and his Secretary for War, Hobart, during the year 1803. It was no fault of theirs that England was not ruined both in a financial and a military sense, so unspeakable were their blindness, their weakness, and their folly. 1814.

The ballot having been discredited, and the recruiting market thrown wholly into the hands of the crimps by these two unhappy men, Pitt took over the military administration in a state of utter chaos. His remedy was to turn parish officers into recruiting sergeants, give them a reward for every recruit that they produced from Imperial funds, and to fine them for every man deficient of their quota, such fines being payable of course out of local funds. Such a system might possibly have succeeded had it been tried at first in time of peace, and become familiar to the parish officers; for, financially,

1814. it was decidedly ingenious. But foisted suddenly upon a nation demoralised by more than twelve months of incessant ballotting for over 100,000 men, it was a complete and dismal failure. Nevertheless, as has been told, it brought the Army into closer touch with the body of the people; and though, upon the whole, Pitt's military administration is a blot upon his fame, yet at the end he did admirable work by his staunch adherence to the Duke of York's principle that every battalion abroad must have a second battalion at home to maintain it at proper strength.

Then came Windham, the great reformer, who held firmly by three sound principles: first, that the Regular Army was the ultimate end for which all our military organisation existed; secondly, that the whole nation ought to be trained to arms; thirdly, that a Volunteer who received anything from the State besides his arms was no Volunteer. His practice, however, fell short of his theory. He was for training the whole nation to arms with practically no organisation; and this was almost a contradiction in terms. He was for using compulsion and yet mild compulsion, ballotting men in turn for a short period of training, yet granting them pay for the few days on which they were to be exercised, thereby ensuring enormous expense with a very doubtful return. In short, his Training Act broke down precisely in the most important province of all, the training, the problem of which was still puzzling him when he resigned office. His idea was that this huge mass of men, to be trained no man knew how, would turn out like the hosts of La Vendée in case of invasion; and that incidentally, through the kindling of its martial ardour, it would furnish an endless supply of recruits to the Regular Army. To tempt such recruits he introduced short service, in which he had profound faith, with increased pay for men who re-engaged for fresh terms beyond the first, and with an increased scale of pensions. His ideal, in fact, would have been a trained nation for defensive, and a Regular Army for offensive service;

with not even Militia intervening between them, and with no man wearing uniform except the Regular Army. His plan failed. Short service proved to be a disappointment as a temptation to recruits. The national training, as he projected it, was impossible; and the one great service which he rendered was the suppression of such Volunteers as were not self-supporting. Nevertheless, his brief administration marked a real turning-point in the history of the war, for he had at least upheld principles that were sound. 1814.

Then came Castlereagh, better known for his work at the Foreign Office than at the War Office, and better remembered, unfortunately, for the Six Acts than for his part either in war or diplomacy. Grasping at once all that was good in Windham's teaching, he started from the postulate that "learning the use of arms should be imposed as a positive duty upon all individuals within certain ages, to be enforced by fine." For the moment circumstances compelled him to maintain the Volunteers for a year; but in his own mind he had sealed their fate. To make national training a genuine institution he established a Sedentary or Local Militia, to be chosen by ballot, without liberty of substitution, from the entire male population between the ages of eighteen and thirty, for four years' service, during which period the men were to be exercised from time to time as companies near their own homes, and assembled once annually as battalions for not more than twenty-eight days. Into this force he swept as many of the false Volunteers as cared to take service, retaining as Volunteers only such as were self-supporting. At the same time, after making an enormous draft upon the Regular Militia to bring the Army to respectable strength, and reinforcing the Militia through the ballot, by an even greater number than the draft, he laid down the principle that a regular supply of 10,000 men should be drawn from it annually and made good as far as possible by voluntary enlistment. He thus returned in some measure to Addington's system, using the Local Militia as Adding-

1814. ton had used the Regular Militia, and the Regular Militia as Addington had used the Army of Reserve, but with this difference—that the Local Militiamen were ballotted without option of substitution and could enlist at any time into the Regular Army, while the Regular Militia could enlist only at stated periods and in large batches.

By these expedients the necessary supply of men for the Regular Army was kept up until the end of the war. That they would have sufficed if the war had lasted for two or three years longer I cannot believe. The Militia, by Castlereagh's own admission, was beginning to fail under the strain; and since 1813 it had been forced to enlist a certain number of boys in lieu of men. Morover, though Ministers asserted that the expense of recruiting soldiers into the Army through the Militia was little more costly than direct enlistment, there was small object in keeping up so expensive a force as the Regular Militia merely as a great recruiting depôt, more especially since the Local Militia had consented to do service outside their own counties. Beyond question some new system must have been found, whether borrowed from Calvert or from some other authority.

Calvert's plan, it will be remembered, was to have one hundred regiments of Infantry of the Line—the first battalions, containing 100,000 men, to be enlisted without limit as to time or place; the second battalions, also 100,000 strong, to consist of ballotted men engaged for home service only, but officered by Regular officers; the third and fourth battalions (for such they were to be, though he did not call them so) to be Local Militia at least 200,000 strong; and the whole to be on a strictly territorial basis. The first battalions would form the "disposable force" for service in any part of the world; the second battalions would be for home defence and would maintain the first at their due strength by means of voluntary enlistment encouraged by bounty; and the third and fourth battalions would maintain the second in the same fashion. Practically 1814. this would have turned the Regular Militia into second battalions of the Regular Army; and, as things were then carried on, the reform would probably have furthered both efficiency and economy. But it would not have overcome the prime difficulty, namely, the fact that only the refuse of the Local Militia ballot would have remained to be gathered in by the ballot for the second battalions. Moreover, the open employment of the ballot to recruit the Regular Army was precisely the thing which had made the Army of Reserve unpopular; and in such a ballot it would not have been possible to forbid substitution, which was the curse of the service.

The question was immensely difficult. Time might have brought the answer if, in accordance with Castlereagh's ideal, every able-bodied man had been compelled to serve his time with the Local Militia upon entering his eighteenth year. But this is no more than to say that things might have been carried on very efficiently if a proper system had been evolved and practised in time of peace, which, of course, is the indubitable fact, though the British nation, in spite of a thousand proofs, steadily refuses to believe it. Improvisations in time of war can never be thoroughly efficient, and must always be unduly expensive. The wit of man can hardly devise a scheme of military organisation for so complex an Empire as the British Empire, which shall be devoid of faults; and it is far better and cheaper to discover and to correct these faults in time of peace.

Incidentally it may be remarked that one special detail of the War Office's plans, which was particularly urged both by the Duke of York and by Calvert, was never wholly fulfilled. To the last there were a few regiments which consisted of a single battalion apiece only, and these regiments were for the most part quartered in the East and West Indies. Nevertheless, there was some method in this omission; the Twelfth Foot, for instance, being supplied with a second battalion when it came home from India. But, on the other

1814. hand, the ideal arrangement that there should be one hundred first battalions abroad, and as many second battalions at home, broke down completely. The second battalions for the most part may hardly be said to have existed, except on paper, until Windham became Minister for War; although there were two of them in Cathcart's force which sailed to North Germany in 1805. Later, there were, of course, many both in the Peninsula and at Walcheren. The territorial attachment of regiments to counties also, though greatly improved, was not perfected; and recruits from the Militia, in not a few instances, preferred another regiment to that which was assigned to them. The favourite corps, as has been told, were those of the Light Division; and it is no more than natural that young soldiers should have preferred to enter regiments which were daily adding to their fame.[1]

Two small points, upon which there is often much loose talk, may be briefly touched upon before I bring this sketch to an end. The first is the enlistment of boys. This was begun in 1805 by sanction of the Duke of York, and he was doubtless wise to permit it early in order that the boys might have time to grow up. The Army of Reserve was in great measure composed of raw lads who drew pay as men. Boys, on the other hand, enlisted as such, received only ninepence instead of one shilling a day.[2] The total number of boys, recruited as such into the Army during the war, did not exceed 20,000, or, roughly, one-twelfth of the whole.

Again, it is often said that the ranks of the Army were filled with the sweepings of the gaols. Undoubtedly convicts sentenced to transportation were discharged wholesale from the hulks on condition of their enlisting, occasionally in batches of five hundred together, but they were all sent to battalions, which were practically penal,

[1] During the late South African war young men flocked from all parts of England to the depôts of counties whose regiments had distinguished themselves.

[2] *H.D.* Palmerston's speech, 26th Feb. 1810.

in the West Indies or the West Coast of Africa, as also were such few soldiers as chose to commute five hundred or a thousand lashes for service in the same much-dreaded quarters. Nor was the principal penal battalion, the Royal York Rangers, a bad one. At first, under an unintelligent commander, it seems to have been a hell upon earth, where the cat was in daily use; but presently it passed into good hands, when flogging became unknown and the men were perfectly docile and well-behaved, earning praise from the Commander-in-Chief. Certainly convicts did not make up one per cent of the recruits. No doubt Deputy-Lieutenants passed a good many doubtful or simply wild characters into the Militia, who were gladly transferred by their Colonels to the Line; but to suppose that the ranks were filled by the criminal class is to assume that we were a nation of criminals. 1814.

Two more fallacies may likewise be briefly dismissed. It is often said that the aristocracy, which governed England at the beginning of the nineteenth century, did indeed, by its high spirit and stubborn resolution to continue the war, fairly wear Napoleon down and bring about his fall, but that it did not bear its fair share of the burden of expense. This is conclusively disproved by the fact, abundantly evident in these pages, that the expense of the ballot, and of the fines and bounties incident to it, except in rare instances, was thrown wholly upon the parochial rates, or, in other words, upon the landed interest. So severe indeed was the pressure upon the landowners, that many of the less wealthy among them were obliged to close their country-houses and retire into the towns.

Again it is averred and believed by many good Irishmen that England's battles against Napoleon, especially in the Peninsula, were fought and won by their compatriots; and not a few Scots are imbued with precisely the same notion with regard to their countrymen. This, of course, is simple nonsense. England produced, as indeed she ought, far more recruits than

1814. Scotland and Ireland put together; and, as a matter of fact, there were English regiments, as well as the Highlanders and Irish, engaged in all of Wellington's actions, though they do not talk so much about it. Each of the three kingdoms, indeed, did its duty; and impartial observers at the time were of opinion that the best regiments of all were those which, like old Ninety-five, contained a mixture of English, Scots, and Irish.

For the rest the broad lessons to be deduced from the foregoing pages seem to be the following:—

England cannot, any more than any other nation, fill the ranks of her Army in a great war without compulsion.

Compulsion cannot be applied for service outside the British Isles.

The admission of the principle of substitution in any scheme of compulsory service leads to ruinous expense, demoralisation, and inefficiency.

Compulsory personal service for home-defence has been tried and not found wanting.

The ultimate end for which all our military organisation must exist is the maintenance of the Regular Army, our only offensive land force. (Windham.)

The true basis of such an organisation is National training. (Windham, Castlereagh.)

"Learning the use of arms should be imposed as a positive duty upon all individuals within certain ages, to be enforced by fine." (Castlereagh.)

A Volunteer who asks more from the State than his arms, except on active service, is no Volunteer. (Windham.) False Volunteers are alike troublesome, expensive, and useless.

England felt the false measures of Pitt from 1793 to 1798, and of Addington in 1803-4, until the very end of the war in 1814. All measures of National Defence and military organisation must be thought out and tested as far as possible in time of peace. Improvisation doubles the cost of war, while imperilling its success.

APPENDIX I

Return of the Number of Casualties which occurred in the British Army during the undermentioned years: distinguishing British from Foreign and Colonial Corps.—Adjutant-General's Office, 13th November 1813.

Period.	Casualties, British.	Casualties, Foreign.	Total.
1803	13,396	2,674	16,070
1804	13,347	2,838	16,185
1805	15,800	2,443	18,243
1806	13,856	3,075	16,931
1807	14,570	2,968	17,538
1808	17,183	3,703	20,886
1809	21,630	2,937	24,567
1810	19,498	3,455	22,953
1811	19,019	3,441	22,460
1812	20,313	5,185	25,498
1813	19,653	4,802	24,455

RETURN of the Number of Men raised for the Regular Army, exclusive of Foreign and Colonial Corps, by ordinary Recruiting, and by transfers from the Militia, etc.—Adjutant-General's Office, 13th November 1813.

	By Ordinary Recruiting.			Raised under the Additional Force Act.	Volunteers from the Militia.	Total.
	Men.	Boys.	Total.			
In						
1803	11,253	...	11,253	...	...	11,253
1804	9,430	...	9,430	1,658	...	11,088
1805	10,180	1,497	11,677	8,288	13,580	33,545
1806	10,337	1,538	11,875	5,834	2,968	20,677
1807	15,308	3,806	19,114 }	...	29,108	61,185
1808	10,477	2,486	12,963 }			
1809	9,675	2,045	11,720 }	...	23,885	44,700
1810	7,367	1,728	9,095 }			
1811	9,532	1,940	11,472	...	11,453	22,925
1812	12,563	1,869	14,432	...	9,927	24,359
Dec. 25, 1812 to Sept. 25, 1813	9,845	1,440	11,285	...	8,834	20,119
Total .	115,967	18,349	134,316	15,780	99,755	249,851

RETURN of the Number of Recruits (distinguishing Men and Boys) raised for the Militia, by Beat of Drum, between 27th May 1809 and 24th October 1813.—Adjutant-General's Office, 15th November 1813.

	Men.	Boys.	Total.
For the English Militia .	23,053	1,464	24,517
For the Scotch Militia .	2,591	252	2,843
For the Irish Militia . .	17,967	703	18,670
General Total . .	43,611	2,419	46,030

[*Commons' Journals*, lxix. p. 635.]

APPENDIX II

EFFECTIVE STRENGTH OF THE ARMY

RETURN of the Effective Strength of the British Army, in Rank and File, from the year 1804 to the year 1813 inclusive; distinguishing Cavalry, Artillery, Infantry, and Militia, and British from Foreign and Colonial Corps.—Adjutant-General's Office, 13th November 1813.

Year.	Cavalry.	Artillery and Engineers.	Infantry.	Total.	Proportions of Totals under		Total.	Militia.	General Total.
					British Corps.	Foreign and Colonial Corps.			
On									
Jan. 1, 1804	16,729	14,113	119,751	150,593	133,554	17,039	150,593	85,519	236,112
„ 1805	20,316	17,109	124,531	161 956	139,581	22,375	161,956	89,809	251,765
„ 1806	23,396	19,546	142,177	185,119	159,076	26,043	185,119	74,653	259,772
„ 1807	26,261	20,951	152,245	199,457	163,641	35,816	199,457	76,159	275,616
„ 1808	26,402	22,250	177,775	226,427	189,210	37,217	226,427	67,677	294,104
„ 1809	27,391	23,563	183,223	234,177	197,230	36,947	234,177	81,577	315,754
On									
Jan. 25, 1810	27,740	24,238	185,474	237,452	199,062	38,390	237,452	72,487	309,939
„ 1811	27,410	23,668	183,516	234,594	194,051	40,543	234,594	84,439	319,033
„ 1812	27,638	23,824	192,423	243,885	198,004	45,881	243,885	77,055	320,940
„ 1813	28,931	25,407	201,538	255,876	203,119	52,757	255,876	71,055	326,931
Sept. 25, 1813	29,504	27,014	204,279	260,797	207,068	53,729	260,797	69,866	330,663

[*Commons' Journals*, vol. lxix. p. 638.]

APPENDIX III

EFFECTIVE STRENGTH OF THE VOLUNTEERS

Effective Strength of the Volunteers of Great Britain only; of all Ranks for years 1803-1808; Rank and File only, 1812

Year.	Great Britain only.			Total.	Ireland.
	Cavalry.	Infantry.	Artillery.		
Dec. 16. 1803	...	...	...	380,193	80,000
Jan. 1804	28,943	341,011	10,304	380,258	70,000
Jan. 1, 1805	32,728	316,079	12,007	360,814	
" 1806	30,927	308,465	12,116	351,508	
" 1807	30,032	293,381	11,297	334,710	
" 1808	29,605	295,768	11,031	336,404	
" 1809					
" 1810					
" 1811					
" 1812	Rank and file 19,207	49,436		68,643	
" 1813				or 30,000 rank and file below establishment	

APPENDIX IV

Memoranda on the Recruiting of the Army

Memoranda.

Horse Guards
6th Feb. 1807.

Army of Reserve

Passed. 6th July 1803.

To be raised by ballot within the year :—

Quotas .	England . . .	33,880
	Ireland . . .	10,000
	Scotland . . .	6,000
	Total .	49,880

Number of men raised within the year (*vide* Return (A), pp. 296-8) :—

England	31,758
Ireland	8,197
Scotland	5,537
Total .	45,492

Deserters : from August 1803 to May 1804 . .		5,651
Of this number .	Ballotted men . .	2,873
	Substitutes . . .	41,198
Extended their Services, and were incorporated in the Line		17,307

The remainder are now serving in the Nine Garrison Battalions, or have fallen casualties.

[*Military Transactions of the British Empire*, i. pp. 60-61.]

RETURN (A)

Accounts of Men raised for the Royal Army of Reserve, in each Month to the 1st May 1804, since the Commencement of the Act passed for that Purpose

England and Wales

An Account of the Men raised in England and Wales for the Royal Army of Reserve, in each Month since the Commencement of the Act passed for that Purpose; of the Number of the same who have engaged for General Service; and of the Number of Ballotted Men and Substitutes who have been enrolled for the said Army; as far as the same can be ascertained.—Inspector-General's Office, London, 1st May 1804.

Periods.	Number of Men raised.	Number rejected, discharged, claimed by Civil Law, etc., etc.	Dead.	Number deserted, claimed as Deserters from other Corps, etc., etc.	Number of Effective Men.	Number due, including the Casualties.	Number volunteered for General Service, included in the Effectives.
Aug. 1, 1803	103	...	...	18	85	33,795	...
Sept. 1, "	19,453	212	2	1,473	17,766	16,029	...
Oct. 1, "	5,168	260	36	1,132	3,740	12,289	1,747
Nov. 1, "	2,117	374	74	371	1,298	10,991	2,014
Dec. 1, "	1,496	172	84	259	981	10,010	2,747
Jan. 1, 1804	956	101	83	181	591	9,419	706
Total .	29,293	1,119	279	3,434	24,461		7,214
Feb. 1, 1804	647	111	81	186	269	9,150	235
Mar. 1, "	707	205	67	147	288	8,862	565
April 1, "	673	82	58	245	288	8,574	348
May 1, "	438	235	45	105	53	8,521	874
Total .	31,758	1,752	530	4,117	25,359		9,236
Number of Ballotted Men	2,531	258			2,273		
Number of Substitutes	29,227	6,141			23,086		

[*Military Transactions of the British Empire*, i. p. 65.]

RETURN (A)—*continued*

Scotland

An Account of the Number of Men raised in North Britain for the Royal Army of Reserve, in each month since the Commencement of the Act passed for that Purpose; of the Number of the same who have engaged for General Service; and of the Number of Ballotted Men and Substitutes who have been enrolled for the said Army, as far as the same can be ascertained.—Inspector-General's Office, 1st May 1804.

Periods.	Number of Men raised.	Number rejected, discharged, claimed by Civil Law, etc., etc.	Dead.	Number deserted, claimed as Deserters from other Corps, etc., etc.	Number of Effective Men.	Number due, including Casualties.	Number volunteered for General Service, included in the Effectives.
Aug. 1, 1803	...	...	...	...	...	...	...
Sept. 1, "	2,984	8	1	101	2,874	3,126	...
Oct. 1, "	999	4	1	77	917	2,209	...
Nov. 1, "	359	3	1	53	302	1,907	...
Dec. 1, "	227	52	1	32	142	1,765	...
Jan. 1, 1804	252	12	2	20	218	1,547	...
Total .	4,821	79	6	283	4,453		...
Feb. 1, 1804	215	7	...	21	187	1,360	482
Mar. 1, "	234	14	2	25	193	1,167	371
April 1, "	193	53	3	25	112	1,055	56
May 1, "	74	8	...	10	56	999	63
Total .	5,537	161	11	364	5,001		972
Number Ballotted	294		8		286		
Number Substitutes	5,243		528		4,715		

[*Military Transactions of the British Empire*, i. p. 66.]

RETURN (A)—*continued*

Ireland

An Account of the Number of Men raised in Ireland for the Royal Army of Reserve, in each month since the Commencement of the Act passed for that Purpose; of the Number of the same who have engaged for General Service; and of the Number of Ballotted Men, Substitutes, and Recruits enlisted for and serving in the said Army; as far as the same can be ascertained. — Inspector-General's Office, London, 1st May 1804.

Periods.	Number of Men raised.	Number rejected, discharged, claimed by Civil Power, etc., etc.	Dead.	Number deserted, claimed as Deserters from other Corps, etc., etc.	Number of Effective Men.	Number due, including the Casuals, to be made good.	Number volunteered for General Service, included in the number of Effective Men.
Aug. 1, 1803	...	...	...	...	...	...	...
Sept. 1, "	1,508	...	...	22	1,486	8,514	...
Oct. 1, "	2,241	25	...	153	2,063	6,451	...
Nov. 1, "	1,367	32	...	200	1,135	5,316	...
Dec. 1, "	1,099	37	...	140	922	4,394	...
Jan. 1, 1804	658	19	1	176	462	3,932	...
Total .	6,873	113	1	691	6,068		...
Feb. 1, 1804	497	20	...	117	360	3,572	1,444
Mar. 1, "	330	18	34	201	77	3,495	24
April 1, "	282	25	3	52	202	3,293	191
May 1, "	215	27	10	109	69	3,224	140
Total .	8,197	203	48	1,170	6,776		1,799
	N.B.—Number of Effective Men			Ballotted .	48		
				Substitutes .	6,528		
				Recruited .	200		

[*Military Transactions of the British Empire*, i. p. 67.]

APPENDIX V

Additional Force Act

Passed. 29th June 1804.

Provided to establish and maintain a Permanent Force :—

Quotas	England	58,285
	Ireland	10,000
	Scotland	10,666
		78,951

Composed by adding the Quotas of the Army of Reserve to the Sup. Militia ; viz. :—

Quota of Reserve	49,880
Sup. Militia of England and Scotland	29,071
	78,951

N.B.—Ireland had no Sup. Militia. Supposing that the Quota of the Army of Reserve had been complete, and the Supplementary Militia also complete, the Additional Force Act would not have commenced its Operation until Casualties had taken place in either of the above.

To be forthwith raised on the passing of the Act :—

England	Reserve Deficiencies	8,302
	Militia do.	6,476
Ireland	Reserve Deficiencies	2,930
	Reserve do.	1,245
	Militia do.	829
	Total	19,782

Brought forward . .	19,782

The period allowed for raising that force was one month from the settlement of the Deficiencies by the Lieutenancy, but was prolonged to the 10th of November 1804.

On the 10th November 1804—

	Men.	Deserted.
England had raised . .	367	37
Ireland ,, . .	342	55
Scotland ,, . .	69	3
	778	95
Deficiency	19,004.	

And the consequent Penalties to be levied on the Parishes at £20 per man is . £380,080

To be raised by the 1st October 1805 :—

To replace men who had volunteered into the Line, not exceeding 9000 annually, for England . . .	England .	9,000
	Ireland .	200
	Scotland .	1,800
Total to be raised by 1st October . .		30,782

The excess above that number being lost, no provision being made by the Act for replacing them.

Men raised by 1st October .	England . .	3,723
	Ireland . .	3,132
	Scotland . .	828
		7,683

Here again an additional penalty presents itself for the deficiencies of 11,000 − 7,683 + 778 Men = 4,095, which at £20 per man is . . £80,950
which, added to the former Assessment. 380,000

is . . . £460,950

Had the penalties been assessed under the Reserve, the amount would be . . £1,843,800

Progress of the Additional Force

The Act undertook to replace the Deficiencies and the Casualties of the Reserve and Sup. Militia by a Return to the Privy Council annually, and a new Apportionment.

These Returns were made, but no Apportionment took place.

The Fines were only partially levied.

The Act continued in force till June 1806, when it had produced :—

England .	8,547	By Parish Officers .	10,907
Ireland .	5,570	By Recruiting Officers .	4,871
Scotland .	1,661		15,778
Total Produce of the Additional Force .	15,778		
Total Desertion . .	3,041		
Volunteers to the Army	8,562		

The remainder placed in Garrison Battalions.

Bounty of Men raised for Additional Force

First Bounty	£12	12	0
Additional Bounty on volunteering into the Line .	10	10	0
For a General Service man thus acquired	£23	2	0
For a man raised at once for General Service at that period	16	16	0
Thus a competition was established, detrimental to the ordinary Recruiting of the Army, giving sum of .	£6	6	0

to those going circuitously into a Regiment.

[*Military Transactions*, i. pp. 61-63.]

APPENDIX VI

Windham's Measures

The Additional Force Act repealed in June 1806, and followed by Mr. Windham's Measure, 24th June 1806.

The Mutiny Act limited the period of Service in the Army.

Men raised by the ordinary means of Recruiting, from 24th June 1806 to 23rd January 1807 .		5,208
Desertions		363
From 24th June to the 28th November	Bounty, £16 : 16s. Men raised	3,282
From 28th November to 23rd January .	Bounty, £12 : 12s. Men raised	1,926

At this period it was thought advisable to employ Officers on half-pay, or who had quitted service, as extra Recruiting Officers.

Recruiting by extra Officers commenced 28th November 1806 :—

Men raised prior to extra Recruiting	3,282
Men raised by extra Officers	163
Men raised since extra Recruiting	1,763
	5,208
Number of Extra Officers	278

[*Military Transactions*, i. pp. 63-64.]

APPENDIX VII

June 1804–1809, State of the Army

(*a*) State of the Army, June 1804

Mediterranean	Gibraltar	2,836
	Malta	5,329
West Indies	Leeward Islands	11,068
	Jamaica	3,857
	Bahamas	560
North America	Canada	1,534
	Nova Scotia, etc.	1,867
East Indies	East Indies	13,500
	Ceylon	5,447
On passage		1,301
United Kingdom	Great Britain	59,785
	Ireland	30,030
United Kingdom Militia	Great Britain	70,918
	Ireland	19,049

(*b*) State of the Army, 1st of June 1805

Mediterranean	Gibraltar	3,318
	Malta	6,680
West Indies	Leeward Islands	11,904
	Jamaica	3,591
	Bahamas, etc.	589
North America	Nova Scotia	2,367
	Canada	1,519
East Indies	East Indies	11,998
	Ceylon	6,870
United Kingdom exclusive of 76,724 Militia	Great Britain	64,614
	Ireland	29,236
On passage		12,442

(c) State of the Army, 1st June 1806

Mediterranean	Gibraltar	4,666
	Malta	4,119
	Sicily	6,647
West Indies	Leeward Islands	11,093
	Jamaica	3,645
	Bahamas, etc.	574
North America	Nova Scotia	3,002
	Canada	1,696
East Indies	East Indies	15,043
	Ceylon	8,739
United Kingdom exclusive of 77,429 Militia	Great Britain	73,857
	Ireland	21,883
Cape of Good Hope		5,058
On passage		13,427

(d) State of the Army, 1st June 1807

Mediterranean	Gibraltar	5,281
	Malta	5,288
	Sicily	11,099
	Egypt	5,074
West Indies	Leeward Islands	12,575
	Jamaica, etc.	4,680
	Bahamas, etc.	673
North America	Nova Scotia	2,831
	Canada	1,539
South America		5,956
With Brig.-Gen. R. Craufurd		4,026
East Indies	East Indies	14,499
	Ceylon	4,736
Goree		226
New South Wales		490
Cape of Good Hope		4,193
On passage		9,366
United Kingdom exclusive of 77,872 Militia	Great Britain	62,569
	Ireland	25,089

(*e*) State of the Army, 1st June 1808

Mediterranean	Gibraltar	5,328
	Malta	4,047
	Sicily	14,947
West Indies	Leeward Islands	12,556
	Jamaica, etc.	5,499
	Bahamas, etc.	2,253
North America	Nova Scotia	4,566
	Canada	3,252
East Indies	East Indies	15,131
	Ceylon	4,645
Cape of Good Hope		7,042
Goree		224
Madeira		1,612
New South Wales		536
With M.-General Spenser		3,704
With Lieut.-Gen. Sir John Moore		10,871
Heligoland		302
On passage		4,454
United Kingdom exclusive of 86,788 Militia	Great Britain	63,355
	Ireland	33,667

(*f*) State of the Army, 25th May 1809

Mediterranean	Gibraltar	3,842
	Malta	3,594
	Sicily	14,716
West Indies	Leeward Islands	15,011
	Jamaica, etc.	4,937
	Bahamas, etc.	1,470
North America	Nova Scotia	4,501
	Canada	3,559
East Indies	East Indies	19,843
	Ceylon	5,115
Cape of Good Hope		5,800
Goree		283
Madeira		913
New South Wales		1,317
Heligoland		270
Detachments on passage		4,223
Portugal		22,623
United Kingdom exclusive of 65,524 Militia	Great Britain	91,999
	Ireland	15,858

(g) "THE EXTENT OF THE ARMED FORCE OF ALL DESCRIPTIONS, MILITARY AND NAVAL, AS BORNE UPON THE ESTABLISHMENT OF THE UNITED KINGDOM, AND OF ITS SEVERAL POSSESSIONS, INCLUDING ALSO THE LOCAL FORCE IN INDIA, ON 25TH MAY 1809."

Last Returns of Population :—

England	9,343,578
Scotland	1,599,068
Ireland	4,000,000
Amounting to .	14,942,646

The force actually maintained by that Population is 786,521, exclusive of Colonial Corps and the East India Company's troops. The whole number of men paid by the Empire amounts to :—

Regulars and Militia . .		285,398	rank and file.
Local Militia		198,534	"
Volunteers	Great Britain .	114,066	"
	Ireland . .	75,340	"
Marines		31,400	"
Seamen		98,600	"
Artillery and Engineers . .		14,261	"
East India Company's Military Force .	Europeans	4,051	"
	Natives	128,418	"
Total . .		950,068	

APPENDIX VIII

25th May 1809.—Foreign and Provincial Corps in British Pay

	Cavalry.			Total.	Infantry.			Total.
	Ser-geants.	Trum-peters.	Rank and File.		Ser-geants.	Drum-mers.	Rank and File.	
King's German Legion .	168	38	2,810	3,016	416	160	7,583	8,159
Do., left in Spain and Portugal . .	11	2	143	156	16	1	515	532
Ceylonese	11	...	56	67	240	68	2,531	2,839
West India Regiments .	...	...	...	...	397	160	7,352	7,909
Pioneers at Jamaica .	...	...	...	...	...	...	305	305
De Meuron's . .	...	...	...	...	27	19	278	324
De Roll's	...	...	...	...	66	19	1,193	1,278
De Watteville's . .	...	...	...	...	50	17	764	831
Chasseurs Britanniques .	...	...	...	...	43	22	879	944
Corsican Rangers .	...	...	...	...	38	16	547	601
Dillon's . .	...	...	...	...	43	21	642	706
Royal Regiment of Malta	...	...	...	...	8	3	148	159
Maltese Provincials .	...	...	...	...	18	5	176	199
York Light Infantry Volunteers . .	...	...	...	...	45	20	580	645
Cape Regiment . .	...	...	...	...	13	20	691	724
Sicilian Regiment . .	...	...	...	...	53	22	1,127	1,202
Sicilians attached to the 61st Regiment . .	...	...	...	...	...	...	19	19
Nova Scotia Fencibles .	...	...	...	...	34	22	474	530
Newfoundland do. .	...	...	...	...	31	22	487	540
New Brunswick do. .	...	...	...	...	42	22	625	689
Canadian do. . .	...	...	...	...	23	22	432	477
Manx do. . . .	...	...	...	...	42	22	721	785
Total . . .	190	40	3,009	3,239	1,645	683	28,069	30,397

N.B.—In the numbers returned in England are included 7,034 Rank and File, who were left in Spain and Portugal by the Army recently returned from thence; viz. 260 Cavalry; 134 Foot Guards; and 6,640 Infantry.

Prisoners of War in France and Holland since the year 1805, not included in above Abstract.

9 Foot . . .	236 R. and F.	
30 " . . .	103	
59 " . . .	65	Accounts have been received of these Men having entered the Westphalian Service.
1 Line Bn. K.G.L.	199	
Total .	603	

[*Military Transactions*, Suppl. to vol. i. p. 148.]

APPENDIX IX

Return of the Artillery for the Years 1803-1809

Royal Horse Artillery

	June 1, 1803.		June 1, 1804.		June 1, 1805.		June 1, 1806.		June 1, 1807.		June 1, 1808.		June 1, 1809.	
	N.C. Officers and Men.	Horses.	N.C. Officers and Men.	Horses.	N.C. Officers and Men.	Horses.	N.C. Officers and Men.	Horses.	N.C. Officers and Men.	Horses.	N.C. Officers and Men.	Horses.	N.C. Officers and Men.	Horses.
Great Britain	925	824	1,248	1,212	1,426	1,318	1,705	1,815	1,635	1,461	1,636	1,435	2,045	1,737
Ireland . .	127	50	171	168	260	234	263	236	300	266	295	285	302	271
Total .	1,052	874	1,419	1,380	1,686	1,552	1,968	2,051	1,935	1,727	1,931	1,720	2,347	2,008

Foot Artillery

	June 1, 1803.	June 1, 1804.	June 1, 1805	June 1, 1806.	June 1, 1807.	June 1, 1808.	June 1, 1809.
Great Britain . .	3,371	4,963	5,562	6,214	7,256	7,380	8,329
Ireland . . .	688	990	1,225	1,240	1,238	1,362	975
Jersey . . .	33	65	62	60	55	113	110
Guernsey . . .	33	61	60	60	58	104	102
Foreign Stations .	2,505	3,033	3,661	3,830	4,516	5,378	5,394
Total . . .	6,630	9,112	10,570	11,404	13,123	14,337	14,910

[*Military Transactions*, Suppl. to vol. i. p. 149.]

APPENDIX X

RETURN OF RECRUITS RAISED FOR THE MILITIA BY BEAT OF DRUM. [*Commons' Journals*, vol. lxix. p. 637.]

Return of the Number of Recruits (distinguishing men and boys) raised for the Militia by beat of drum, since the 27th of May 1809, the date of the Act of Parliament under which the Regiments of Militia were authorised to raise recruits by that means.—Adjutant-General's Office, 13th November 1813.

	May 27, 1809, to Dec. 24, 1809.		Dec. 25, 1809, to Dec. 24, 1810.		Dec. 25, 1810, to Dec. 24, 1811.		Dec. 25, 1811, to Dec. 24, 1812.		Dec. 25, 1812, to Oct. 24, 1813.		Total.		
	Men.	Boys.	Men.	Boys.	Men.	Boys.	Men.	Boys.	Men.	Boys.	Men.	Boys.	General Total.
England . .	5,320	1	4,577	10	1,508	328	4,974	569	6,674	556	23,053	1,464	24,517
Scotland . .	600	11	761	3	126	15	506	80	598	143	2,591	252	2,843
Ireland . .	3,718	...	6,074	...	2,789	11	3,214	223	2,172	469	17,967	703	18,670
General Total . . .											43,611	2,419	46,030

APPENDIX XI

TABLE OF DATES OF THE ADDITION OF 2ND BATTALIONS TO REGIMENTS OF THE LINE

Regiment.	Date of 2nd Battalion.	Act of Parl. by which added.	Regiment.	Date of 2nd Battalion.	Act of Parl. by which added.
†1st (4)	Dec. 15, 1804	A. of R.	28th (2)	July 21, 1803	A. of R.
2nd (1)	*None*		*29th (1)	*None*	
3rd (2)	July 21, 1803	A. of R.	30th (2)	July 21, 1803	A. of R.
4th („)	April 24, 1804	A. F. A.	31st („)	Oct. 1, 1804	A. F. A.
5th („)	1804	„	32nd („)	„	„
6th („)	„	„	33rd (1)	*None*	
7th („)	„	„	*34th (2)	May 11, 1805	
8th („)	April 24, 1804	„	35th („)	„	
9th („)	Oct. 1, 1804	„	36th („)	Oct. 1, 1804	A. F. A.
10th („)	„	„			
11th („)	July 15, 1808		*37th („)	June 11, 1813, possibly never formed	
12th („)	Jan. 6, 1812				
*13th (1)	*None*		38th („)	Oct. 1, 1804	A. F. A.
14th (2)	Oct. 1, 1804	A. F. A.	39th („)	July 21, 1803	A. of R.
15th („)	„	„	40th („)	Oct. 1, 1804	A. F. A.
*16th (1)	*None*		*41st (1)	Sept. 2, 1812	
17th („)	*None*		42nd (2)	July 14, 1803	A. of R.
18th (2)	April 24, 1804		43rd („)	Oct. 1, 1804	A. F. A.
19th (1)	*None*		44th („)	1803	A. of R.
20th („)	*None*		45th („)	Oct. 1, 1804	A. F. A.
21st (2)	Oct. 1, 1804	A. F. A.	*46th (1)	*None*	
22nd („)	Feb. 12, 1814		47th (2)	July 7, 1803	A. of R.
23rd („)	April 24, 1804	A. F. A.	*48th („)	July 21, 1803	„
*24th („)	Oct. 1, 1804	„	*49th (1)	*None*	
25th („)	„	„	50th (2)	Oct. 1, 1804	A. F. A.
26th („)	July 21, 1803	A. of R.	51st (1)	*None*	
27th (3)	2nd Battn., Oct. 1, 1804	A. F. A.	52nd (2)	Oct. 1, 1804	A. F. A.
			53rd („)	July 21, 1803	A. of R.
	3rd Battn., Sept. 2, 1805		*54th (1)	*None*	
			55th („)	*None*	

* A recruiting company was ordered to be added to these regiments, whether of one or of two battalions, on 12th June 1809.—S.C.L.B.

† This regiment had always two battalions; 3rd and 4th raised 15th Dec. 1804.

Regiment.	Date of 2nd Battalion.	Act of Parl. by which added.
56th (2)	Oct. 1, 1804	A. F. A.
57th (,,)	July 21, 1803	A. of R.
*58th (,,)	1803	,,
59th (,,)	Oct. 1, 1804	A. F. A.
60th (6)	July 1806, 7th Battalion, 3rd not formed	
61st (2)	July 21, 1803	A. of R.
62nd (,,)	Oct. 1, 1804	A. F. A.
63rd (,,)	,,	,,
64th (1)	*None*	
65th (,,)	*None*	
66th (2)	July 21, 1803	A. of R.
67th (,,)	1803	,,
68th (1)	*None*	
69th (2)	July 21, 1803	A. of R.
70th (1)	*None*	
71st (2)	Oct. 1, 1804	A. F. A.
72nd (,,)	,,	,,
73rd (,,)	Dec. 29, 1808	A. of R.
74th (1)	*None*	
75th (,,)	,,	
76th (,,)	,,	
77th (,,)	,,	
78th (2)	Apr. 19, 1804	A. F. A.
79th (,,)	,,	,,
80th (1)	*None*	

Regiment.	Date of 2nd Battalion.	Act of Parl. by which added.
81st (2)	July 21, 1803	A. of R.
82nd (,,)	Oct. 1, 1804	A. F. A.
83rd (,,)	,,	,,
84th (,,)	May 6, 1808	
85th (1)	*None*	
86th (2)	Feb. 12, 1814	
87th (,,)	Oct. 1, 1804	A. F. A.
*88th (,,)	,,	,,
89th (,,)	,,	,,
90th (,,)	,,	,,
91st (,,)	,,	,,
92nd (,,)	July 21, 1803	A. of R.
93rd (1)	*None*	
94th (,,)	*None*	
95th (3)	2nd Battn., May 14, 1805; 3rd Battn., 1809	
96th (2)	1804	
*97th (1)	*None*	
98th (,,)	,,	
99th (,,)	,,	
100th (,,)	,,	
101st (,,)	,,	
102nd (,,)	,,	
103rd (,,)	,,	
104th (,,)	,,	

* A recruiting company was ordered to be added to these regiments, whether of one or of two battalions, on 12th June 1809.—S.C.L.B.

A. of R. signifies Army of Reserve. A. F. A. signifies Pitt's Additional Force Act.

APPENDIX XII

Strength of Forces at Disposal of District Commanders in Great Britain, January to March 1804

District.	Contents.	G.O.C.	Regulars: Militia included. Effective Rank and File.	Volunteers and Yeomanry. Effective Rank and File.
Southern	Kent, Surrey, Sussex (exclusive of London)	General Sir D. Dundas	32,406	11,778
Eastern	Norfolk, Suffolk, Cambs, Hunts, Essex	Lt.-Gen. Sir J. Craig	28,720	21,561
London	(Including Surrey within the bills of mortality)	Lt.-Gen. Gwyn	5,068	28,383
South-West	Hants, Wilts, Dorset	Lieut.-General Gardiner	10,935	11,771
Western	Devon, Cornwall, Somerset (exclusive of Bristol, Bath, Troubridge, Uxbridge, or other places garrisoned from Bristol)	Lieut.-General Simcoe	9,518	26,043
North-Western	Cheshire, Salop, Lancs, N. Wales	Lt.-Gen. Prince William	805	9,806
Northern	Northumberland, Cumberland, Westmoreland, Durham	Lt.-Gen. Sir H. Dalrymple	5,466	14,126
Yorkshire	Yorkshire, Lincs	Lt.-Gen. Lord Mulgrave	5,628	16,788
Isle of Wight	...	Major-General Hewett	4,171	1,870
Severn	Glos., Worcester, Hereford, Monmouth, S. Wales	Lt.-Gen. the Duke of Cumberland	1,542	7,945
Home	Middlesex, Herts, Berks	Lt.-Gen. Lord Cathcart	4,942	...
North Inland	Derby, Notts, Staffs, Leic., Warwick, Rutland	Lieut.-General Gardiner	414	...
South Inland	Beds., Oxon, Bucks, Northants	Lieut.-General Gwynn	Nil.	...

RESERVES OF VOLUNTEERS, ADDITIONAL TO THE ABOVE

Wakefield	14,303	Chester	2,200	Reading	6,566
Salisbury	5,042	Liverpool	3,287	Aylesbury	9,683
Bristol	8,495	Lichfield	29,140	Brentwood	10,738
Gloucester	12,451	Northampton	8,247	Dorking	7,299
		London	28,283		

Stations for carrying troops by post: Guildford, Andover, Marlborough, Bedford, Banbury, Daventry, Northampton, Kettering, Stilton, Cambridge.

[*Record Office*, W.O. Divn. 30, vol. lxxvi. 1st Jan. to 27th March 1804.]

INDEX

Printed by R. & R. CLARK, LIMITED, *Edinburgh.*

www.ingramcontent.com/pod-product-compliance
Ingram Content Group UK Ltd.
Pitfield, Milton Keynes, MK11 3LW, UK
UKHW041848190726
13854UKWH00002B/778

9 781843 421818